SOURCE OF
THE DREAM

SOURCE OF THE DREAM

My Way
to
Sathya
Sai
Baba

ROBERT PRIDDY

SAMUEL WEISER, INC.

York Beach, Maine

First published in 1998 by
Samuel Weiser, Inc.
Box 612
York Beach, ME 03910-0612

Library of Congress Cataloging-in-Publication Data

Priddy, Robert.
        Source of the dream : my way to Sathya Sai Baba /
    Robert Priddy.
            p.   cm.
        Includes bibliographical references and index.
        ISBN 1-57863-028-2 (paper :   alk. paper)
        1. Sathya Sai Baba, 1926– .   I. Title.
    BL1175. S385P75   1997   97–25620
    294.5'092—dc21   CIP

MG

Typeset in 10 point Galliard

The photo of Sai Baba on the cover is a well-known photo used
everywhere in India. We do not know the photographer.

Printed in the United States of America

05   04   03   02   01   00   99   98
10   9   8   7   6   5   4   3   2   1

The paper used in this publication meets the minimum requirements
of the American National Standard for Permanence of Paper for
Printed Library Materials Z39.48–1984.

CONTENTS

FOREWORD

In this book I recount experiences that eventually led me into the sphere of a very great being. They are like a lens, and at the focus of interest is Sathya Sai Baba.

Facts are, of course, ultimately only meaningful when related to personal experience. Our own experience is what each of us can know best, as we are the sole witness and final coordinator of it all. However poor my self-knowledge may happen to be, I still necessarily know myself more intimately than I do any other person. Though self-knowledge and knowledge of others are doubtless related, it is to myself that I am closest. Short of possessing supreme intelligence, to know and understand any other person fully and truly seems to be beyond anyone, not least when I consider how difficult it is to know myself in the deeper sense of understanding my whole being.

When the atomic scientist Dr. Bhagavantam asked Sathya Sai Baba why he still could not fathom him at all, after having been many years in his presence, the reply he received was that he, Bhagavantam, had been himself from birth . . . but did he therefore know himself? Sai Baba told him, "First try to understand yourself, and leave me to myself." Sai Baba has also asserted that we can never "know" him and that his nature as an avatar is far beyond the reach of human understanding.

This book deals with what have so far been unquestionably and by far the most important matters in my experience, but it is no autobiography, in that it concentrates only on what relates to my way to Sathya Sai Baba and how he features in my life. I am obviously restricted to writing about my relationship to him. I recount some experiences preparatory to my first encounter with Sai Baba because of the extraordinary combination of intricate means by which this was brought about.

I am very much aware that my personal experiences are of limited importance to the whole scheme of things over which Sathya Sai's direct influence operates. Anyone who reads a fair selection of the many hundreds of personal stories already available from people whom Sathya Sai Baba has attracted and transformed will perceive that my "story" and person are not exceptional. Likewise, Sathya Sai's influence has been at work in many people's lives (invariably unbeknown to them) long before they meet him in person or even become aware that he exists. Yet, like anyone else, my background and experiences are in some ways unique, and provide a personal setting for the same basic search in which I believe we are all somehow engaged.

In the interests of objectivity I try to record both the most relevant objective events and my subjective anticipations, interpretations, and reactions to them. Many years of working in philosophy and other subjects have convinced me that nothing can be described with "sheer objectivity" independent of personal and subjective perception and thought. No scientist, no observer, and no writer can ever avoid selecting and interpreting his subject matter, shaping and filtering it through the aperture of the personal mind. Individual aspects of understanding lie behind even the very driest of apparently-neutral facts and figures, and this is often the insidious deceptiveness of what would claim to be nothing but "descriptive," but is actually always partly a product of subjective design.

For the above reasons, I try to give a truthful and accurate description and analysis of the mental and emotional processes through which Sai Baba drew me to him. This "phenomenological method" allows the reader to judge the so-called objective facts by understanding their personal or "subjective setting" and my approach to them.

I chose the outlined approach in the hope that people who may not be able to visit Sathya Sai Baba will be aided in seeing how he may communicate with anyone, even from great physical distance.

I shall consequently avoid "hearsay evidence" almost entirely, making it quite clear whenever I may report any that I regard as reliable and accurate. There are very few occasions when second-hand observations seem to be of much genuine value. Reproducing verbatim quotes of reported speech are acceptable, but indirect accounts culled from other sources, especially when re-worded, are a constant danger to the truth and may be a rich source of confusion and misunderstanding. Therefore I do not attempt to give any resumé of the life of Sai Baba, amazing and fascinating as it most certainly is.

Any fairly persistent observer knows that the achievements of Sri Sathya Sai Baba are monumental. The account I give is only one fraction to add to the hundreds of books already published around the world of people's experiences of Sai Baba. The sheer volume of these is, itself, a striking and helpful phenomenon.

I have tried to recount judiciously and descriptively rather than giving outright expression to devotion or poetic enthusiasm. Likewise, I have avoided the use of capital letters for nouns and pronouns referring to Sathya Sai Baba, which may have pleased the converted but alienated other serious seekers. Some may wish to know that Baba has nevertheless blessed these writings by touching the materials on two occasions before the final draft, which he has also since given me permission to publish.

I am fortunately placed in having been shown, through indubitable insights into the meaning of many events that occurred in my life, how a guiding and protecting hand really has been with me, even during years when I would have rejected such an idea on supposedly very sound rational grounds. As will become evident from the more extraordinary happenings themselves as recounted here, they came about through Sri Sathya Sai Baba's agency—sometimes directly, sometimes less evidently.

I would also add that the facts referred to here have been continuously researched, rechecked, and corrected through a period of seven years, and the text has been reworked in the interests of precision, accuracy, and truth, time and again.

I clearly owe my deepest thanks to Sathya Sai for all the essential "subject matter" of this book—the experiences that were granted to me and that I record.

ACKNOWLEDGMENTS

Thanks are due to Sri Sathya Sai Books and Publications Trust, Prashanthi Nilayam, for quotes from books and journals by Sri Sathya Sai Baba, and from *Loving God* by Professor N. Kasturi.

Thanks also to E. Fanibunda for brief quotes from *Vision of the Divine*; to R. K. Karanjia for a quote from "*Blitz*" magazine; to Samuel Weiser (York Beach, ME) for a passage from *Sai Baba: The Ultimate Experience* by Phyllis Krystal; to Birth Day Publishing (San Diego) for brief quotes from *My Baba and I* and *Conversations With Bhagavan Sri Sathya Sai Baba* by Dr. John Hislop. Robert and Rita Bruce have provided both moral and computer support, for which I am very grateful.

Lucas Ralli (London) and Ruth Boxall read the manuscript in its earlier stages and gave good help and advice. I am also very grateful to my friend, V. K. Narasimhan (Prashanthi Nilayam) for reading and helping to correct the text and some of its factual contents. Thanks to my son, Kai Priddy, for unlimited computer aid. Above all, I have had the untiring support of my wife, Reidun, for very deep-reaching analysis and constructive critical comment, as well as perceptive spiritual, excellent editorial, and other assistance throughout the long writing process.

1

MY "PASSAGE TO INDIA"

Since being brought into the sphere of Sathya Sai Baba, I have had the great benefit of meeting a number of other people who have told me how they have been drawn to him in remarkably different ways, yet often just as unfathomably as in my case. In quite a few instances, people have come to learn how Sathya Sai has been protecting them, or how he has otherwise been involved in their lives, long before they first came to him, and sometimes before they ever heard of him.

One feature that is common to many of these accounts is the combination of subtlety and intricacy of events through which Baba draws followers to him and eventually makes himself known to them. Though no two personal histories are identical, I shall recount some typical milestones on my way, hoping to convey what I now know of the underlying "drama of destiny," in which I was the player but was certainly not the director. I shall present evidence for my confirmed belief that it was Sathya Sai Baba who, unbeknown to myself, guided me on the course of my life.

The inner journey toward India began long before I realized that it was underway or where it was leading. An "internal review" of everything informs me unequivocally that it was not simply some set of chance developments. Through about forty years, the way was strewn with events that became gradually more extraordinary and more meaningfully interrelated, especially from about age 35 onward. These included the quite common fortuitous coincidences, or events, that defy all statistical laws of averages—those that C. G.

Jung called "synchronicities"—wherein deeply-felt or long-held wishes of spiritual significance can be fulfilled as if by a miracle. It is interesting that Aldous Huxley's writings confirmed such things when he wrote that, "the divine mind may choose to communicate with finite minds either by manipulating the world of men and things in a way which the particular mind to be reached at that moment will find meaningful, or else there may be direct communication by something resembling thought transference."[1]

My fascination for India began during a period of some turmoil and suffering while at an English boarding school in my boyhood, after my father had left our family for South Africa, when the make-believe world of two books became a consolation to me. The first was a wartime edition of *Jungle John*, by John Budden, the story of a boy, told in authentic detail with the aid of pen-and-ink sketches. John was called to live with his father, a forestry officer, in the wild jungles and plains of central India, where he was looked after by a sort of guru, a most kindly elderly tribesman, wise in local lore and in the ways of animals.

The second book, *My Friend Mr. Leakey*, was about a fabulous magician who could transport himself (and any acquaintances he chose) across cities and continents at will. Among other fanciful flights, he took his young friend on a magic carpet tour of the Far East, including a visit to India, where he learned a Sanskrit formula as a magic mantra. He materialized whatever was wanted, even taking out-of-season fruits from a tree that grew on his table! This is the sort of impossibility all children wish to believe in, but it took about forty years to discover that this is not impossible!

The spiritual interests of the author, the once-famous genetics professor J. B. S. Haldane, are evident in that he once said that the Gayatri Mantra (into which it so happens that Sathya Sai Baba initiates young boys at the thread ceremony) ought to be carved on the doors of every laboratory in the world to save man from perdition. Haldane left Europe to live in India in his latter years, humorously commenting that "fifty years in socks is enough."

It is extremely difficult for most persons who have no direct experience of Sathya Sai Baba to credit what is, however, a well-documented fact: that he once very frequently used to produce, for the wonder and joy of those who were still in the process of becom-

---

[1] A. L. Huxley, *The Perennial Philosophy* (London: Triad Grafton Books, 1985), p. 49ff.

ing his devotees, edible out-of-season fruits from the so-called "wish-fulfilling tree" on a hill in Puttaparthi. Yet, like hundreds of thousands of others before me, I have myself witnessed how he is still fully active as the wish-fulfilling tree himself, producing both material and immaterial boons for those who come to him, including my wife and I. Now and again he is reported by persons whose integrity is beyond question actually to "pick" the occasional fresh fruit out of the air in the relative privacy of the Prashanthi Nilayam interview room. Of course, I do not think of Baba as a magician, amazing as his manifestations and his many types of extrasensory and paranormal abilities are in themselves, because finding this holy, universal teacher means far more to me than the realization of childhood dreams and the longing for the miraculous to come true.

Though I never forgot those books or their titles, their effect on my conscious mind gradually wore off, of course. Yet now and again during adult life I would wish to find these books again, having left them behind somewhere long ago. Occasionally while visiting England I would search through a secondhand bookshop for them.

Not until I was 42 years old, in 1978, did I again come across *Jungle John*. By then, on my search for truth I had more or less emerged fairly unscathed from many years of intellectual discipline, which had burdened my mind with all kinds of science and philosophy, Marxism and philosophical anthropology, existential psychoanalysis, metascience, and so on—an almost endless list. One day, I was in a bookshop in Stratford-upon-Avon when something prompted me to think that, if I were to reach out for the very first volume I could lay hands on, it would be that book.

I reached out a hand blindly and—believe it or not—it was *Jungle John*! It was a fine, first-edition, hardcover volume. Its appearing just after coming to mind may seem to many to be no more than coincidence. To see it as evidence of the workings of a higher power would, for many people, be regarded as make-believe. For me, however, this instant connection of thought and its literal manifestation fitted remarkably into a larger pattern of events that were evolving in my life. At the time, such occurrences helped me to sustain some faith in the possibility of interventions in worldly affairs by supernatural agency. I never entirely lost openness to the mystical, despite all the ingenuities of scientific arguments.

That book proved to hold true-to-life descriptions of Indian life and an intensity of subtle reminiscences for me. Though the naturally inexplicable manner of its appearance was perhaps of minor significance in itself, it was one of many such incidents that began to build up, one upon another, in subsequent years. (And the moment I wrote the word "many" in the above sentence, the phone rang. It was a friend who wanted to tell me of a book called *Miracles Are My Visiting Cards*, by Erlendur Haraldsson. The above sentence's meaning as a whole was therefore instantly and concretely demonstrated, confirming the sentence I was writing when it occurred! Haraldsson's book deals with miracles by Sathya Sai Baba.)

Due to my parents' breakup, and so I could finish my schooling, I was taken in by an aunt and uncle because they felt a duty, being my godparents. They were Anglicans and made me attend church weekly. The grammar school environment and my own observations caused me to lose faith in much of the Christian doctrine. Once, when I was very confused and downhearted about all this, I found that all I could pray for was to not be one of those who, according to a Canon Collins who preached at Hornchurch, would be too hard-hearted to recognize Jesus if he were to come again. Thereafter I had a dream that seemed to promise something so amazing that my spirits were lifted greatly. I can no longer properly recall its contents, but I have somehow been increasingly prompted to recall that I was visited by some figure who reassured me and said that he, Jesus' Father, is himself here on Earth and that I would see him one day. However, as clear and intense as the experience was, I soon realized instinctively that if I were to tell my aunt or anyone in the church, I would be corrected, possibly ridiculed, and the dream might even be taken as an evil and demonic visitation. So I never told anyone about it.

The memory of that reassuring and amazing dream faded; maybe I could not really believe in it myself—but I first recalled it decades later, some time after Sai Baba spoke to an elderly gentleman who was present with us during an interview. Turning toward us where we sat together, Baba said to him, "I have been with you for forty years." The man literally started in surprise! Baba knew that he had read about Shirdi Sai Baba forty years previously in a book, which I think was *The Life and Teachings of the Masters of the Far East*. Baba began to quote the title, too, whereupon the astonished man remembered and joined in to recite it together with him.

While not ostensibly addressing himself to me, Baba's words reactivated my memory. It so happened that my boyhood dream had occurred very close to forty years prior to that time. Persons have often reported how Baba says something to someone that also applies with equal meaning to another within earshot. This he has sometimes confirmed later. He even has addressed people who can make no sense whatever of his words, while someone beside them immediately sees its meaning and knows very well that it is addressed specifically to them. I have not so far had the opportunity to ask Baba personally about my boyhood dream, for the time with him is precious and only for vital matters.

The first time I heard speak of the Sai Baba avatar,[2] to the best of my knowledge, was when I was at sea. Likewise, my first social encounter with the East came at age 17, when I joined the British Merchant Navy as an apprentice deck officer in 1953. As my mother was ill and unable to house or keep me, going to sea seemed to be the only safe option for getting board, lodging, and perhaps developing future prospects.

My first encounter with the Indian crew on this ship was felicitous! While boarding the tanker *London Glory*, riding at anchor in the Mersey, a traveling companion and I were helped by the assembled Indian crew in such a genuinely loving manner that I can still feel the afterglow! I think the lasting effect of that heartfelt welcome illustrates how loving friendship that springs from natural spirituality can strike an undying chord, as it did in me. The Indians' interest in us, and their blessings for our futures, was quite unprecedented in my brief experience, and it really helped to allay my misgivings and nervous anticipations about what lay ahead.

We were asked if we were Christians, to which I could reply "yes" with some truth. Though I had shunned the Anglican church once I was away from the care of my godparent aunt, I still felt at-

---

[2] *Avatar* here refers to an incarnation of Divinity in human form. God descends to Earth. The word "avatar" is derived from the Sanskrit word "to descend." Indian history records the existence of many avatars, major and minor, from the very short-lived to the very long-lived. Of these, sixteen are the major ones of the present cycle of the ages. Many Indian scriptural texts discuss the nature of avatars, classifying in much detail the various types of superhuman powers and miracles they may exercise, their qualifications, their tasks and activities, and the mysteries of their births into deserving families. Among the most prominent of the ten greatest avatars generally recognized in Indian tradition are Narasimha, Vamana, Rama, and Krishna.

tached to the essentials of the teachings of Christ at that time, though not to very much to Christian dogma.

The stewards were Goanese Christians, and, apart from a few Muslims and Sikhs, the deck crew were mostly Hindus, all of whom bore themselves with an air of humble dignity and respectfulness for others, which I realized was not mere servility to *sahibs*, as the English officers still saw it in 1953, despite several years of Indian independence.

It was soon clear to me that Indians were very religiously inclined, both in worship and in daily practice. Strange as the mixture of religions aboard ship was, there were no conflicts, and I learned that Indians are extremely tolerant of others' opinions. They also made me feel at home wherever I met them on my duties about the vessel. I would be invited to "down tools" and share a rice and curry, crouching about a communal plate on the teak deck near their cooking galley—quite unlike the somewhat formal dinners in the officers' mess. I now and again visited them in my leisure hours for tea, sweetmeats, and some Indian music.

The best English-speaker among them was a young man of about 20 called Hari, with whom I became friends on account of a shared interest in Aldous Huxley. He held a B.A. in English from an Indian university. As I was in charge of the ship's library—a ragged collection by charity of "The Flying Angel Mission to Seamen"—he asked me to lend him some mind-improving literature for his leisure hours. Unfortunately, those who made the company rules assumed that all foreign crew members were potential thieves and thus banned them from the services of the lending library.

The Second Officer saw me exchanging books one day and soon ordered me to restrict lending, telling me that the service was only for officers. I explained that the borrower was above suspicion and that he had a B.A. in English. This was my mistake. The Second Officer's pride was badly wounded. He swore in anger that he might just as well be a "BF," too ("bloody fool"). He strongly forbade me to lend out even a tattered volume.

To save Hari's feelings—and to avoid unpleasantness myself— I told him nothing and still lent to him on the quiet by taking books down to his cabin. We were not close, but there was genuine friendship. He told me once that there was a "wise man" aboard the ship, a yogi of whom he spoke with real respect. He said that this guru had spoken of me in a positive way and had said that I could meet him if I wished. As I recall it, the claim was made that this man could do things such as see people's spiritual natures, read minds, and even foresee future events. Hari would not tell me, however, which of the crew this person was. If I wished to see him, then I would find out; otherwise he would not tell me.

I was naturally curious, though quite unconvinced of the claims, the likes of which I had come across only in fiction. The matter was not pressed, but Hari mentioned it a few times casually later on. He told me about yogic breathing to the mental accompaniment of *So-Ham* (literally "He is I") saying *So* (meaning "He" or "Divinity") on the intake of breath, and *Ham* (meaning the individual "I") on the out-breath, as a means of reaching spiritual wisdom, if it is done nonstop. I soon objected that this would stop one from doing anything else whatever. He replied along the lines that the brain could handle its other tasks at the same time, for it has a potential double-function. This I tried, but I did not find it as easy and enjoyable as he said it was, and—since it gave no results for me other than tedium—I soon decided it was rather a "mindless" practice.

At that time I did not understand that it was supposed precisely to make one "mindless," by stilling both the rational and irrational processes of thought so that the suprarational could enter awareness. Most of this I assume he had from the supposed yogi, who may or may not have been instructing him to pass these ideas on to me.

I also recall my skepticism when Hari told me about the Indian concept of "avatars," and especially that there had been many of these supposed incarnations of God. Though I no longer accepted the likelihood of Christ having performed miracles, I could just about agree, after some argument, that he might be regarded as an incarnation of a divine spirit. The only doctrine I knew then was that Christ was the son of God, but that he was not himself God, who was essentially either the Father or the Holy Spirit.

I was quite unprepared to cope, therefore, with the sophisticated conception of avatarhood that Hari espoused. He held that both Krishna, Rama, and at least several others were actual incarnations of the Holy Spirit, having come down to Earth, as God, by voluntarily taking on various human forms. He asked me whether it were not so that Christ was born a human being and was thus a "son of God." Then he added that, although Christ's incarnation was surely similar to that of Indian avatars, the Indian avatars were actually born as God Himself in human form. Sathya Sai teaches just this, that Christ's realization of unity with the Father God was attained during his life and was thus unlike the cases of Rama and Krishna, who were born as full avatars of God.

This view provoked me, I recall, because it somehow put Hinduism above the religion with which I was familiar, despite my having already largely fallen by its wayside. It rather implied that India and Indians were better, or somehow superior or privileged spiritually. This I think I would not admit, though privately it confused me somewhat. Incidentally, his own name, Hari told me, was of one of the forms of God (of Vishnu or Narayana), which was clearly why he—a Brahmin—was offended by the English nickname of "Harry," which I found easier to recall but to which he flatly refused to answer.

I had almost forgotten about that young Indian seaman telling me eagerly that there were those on the ship who believed that God Himself had taken on human form in India again. I do not remember if this alleged avatar's name was given me, but I was told that one could best visit him from Madras and, if one had the good fortune to find him at the village where he mostly stayed, one might see him perform many wonders, such as reading people's thoughts and producing physical miracles. In those years Sathya Sai Baba is known to have moved about unpredictably near Bangalore, Madras, and elsewhere in South India. Well, the idea of having my thoughts read like an open book did not exactly appeal to me! Besides, I privately scoffed at the idea of going all the way to India, then trawling the villages for some elusive person, of whose abilities—and especially of whose divinity—I was most skeptical anyway.

I did not have the good fortune of going to India at that time, for I was still a 17-year-old with no money and stuck on that ship, though several of the kindly Indians invited me to visit them at home in Madras, Goa, or Bombay, assuring me I would love India's spiritual people and that everyone would be kind and pleased to house me. Not until thirty years later was I able to see for myself that what was promised was still much the case in India! Sai Baba has often fulfilled, by many different means, the longings of persons to visit him, even when to all outward appearances their making the journey seemed an impossibility. Knowing what I do now, I can only reflect that he somehow would have made the opportunity arise, had I been ready and burning with yearning faith. Wiser after the event, of course, we can all always say that fate had decreed that it was not yet to have been!

That I could not accept the idea of a truly wise man, let alone one aboard the same ship, was largely due to my already being a victim of the Western egocentric belief in the superiority of European civilization, which overwhelmingly rejected all such Eastern claims as superstitious nonsense. Being an unwitting product of this unilluminating background, being "born ignorant" about yogis and realized saints, so to speak, I probably lost a chance of shortening the long, painful search on which everyone is embarked, even despite themselves.

At one point Hari gave me the guru's message, or at least reported his words, that I would one day see God. I recall vaguely that this seemed both wonderfully flattering and yet somehow preposterous. Nonetheless, this prediction has proven to have had real meaning. Even though I have since then had ample proof that accurate foreknowledge of certain specific events is possible for some people, I naturally still look back in wonder as to how far the holy man on the ship was aware that I was destined to be slowly drawn toward the avatar, Sri Sathya Sai Baba. (I must even now sometimes wonder if the "wise man" might not have been Hari himself.)

What is more, Hari thought it would be a good idea for me to seek out this young holy man, so that I could be the first person to write a book about him to make him known to the English-speaking world. Not only did I not think I could write such a book, but I pooh-poohed the idea altogether. Nevertheless, here I am at last, writing that book, I feel, if somewhat belatedly perhaps!

My surreptitious book-lending to Hari was discovered when the Second Officer made a surprise check on the library. The library keys were taken from me, and books could only be exchanged thereafter under surveillance. No longer could I save Hari's feelings. Having lacked the courage to tell him the Second Officer's orders openly and explain the racist reasons given, my behavior must have seemed very odd. He failed to grasp the situation I was in, for I had by now been ordered formally by the Captain to avoid all contact with the crew except when strictly necessary on the job. As a first line of punishment, my main source of pleasure on that vessel, my precious guitar, would be impounded for the rest of the voyage if I continued to sneak off aft to the crew's quarters after dark.

Hari was naturally very upset by this discrimination and, bit by bit, he urged me to oppose the whole ship's system. Before long it was a question of either that or our friendship; he insisted on me taking a stand for what was right. Faced with this dilemma, I felt weak at heart and in spirit before the formidable challenge: one boy against the entrenched views of a dozen adult officers, on whom I was dependent for everything and under whose definitive orders I must sail. Even in the Merchant Navy, I knew that refusing to comply with Captain's orders was formally defined as "mutiny," and I had no inkling of my actual rights, if any, for these were a mystery ruled over by the Company and the Captain. The result was really a foregone conclusion: I capitulated.

That was the end, virtually, of that spiritual companionship on my first apparent "passage to India" (recalling here the essential contents of E. M. Forster's famous novel about India's mystery, spirituality, and also its interracial problems, *A Passage to India*). Some months later the Indian crew were relieved by a new complement, and I was never able to take up any of the various genuine invitations, as the nearest our ship's passage took me to India during its far-flung voyages was Colombo in Ceylon.

Shipboard loneliness and great distances really did make the heart grow fonder, and it also added to the intensity of longings. I had to learn a good deal about how to live with myself when cast on my own mental resources. In the fifteen months during which I had daily contact, however curtailed, with a variety of Indian people, I feel that something of their being, some of the essence of their ancient culture was subtly awakened in me, perhaps by some deeper affinity. I could follow the idea, so rooted in Indian life, that whatever one's country or background, each person somehow shares in the selfsame spirit or higher soul and thus always deserves others' respect. The loving kindness I could feel in some of them, and see in their faces, imparted in a natural way a genuine sense of spirituality.

All this added to my sense of personal expansion and of becoming more of a "man of the world," in a literal sense. More important, I had my first glimpse into the heart of another culture. At that impressionable and formative stage in my development, something of the all-inclusive spirit of Hinduism rubbed off on me. I now realize that those who grow up in India, as did Hari, are able to share in the richest and most ancient religious culture known in history, even though millions of modern Indians have turned their backs on the values of their own culture.

In doubt as to whether or not I should include my early meeting with Indian culture in this present chapter, under the heading

"My India," I went out to consult my wife who was clearing out the cellar. As she was cutting up a large cardboard carton that we had once used for packing books, I caught sight of a tiny piece of paper among the scraps and dust in the carton. On it was printed, in capitals, the single word, INDIA. I recognized at once that it came from the spine of a well-worn, wartime Penguin paperback copy of *A Passage to India*, which I had long possessed!

I cannot explain it, but this find released a great surge of emotion within me. Many long-buried memories of times and people I have known across the world mingled in an inner panorama of both sadness and joy. Besides, this "coincidence" was an unmistakable *leela* (literally, divine "sport" or "play"), which decided that I should include this chapter as "My Passage to India."

Though I had been tempted to travel as a seeker to India in the 1960s, I did not, partly out of a sense that it would be self-indulgent to travel as a mere tourist and live in a poor country on local resources when I had nothing useful to offer in return, partly due to my ties at home, and not least due to a chronic lack of funds. In 1968 an American student called on me. He had heard from a professor at Oslo University, where I was finishing my philosophy degree, that I played the sitar and was interested in India. He eventually told me about a certain Sathya Sai Baba, insisting that this holy man often went out on the sands and materialized golden statuettes, rings, and so on.

I was a budding (or even blooming) Marxist at the time, and I thought he was either putting me on or else was slightly deranged. Perhaps he simply wanted to make himself interesting. I politely ignored his accounts. I remember clearly some of his words: "Why don't you go there. I'm sure he'd make you a ring—or anything else you want!" The very idea of leaving my wife and baby son behind while going all the way to India at great expense for something like that seemed absurd, for it was so clear that rings could not just be made out of thin air! In the end, he gave up, saying that he could see I didn't believe him and thought him cracked. He did not visit us again, so I suppose he gave me up as a hopeless case. In any case, my *karma* was evidently not ripe. It now seems as if Baba was playing with me. Sai Baba of Shirdi sometimes insisted, too, that those he was drawing to himself were like chickens with a string attached to their legs, by which he slowly but inevitably pulled them in!

Now I can sympathize with that poor fellow—whose name I promptly forgot—and his effort to convey his priceless secret to me, for I have since been in his position time and again. In fact, very few of my longstanding acquaintances have much or anything at all to do with me now, apparently on account of my incredible "beliefs"!

One further incident: around 1980 I was lecturing at Oslo University on Spinoza and discussing his view that miracles cannot occur, because that would be a contravention of the laws of nature that God has instituted. An elderly Indian gentleman attended that one lecture (midway in a fourteen-lecture series). Afterward he came up to me and politely told me that he disagreed with Spinoza, as he had seen many miracles in India, on a daily basis! Concerned with my teaching duty of preparing for exams, I politely explained how it was a matter of definition—what some call miracles may be an expression of as-yet-unknown natural laws.

This sweet but somewhat imprecise gentleman tried to explain about materializations he had experienced and asked if I believed in that. I answered that I had not had that experience, so I could not myself believe in it—but I did not show any interest in finding out either. It may well be he took this implicit rejection to mean that I thought he was either a naive fool or simply telling an untruth. Presumably, he gave up on me at that point. Once again the opportunity had come to me to find out about the maker of these miracles. There is little room for doubt that the gentleman was referring to Sathya Sai Baba, for he must be about the only person whose materialization miracles can actually be observed daily. By this time I was fascinated by all paranormal phenomena and was open toward investigating them, surprising as this may seem, considering how I was unable to pick up the trail when it came through the unexpected guise of a supposed "student."

As far back as human memory reaches, and doubtless very much further than historical research is capable of establishing through observation of records and dating of artifacts, India has had an unbroken continuity of religiosity and deep spirituality that has produced countless people recognized as realized saints and Sons of God of the highest order. This has always exerted a subtle pull on many serious seekers from everywhere, a numinous enchantment that bears no relation to merely mundane purposes and goals.

Today the intense, soul-magnetic power of the spiritual love of Sathya Sai Baba, moving in previously quite unheard-of ways, is causing a huge and ever-swelling pilgrimage, surpassing by a large measure anything recorded in known history. Sathya Sai certainly appears to be the very fulfillment of the promises of a whole history of Indian mysticism for this age. The "open secret" that he is revealing judiciously, to opening hearts globally, is that his supreme ability bestows such experiences of love and joy as to actually transform us from our core and lead us on to greater conscious realization of our origin and most ultimate destiny.

WHEN THE SOIL IS READY

If or when it comes, the "thirst for liberation" surely arises in many ways, depending on one's background or culture. Since meeting Sathya Sai Baba I have become convinced that anyone who has had spiritual yearnings, whether within the context of a religion or not, may be assured that these will eventually be fulfilled. My own yearnings began at last to flower steadily from about my 50th year, as I had come to be much more cognizant of the process in which I had been involved. My perspective on the previous events of my life was marvelously shifted, bit by bit, by Sai Baba's agency, until my mind and all it held became refocused, and I saw many a previously-unseen thread and the hand that has held them. I now also know personally many others who have experienced the same.

> When the thirst for liberation and the revelation of one's reality is acute, a strange and mysterious force in Nature will begin operating. When the soil is ready, the seed appears from somewhere! The spiritual Guru will be alerted and the thirst will get quenched.[1]

Sathya Sai Baba has drawn me along the way of realization, mostly through various other means than the "normal" personal contact or conversation. Plenty of good grounds exist to say that similar experiences are open to anyone who truly wishes them and is willing to

[1] Sathya Sai Baba, *Sathya Sai Vahini* (Prashanthi Nilayam: Sri Sathya Sai Books & Publications Trust, n.d.), p. 97.

engage in the spiritual experiment with full commitment, even though one may be unable to travel to India.

Here I shall disclose spiritual facts that I once would not completely believe could occur, through lack of proof at the time. Please know that I am choosing my every word here with extreme caution and on the basis of experience and critical examination of many, thoroughly-investigated facts. These facts have been manifested for me through an increasingly-absorbing relation to Baba, who is now to me the greatest of incarnate spiritual beings. However, the documentation of his huge and unprecedented life and works, and their vast and demonstrable significance in relation to the history of avatars in the scriptures of the Hindus and the other main religions, I leave to others.

Spiritual seeking can occur in many guises. Though we may all differ in externals, such as circumstances of birth and the course of our lives in society and the world, it is "the internals" that draw us universally toward spiritual opportunities and truths. My need to know how to discover the true self grew out of the natural desire to know and understand life and the many and variable experiences to which that leads. There is always a temptation in memoir-writing of eliminating one's own earlier self-contradictions. Though I went through more than my fair share of them, the danger of boring the reader with them seems great, so I'll be brief.

By my 20s, a constant shifting of schools, homes, social classes, and occupations already had made me an outsider, and I had probably gone through more self-questioning than was normal. The people I knew in the 1950s and 1960s mostly viewed any kind of thought about spiritual searching as abnormal anyway, as strangely threatening or even somewhat crazy. I had not been a believer in any religious creed or church for years. In my mid-20s, I moved to Norway where I subsequently studied social science and philosophy. I was keenly interested in all the world's cultures and civilizations, not excluding accounts of religious experience, Zen mysticism, and a wide range of esoteric theories and phenomena, past and present.

A totally mind-shattering and subsequently most wonderful and intensely ecstatic experience befell me one day, as if from out of the blue. Much could be said on the subject, as it is an almost entirely misunderstood one and thus very controversial, but I do not believe doing so would appreciably enlighten anyone who has not actually had the very same experience. I am certain that no words can capture the vital nature and truth of such an experience of transcendental consciousness. I mention it because, without its having befallen me, I cannot guess how I might otherwise have been able to realize the value of pursuing spiritual development and exerting any measure of the determination, and one-pointedness that such a course eventually requires. The experience probably did not improve me much outwardly, if at all, but inwardly it altered my life in various quite crucial ways. I could simply no longer manage to regard normal worldly experience as the be-all and end-all of life. Having been forced to see my usual self and the mind literally from outside, with merciless clarity, through knowing and temporarily becoming the sheer all-pervasiveness of a sanctified joy, peace, and unrestricted awareness that underlies everything, I later came to know how that experience both consoled me and yet set me apart. Like a two-edged sword, it strengthened my insight, yet isolated me for many years in loneliness, for I had the burden of both incommunicable experience and a certain spiritual pride.

When I fell asleep the night after that experience, I dreamed vividly that I was climbing the last ridge toward the top of Mount Everest, where high winds blew across the huge heavens. Then at last I stood on the summit, but there was a final mound, a few feet in height, which I did not ascend. A voice of perfect authority, resonance, and certainty, which I knew immediately as God's own, said, "I have brought you here, but you must find the way down yourself."

As to the last mound on the peak of the world, I later remembered having read that early expeditions to Everest had taken vows with Tibetan lamas at a monastery below to place food offerings to God at the foot of a mound that they would find on the peak! On no account were they to mount it, for it was revered as "the home of God." In retrospect I can see how risky a process my "descent" from that transcendental experience was, and very painful too, especially as—day in and day out—I wanted only to reascend. From then on, dreams and their many possible meanings always held great interest for me.

For about two years after this decisive event I became intensely involved in attempting to discover a means of regaining the universal blissful awareness in which I had been immersed and dissolved. But various events, including the birth of my son and other dramatic dreams, were fairly decisive in helping me to understand that "the soil was not ready" and that I had yet to work my way through many more of the challenges of life and shape myself through them, before I might hope to benefit properly from transcendental transports.

Though I had "been and seen," I definitely had not conquered. How to do so became an obsession, though even this did not cause me to do very much in the way of spiritual practices. For example, I joined the international Subud movement which originated in Java. As I learned more about it and went through the "opening" ceremony, I found that the members regarded Pak Subuh as a guru (*pak* means "father"), and I observed clearly that, despite all the denials, it was in practice run on authoritarian paternal lines and my interest quickly cooled to zero. Accepting a father-figure type guru was *certainly* not in my line at all! I left the movement for this and other reasons. This incident helps demonstrate that I was not seeking any "father substitute." Moreover, I have since learned how all earthly fathers are only imperfect earthly substitutes for the perfect Divine Father of All.

After I had been studying, researching, and teaching philosophy and social science for about ten years in Norway, my personal search for the meaning of life seemed to come to a dead end. The mundane and mental world of the Western university intellectual environment, with its ingrained and universal assumption of materialism or physicalism, is not in the least bit conducive to spiritual life or to real philosophical investigation. It is difficult even today for people to grasp how very spiritually arid modern societies actually were back in the 1960s. This was most excessive in Norway, where an oppressive mental climate clouded all, and one was universally regarded as frivolous or even lunatic if one was even open-mindedly nonjudgmental toward things "esoteric"—such as, say, the theory of reincarnation, spiritual energies or the idea of an unseen reality beyond physical appearances. Were it not for my marrying a Norwegian and receiving a son, I would surely never have settled here.

Though everyone is unique, many people today are still going through a fairly typical process of trying to rediscover the spirituality lost to modern civilization, just as I have had to do. I had long since despaired of the various confused dogmas of religious exclusivity, of oppressive orthodoxy, and of serious shortcomings of one sort or another in all established Western churches and movements. For many years I delved into Western science, philosophy, culture, and art, which, however, never sufficiently satisfied the underlying desire for living, knowing, and experiencing joy that I came to see as the underlying spiritual motor in all human endeavor.

Also, various schools of esoteric Buddhism had become available in the West and interested me a good deal. On the basis of what I had myself already witnessed in full clarity at least once, however, I could not help but find their followers either overly-sophisticated or insistent on mystificatory mumbo jumbo, and sometimes both at once! Then I discovered Madame Blavatsky and the various esoteric traditions she inspired. Even though much of theosophy, and its many sorts of New Age offspring, is either impracticable, misguided, or lacking in complete authenticity, her works did cast a searchlight on the loss of insight of much of Christian and other religious doctrine.

In retrospect I know that a decisive signpost pointing out my future direction was Romain Rolland's biographies of Paramahamsa Ramakrishna and Vivekananda, which I first read in 1970, when I was 34. The wonderful story of Ramakrishna's life was the key that turned me toward religion again, even despite the guru-disciple relationship between Ramakrishna and his followers. My readiness to investigate the question of whether gurus really knew and could teach anything worthwhile represented a turnabout from practically all that I had been involved in previously. Due to an underlying faith that came of the transcendental experience that had thrust itself upon me, I felt it most likely that somewhere there must be people who really did have superior knowledge and who had attained stable conscious powers far beyond anything recognized by our sciences or academic intellectuals today. Moreover, I had received a clear understanding of what such people would be like . . . a basic perception reinforced many years later by my first coming into quite close contact with such a person.

After all, nothing short of totally universal, nonsectarian, and dogma-free spirituality would appeal to me, although I did not know this at the time. I knew of no one who taught any such approach authoritatively, although I had gleaned many a spiritual book and examined the peculiar ideas and antics of a variety of would-be gurus.

Ramakrishna's example demonstrated that ideal to my great satisfaction. It was clear that the established churches of most religions were each dependent on parroting their exclusive doctrine, all so institutionally rigidified or dried up as to be stifling to the discerning mind. The vivifying example of Ramakrishna's life, though quite unattainable in its saintliness for me, nevertheless bore out how essential it is never to deny one's own experiences and, rather than rely on any sort of catechism, to pin one's faith exclusively on Divinity.

Eventually the recognition forced itself upon me that, if I were to get anywhere, I needed to find someone who was self-realized, or at least highly spiritual. What I sought to learn was evidently not to be found in any university or by ordinary means.

Because of my own transcendental experience, it seemed almost certain from the start that the ecstasies reported of Ramakrishna must have been genuine. I also saw that practitioners of at least several fully developed spiritual approaches existed, in India, yet the devotional tradition was difficult for me to adjust to mentally. I found it fascinating to read about India's saints. Above all, though, Ramakrishna's simple, loving wisdom and deep vision of universality strongly moved something in me.

The problem was, of course, how to strengthen my faith in theory and practice and move toward some realization of divinity. I was virtually convinced that there was no one remotely like a true spiritual teacher in Norway and, for all I knew, there may have been none in the whole of Europe. This was in the early 1970s, the era of widely-known Eastern gurus. Many were actually selling spiritual truth for money, which to me was the "first sign of badness." I had reliable information from friends about various Buddhist and Hindu gurus who practiced seduction with female aspirants—even quite openly at times—adjusting their versions of the doctrines to accommodate it all! In short, what Ramakrishna warned against as the two great spiritual pitfalls—the lusts for "women and gold"— were part of some "gurus" very stock in trade!

For a long time it looked as though the only solution was to take refuge in the adage that the best guru is oneself. Since the passing over of Ramakrishna in 1886, it seemed that no religious figure of any comparable stature had arisen. Little did I know how far this was from the truth! More and more, I felt that having an enlightened saint as a teacher must be a great advantage, even a necessity, for reaching a stable inner illumination and the many boons it gives.

I began to follow at least some of the spiritual guidelines discernable in Ramakrishna's words, if only fitfully, I admit. Though the account of Ramakrishna's amazing doings and sayings could bring the warmth of happy tears to my eyes, nevertheless I felt that the standards of purity, selflessness, tolerance, and seemingly inhuman endurance he set were inordinately high. By comparison, I had to suffer the discovery of how feeble my capacity was for detachment from worldly goods and desires, especially when considering making any real sacrifices. Still, I hoped that a genuine guru in the spirit of Ramakrishna might come forward from somewhere.

The first sign came some months later that year, where I met some people in London who had just become followers of an Indian swami. This person was, it seemed, often clairvoyant and very unusual in many other ways, if their accounts were true. An old friend of mine was also charmed by him. Therefore, I decided to visit him. I went to the address at which he was staying, but no amount of knocking on the door brought any response, even though I had been assured that there was someone there. My time in London ran out, and I had to return to Norway, my family, and work. However, I occasionally meditated on meeting this guru, and I sent out many deeply-felt mental requests for that privilege.

Nearly one year later I was involved in arranging a charity concert in Oslo. Much to my surprise and pleasure, the visiting band from England all turned out to be devotees of that same swami. Since I was living in a large house at the time, I offered to house them for their week's visit. This Indian swami was not well known, nor did he have many followers. Unlike the gurus of whom we could read, he carefully avoided prominence and publicity, and no guarantees at all could be given that I could meet him, even when I next came to London.

None of his followers seemed to doubt that the swami sometimes displayed considerable psychic powers. It was rumored that he no longer slept at night, only meditated. He was always talking about spiritual matters and the divine, calling on God in various forms, and sometimes going into deep trances. He was an accredited swami of the Ramakrishna Math, a very genuine and selfless service organization that has international branches.

Another year passed without any chance of my visiting this swami. Doubts as to whether he really could be an illumined master alternated with longing for advancement on the mystic way by a God-sent yogi. Being of a down-to-earth and yet questioning turn of mind—and with my training in critical thinking—I thought much about how I might discover if this swami was authentic. If he were an advanced yogi, he must have certain powers, which by all accounts his followers seemed to have witnessed. So I set up a difficult test of at least one of his alleged powers—the ability to read minds—a test that I never mentioned to anyone at all. The test was that, if I should meet him, he should tell me without my asking him, exactly why my call at his door had not been answered when I had come to see him two years previously.

At the same time, and at least partly as an experiment in devotion, I directed my heartfelt inner yearnings for further spiritual enlightenment toward this swami. Finally, during a gathering known as a *sankirtan,* at which there were readings, singing, and talks, I at last met the swami in London. He welcomed me and asked me to sit on a cushion near him. He was facing the group of his followers, about forty of whom were present.

Soon after I arrived he pointed to a picture of the Indian saint Shirdi Sai Baba on the wall beside him, saying, "That is God, do you know?!" Inadvertently I replied, "Yes," an answer that perplexed me then, and for that matter, still does! I had previously only heard a little about Shirdi Baba from the other devotees and had seen his picture.

The swami's behavior was certainly unusual. Sometimes he talked very intensely, often leaping confusingly between religious subjects and personal comments to his followers. He appeared to go into a state of trance or *samadhi,* his eyes rolling upward to show only the whites, his speech becoming disconnected and slurred. He cast wild glances about, seeming to be looking through everything and everyone. It was quite a disturbing experience. Then he would be most charming or funny. At one point he referred to his own behavior as "divine madness," which was what Ramakrishna had always called his own intensity of longing for ecstatic absorption in the Godhead.

Without my noticing it, he soon brought up the subject of my first attempt to visit him. He said that he had been ill at that time and, besides, I could not have accepted the group then, either. In fact, I was told by others, he had been fasting for about 45 days and had contracted influenza at the very time I had called at the house. That he passed the test I had set, which I quite forgot throughout my visit, occurred to me only days later.

Before I left my first meeting with the swami, two things of special note occurred. Suddenly, during a general talk, he looked up with a most unusual expression, as if seeing through inner space, and slowly said: "A powerful Indian is looking after you. Very powerful indeed!" I had no idea as to what this meant then, taking it perhaps to be an indirect allusion to himself; that he perhaps was hinting that he had taken me under his care. This was actually a mistaken interpretation because, over a decade later, various events, which I shall describe in due course, established beyond any reasonable doubt that it was Sathya Sai Baba who was indicated.

I seemed to get no chance to collect my thoughts and question the swami to clear up ambiguities or elicit straight answers from him, such was the dominance of his presence amid his group of followers. At one point he let out an awful and soul-piercing scream of pain, the likes of which I have never heard before or since. He cried out: "Such a long, long time!" He was actually very upset, but after a while this passed, and he said, "Back to normal," in a funny way. I felt it had to do with me somehow, and it was rather disconcerting, to say the least.

The swami also took me a bit aside and told me some all too flattering stuff about myself, concerning a past life and future events in which I would have liked to believe. Nevertheless, I was torn between attraction to his fascinating presence and nagging uncertainty about the extent and reliability of his spiritual competence. He was not at all what I had expected; he seemed just too "spaced out," as a friend of mine put it. That night I awoke from a very clear but brief dream in which the swami came to me, spread his arms wide, and said directly to me: "You need look no further. Here I am, I am the master!"

But I was not ready for such a guru after all, I decided. This was too much of a good thing! Despite this dream visitation and the subtle way in which *"swamiji"* (as he was always addressed) passed my predetermined test, I was put off by his dramatic, irrational style. Some of his followers seemed to me to form a too-passive captive audience and trusted too blindly in anything he said. Yet the meaning of all the peculiar things he had said and done in those few hours took a long while to mature in my mind. I did not visit the swami again for six years.

3

LOST AND FOUND?

In the spring of 1979, I visited friends in London who still followed the swami, and I accepted an invitation to meet him again, not having seen him for nearly six years. The atmosphere was as intense and unusual as it had been on my previous visit. The swami came very close to me and looked into my eyes from only a few inches away, which gave me a peculiar feeling; then he said that I was torn between England and Norway, duty to my mother, and duty to my son. This was true indeed, being the very nub of many related problems that caused me great difficulties. I was certain he had no normal way of knowing this so well.

He asked me to hold a bunch of incense sticks while someone else lit them, adding in a commanding tone, "Don't drop any!" I found this provocative and unnecessary. As before, he still dominated all around him. Not a minute later, I swapped the incenses to the other hand, and one stick fell on the floor. The swami had his back to me, making an Indian sweetmeat, but he straight away said, "You dropped one?" This caught me off balance, and I had no answer. I decided I would not let this happen again, whatever he said, all the while puzzling over what had happened.

Five or ten minutes later, the swami was rapidly moving among those present, serving food, when he suddenly and very swiftly turned to point at the floor at my feet, exactly as another stick of incense fell from my hand to that spot! He gave me a penetrating and knowing look, as if to say, "Didn't I tell you so?" It took me some time to realize what had occurred. I was certainly astonished and rather disturbed by this apparent usurpation of my will, which I had in a sense pitted against his. What actually happened, whether it was mind-reading or what, I cannot say.

In accordance with the custom, I, like everyone else, had brought a bunch of flowers that the swami had said we ought to offer to the Divine Mother. He had directed me to put the bunch I brought before the house's shrine, saying, "Let them stay there!" I had felt a bit "bossed about" then, too, and my ego was quietly preparing to rear its head. When the children's part of the program was over, the adults threw the flowers they had brought to the children. I reached for "my" bunch, too, but they were daffodils with strong stalks, so instead of throwing them, I handed the bunch to one of the children running out of the room. But one flower was dropped in the hand-over. Just a second too late, the swami came rushing from an alcove where he had been sitting, to try to stop me from handing over the flowers. In a trice, he pointed at the flower that had fallen, as if it were a calamity, which created a dramatic atmosphere. Then he shrugged his shoulders expressively, saying he was very sorry, but it was too late. He gave me no further explanation, and I was too nonplused to think of asking for one. It is sufficient here to note that, months later, something causing me much emotional pain happened, in which a yellow flower was peculiarly involved.

Later I sat on a sofa, close to where he sat on the floor. He sang songs, accompanying himself on the harmonium and created a loving and also very inspiring atmosphere, spicing his singing with hilarious comments or sudden advice to a devotee. At one point he asked a lady present to read from a book about Sai Baba. The reading contained accounts of someone who had been revived from death by Sathya Sai Baba. I had not then heard much about Sathya Sai Baba being a present reincarnation of Shirdi Sai Baba, who had passed on in 1918, and I tended to confuse the two figures. Sai Baba was just the name of yet another Indian saint to me then.

Most of the swami's long-term followers were known by a spiritual name that he had given them. This is a common practice in India, one of the purposes being to perceive oneself more spiritually and to identify with the divine within by being reminded every time anyone says your name. I had once wished to have such a name, and I knew which name I would choose. After reading Paramahansa Yogananda's *Autobiography of a Yogi* I was fascinated with his account of the Himalayan saint known as Babaji. Without giving any notice, the swami looked up from his music and announced, "Bob can be Baba."

Never had I told anyone at all which name I would have liked. However, the sound of the name Baba is close to Bob, and I knew that the swami apparently now and again gave names sounding like one's own, the most striking instance being a devotee called Harry Ball who had received the spiritual namesake "Hari Bol" (i.e., "God's Name"). Later, the swami joked around with my name, writing that Bob Priddy could become Baba Shriddy. Later he modified this to Baba Shirdi. He thus linked me not to Babaji, but to Sai Baba yet again, which I now see was another indication of things to come.

People in the ashram now began to call me Baba, and I even used the name myself, if only in letters to them. When I left that evening, the swami marked my forehead with holy ash (*vibhuti*) and gave me some to taste. From where it came or quite what it represented I did not learn until years later. It was *vibhuti* from Sathya Sai Baba's ashram.

In the following months I corresponded with the swami, and among the peculiar things he wrote was a provocative reference to my "future wife." I was by now divorced from my first wife, and had been living with Reidun for five years. We were firmly determined not to marry, she more so even than I. At that time, we thought of marriage as a last recourse for those who were unable to live in harmony together, for those who could not solve the problems of genuine sharing. Since cohabitation is accepted as quite normal and legally recognized in Scandinavia, marriage seemed to us to be a ritual having real significance only for public authorities, like the tax man.

During my spring visit, I had seen a photo of the swami, supposedly picturing him during *samadhi* or superconscious trance while visiting the Himalayas. It was a most attractive, largish photo. As time went by, I wished I had a photocopy of it, and wondered about asking my friend R. R. for one. A week or so went by, and my ex-wife sent a message to ask me to remove all my old papers from the dusty attic in the house that was now her property. Among those papers were some I had received from the visiting band before I had actually met the swami, and there was the exact photocopy I was wishing for!

That summer, while on a visit to England to see my mother, we attended a big fair near Newcastle. Reidun had never had her fortune told by a Gypsy before. She came laughing sardonicaly from the gaudy caravan because the fortune she had been told by the daughter of Petroleigo had ended with the news that Petroleigo herself was in another room and would read her fuller fortune for a few more pounds! One item that had made her most skeptical, however, was the prediction that there would very soon be a most happy event in the family, within some weeks. This, we were sure was out of the question, as no births, marriages, or other happy family events were pending.

When we went down to London, Reidun was able to attend a *kirtan* and meet the swami for the first time. As usual, he was unconventional, nodding "hello" to us while sitting to sing at the harmonium. He looked up at Reidun, and his first words to her, between two melody lines, were: "Gypsies can't tell you anything!"

During that meeting the swami took me aside to talk in the privacy of a side room. He asked me if I would mind reading aloud for the group some things he had written that had to do with Sai Baba. He explained that he had written it, not knowing I was coming there, but feeling sure that it had all been arranged by a higher power. Both Reidun and I read part of the invocation, and very drawn-out and peculiar it was.

Later the swami almost transfixed me by his intensity in a half-hour conversation in the middle of the room, during which he insisted that it was best for me to get married to Reidun—at least, I should if I wished to continue on the spiritual path with him. I was rather obstinate, as one might understand. I marshaled my objections in haste, but to each of them he seemed to have an answer that I had not really considered properly before. My strongest card was the final, "But *she* won't!" (I had actually asked her some years before.) "Oh! Never mind. She will!" was his completely confident reply.

Through all this Reidun sat, unable to say a thing, while people who were waiting to get the swami's attention listened to it all. I had to laugh when I thought about what Reidun's women's liberation colleagues would have made of it. One truly strange thing the swami did was to suddenly and dramatically adopt an extraordinary stance, pointing up with one hand and down with the other and saying in a strong voice, "*He* blesses you!" When he became normal, so to speak, he explained that God had blessed us through him, and that it had surprised him greatly because of our unmarried state. I did not know *what* to make of that! Such behavior was rather too far-out for me to judge. Incidentally, I later recalled that the stance he had adopted is one that traditionally represents the connection of heaven and earth, such as in the tarot card deck.

To cut the long course of our deliberations short, we decided to get married within 24 hours. The swami sounded delighted on the phone. No one in my previous experience could have changed my mind like that on such a vital question, or get us to marry in church, which was anathema to both of us—for I was convinced that he had also added the improbable condition "in a church." It was characteristic of the atmosphere he created that I didn't want to call him to ask him why or even whether he really had said that! Oddly, though, the friend with whom we were staying in Hampstead was very keen on a church wedding because he knew of a Unitarian chapel where we could have a wedding with any type of arrangement, regardless of denomination. In looking for someone licensed to marry us, we met a near-blind lady minister, with whom we arranged a short ceremony to our liking, and within ten days we were married. So the Gypsies had known something, after all, though the swami doubtless meant that they had only psychic abilities, not spiritual wisdom.

Some days after the ceremony we met some people who had been with the swami in the West of England while we were being married in London. He had given a running commentary on the events to them, so they said, and they were most intrigued to know whether we had used incense sticks, for the swami had suddenly become upset and called out about the incense. I recalled that a guest had accidentally kicked the incense holder on the floor and scattered the incenses everywhere. "Did M. L. pick them up?" they wanted to know. Indeed, she had! They told me that the swami said she had done so at the time.

The swami came to London for a *kirtan,* during which he performed for us what he called a spiritual marriage. This was an unconventional event with Hindu overtones and what seemed to be his quite spontaneous directions. Later he gave us his papers with the outline of the ceremony he enacted. Quite a number of his words and actions, which were meaningless to me then, proved very meaningful indeed in terms of events that took place much later.

Someone told me that he very seldom accepted gifts from anyone, and only if they were given from the heart. I had at our previous meeting offered him a small candle that was molded in a red,
heart-shaped tin. I had a specific intention in doing this, and the gift
was a symbol of something that one would in fact be very hard put
to guess its meaning! During the spiritual marriage proceedings, the
swami returned the small tin to me, asking me if it did not represent
exactly what it in fact had. He did this in a way that kept this meaning quite private. He had burned the candle, and it now contained
ash that he said had just been brought from the shrine of Sai Baba
in Shirdi, India. He also gave us each a dried rose petal from that
same shrine.

There I also met briefly a young Indian who had just come
from India and apparently had brought these things with him, some
from Shirdi and some from Puttaparthi. He told me that since
Sathya Sai Baba had entered his life, everything had changed vastly
for the better. A week later some of the devotees gave us a box of
fragrant *vibhuti,* as the swami had told them. He had also told them
it was from Sathya Sai Baba and had somehow issued from a picture
of him somewhere. Six years later it transpired that I actually received a lot more of this same *vibhuti,* with its unmistakably unique
fragrance, from a picture in a Sai Baba temple in India.

At another point in the spiritual marriage ceremony, the swami
asked someone to hand him a carrier bag he had with him. He drew
out a garland made of sandalwood shavings, looking very surprised
as he did so: "There were two, but now they are joined together
into one!" he said. "But then, Sai Baba does many wonderful
things. It's not *my* doing!" He placed the garland around both our
necks together. "It is from Sai Baba. You understand?" Yet I did not
grasp whether it was from Shirdi or Puttaparthi, nor did I know
whether he meant this figuratively or literally. Everything was happening too fast for me to figure it out. I was not at all sure where I
had this swami—or for that matter, where he had me.

The symbolic meaning of the "unification" of two garlands to
one I understood from the swami, who declared that from then on
Reidun and I were made as one by God. This was eventually illustrated to us by what happened in our relationship years afterward,
and most adequately, too, as will become evident. He reminded us
how we had been "blessed by the Great One, the Almighty One
Himself," and "as He spoke, it was made and sealed," even

though he had been surprised considering our having lived together unmarried.

The whole experience was very felicitous for us. In arranging the day, the swami said he had taken account of planetary movements that he could not explain to us. We later found it to have been the auspicious day of the new moon. Also, though it was a very sunny, hot, and almost cloudless July day, a very fine rain fell for just a few minutes when we took a pause in the garden after the ceremony, which supposedly is a very good sign. It had also rained after the church ceremony. Altogether, many difficult practical matters that seemed to be insoluble hindrances to our getting married, such as a missing certificate of divorce, airline reservations, and the booking of the chapel all fell exactly into place, just in time, most remarkably.

One day a friend who knew the swami came wearing a red corduroy cap and I realized it was a favorite cap that I had lost the last time I was in London. He immediately said that the swami had passed it on to him, saying he had found it. When my friend asked him what to do with it, the swami had said, "Give it to lost and found." This had seemed difficult, for where in London was a lost property office where one might deliver a cheap holiday hat? Before he could decide what to do, I turned up to claim it. I had left it at the *kirtan* with the incense sticks and flowers the previous Easter. In a deeper sense, of course, it was I who, from the swami's viewpoint, was "lost and found."

That incident was similar to many others involving the swami. He was not a person one could tie down to straightforward discussion, for the atmosphere he created about him simply made one's own intentions slip away or feel irrelevant. Once I saw his eyes shine "like burning embers," as someone most aptly had tried to describe it. They shone with a fascinating light that was entirely out of the ordinary, showing a depth and mystery that I have never seen before or since.

NOT TO FOLLOW BLINDLY

My relationship to the swami seems to have served as an invaluable preparation that smoothed the way on the path toward Sathya Sai Baba. It reduced the mental, cultural, and spiritual hurdles I first had to surmount, which is why I find it relevant to describe here. I cannot judge to what extent the swami knew of my future course or—if indeed, it was inevitable to some extent—whether he was consciously helping me to secure it.

The swami said things about the future that sounded like predictions or sometimes like instructions. Among these was his pronouncement that we would have "lots of children . . . and very spiritual ones." Hardly anything else could have been further from our intentions or desires. He also said I would stay in Norway and work for a long time, but that we would visit the U.K. for a long holiday. Our own plans were for a more or less permanent move to the U.K., as soon as circumstances made it feasible. Somewhere along the line he threw in, "Don't go to India!" and several other "woulds" and "mights," including a question about my health, particularly as to how my back was. It was fine and I said so.

As I write this, fourteen years later, I can add that we have not had any children, nor will we have any. However, our plans for a permanent move to Britain proved impossible, not least due to spinal problems that I began to have, though we did manage to stay for as long as a whole year in 1981–1982, when I took an unpaid year off from Oslo University.

Upon our return to Norway, the relationship with the swami was kept up by letter and once by telephone. I became more and more intensely involved in the matter, despite the physical distance, or even perhaps because of it. Not surprisingly, there were many unresolved questions in my mind, some of which made me feel dubious again. Altogether I had heard a considerable amount about him and had listened to his every word with concentrated interest and desire to learn. That he had something to impart beyond what any ordinary teacher could give, I was convinced. Still, much of what he said was unclear to me, and much about what he stood for came to me secondhand through the interpretations of his followers, because of his avoidance of ever being buttonholed and his general air of inscrutability. I could not get over a number of inconsistencies in what he said, and even after my most thorough concentration and soul-searching, some of his views jarred too much with what I found acceptable,

Despite the powers for which he clearly could be a channel, I could not submit my will, willy-nilly to his directions, nor could I see him in the way the Hindu guru of tradition is supposed to be seen—as an infallible God-man whose every suggestion must be taken up and fulfilled with eager obedience. Though I could accept that some very, very few persons (such as Ramakrishna) had reached saintly pefection and become pure channels of divine will and powers that one regards as miraculous, I was uncertain whether the swami was of any comparable spiritual infallibility. I was still in a considerable flux of doubt about the wisdom of putting my fate in anyone else's hands. This point is surely often crucial for many educated, rational people, even those who have strong spiritual leanings, because it strikes at the root of all that a supposedly enlightened education has made us struggle to achieve.

This attitude was later confirmed when I read Sathya Sai Baba's words: "Faith is natural to each person. Each person has some faith in himself, some confidence in himself. And the core of his being, of himself, is Atma. From this is the foundation of faith in himself."[1]

What I wanted was definitely not a father substitute or an overpowering master, even though spiritual gains might be the promise. I did not wish to risk gambling away by acts of blind faith what inner strength I had gained in life. I could only trust fully in a teacher who would not only demonstrate the higher truth through

---

[1] Sathya Sai Baba, quoted in John S. Hislop, *Conversations with Bhagavan Sri Sathya Sai Baba* (San Diego: Birth Day, 1978), p. 54.

exemplary actions, but who also could explain it with some clarity. It was not a question of disbelief in the reality of the goal itself or the desirability of personal perfection and exceeding bliss.

In order to have learned more, I would have had to have made a commitment to the swami, to have complete faith in his advice, because in spiritual matters, I felt that half-measures were little better than none at all. However, I did not feel that I could accept such a relationship, despite all that had occurred. Moreover, some of his followers openly worshiped him as if he were, himself, a divinity. Though he never claimed anything like this, to my knowledge, and spoke as if God were independent of himself, he did say that he was "one with God." As this was also what Jesus meant when he said, "My Father and I are One," I found it difficult to accept and satisfactorily comprehend.

A good deal of confusing ambiguity is possible when dealing with the sort of monistic faith involved here. According to the Vedic tradition, everyone is divine in origin and destiny. More than that, whatever our goodness or sinfulness, whatever our stage of development, divinity is in every one of us and equally so at all times. It is said to be "nearer than the nearest." A chief difference between an illumined master or true yogi and the person who is still a seeker and an aspirant is that the master inherently and fully recognizes the divinity in himself and in everyone and all else, realizing it continuously and never for a moment losing that blissful consciousness.

However, how can a seeker know enough to be fully confident that one has found just such a master? Were a straight and general answer to this possible, or even a lengthy one that served as a completely reliable test a seeker could apply, the world would surely be quite a different place. Because of one's own relative ignorance, therefore, some degree of faith and openhearted, open-mindedness are necessary ingredients.

To have knowledge is not the same as to know from direct experience, as I knew all too well already. "To know" in the bookish or even scientific sense is only to hold an abstraction, to be a conscious subject possessing a mental grasp and conviction about some objects of thought, whatever this knowledge may enable one to do in the physical realm. But such knowing is a dry and tasteless experience, compared to the intense joy of being, and the actual bliss I had already experienced.

Another problem was that, if I were to make a decisive commitment to follow this guru in all things, I might in time come under the sway of a very powerful social and psychological dependency. In fact, I already had something more of a dependency than I knew, which I did not feel or recognize properly, until after the tentative bond between us was severed.

Nowadays, one frequently hears doubt praised as the very basis of any reasonable approach to the world, and as a palliative against dangerous convictions and fanaticism. While in earlier eras it was widely believed that lack of faith was the worst of illnesses, nowadays, it is often thought that lack of doubt is a pathological condition. There is much to support this, too, for the cocksure and the ignorant usually go together. Where there is belief, the possibility of doubt is always close at hand—for belief can only arise where there is neither definitive knowledge nor genuine bedrock faith based on direct intuition and life wisdom.

My background in systematic, critical thinking had obviously tended to push me repeatedly toward caution rather than acceptance of all I heard, so I had a very intensive struggle in sorting out all the facts while also balancing the many and crucial issues and decisions involved. On the one hand, I might lose marvelous opportunities for self-transformation, while on the other, I was in danger of beguiling myself into a diverting set of spiritual and social entanglements that would turn out, when it was too late to go back, to be contrary to my temperament and perhaps even contrary to my best spiritual interests.

Though I was confident that the swami was a person who could never condone any form of violence whatever, the fact that such things did happen when people wished to leave certain guru-dominated movements, occasionally with disasterous consequences, reminded me of the caution needed in entering any sort of close-knit group relationships. The inherent power of any tight social network can become very difficult for the individual who gets deeply involved. Extrication can sometimes be traumatic, even impossible. It did not feel right to me to get into that sort of social gridlock, not least because I knew myself on that score. As the swami also clearly had the final say on who joined the group, we would therefore no longer be able to decide who our close associates would be. This was confirmed a year later when, while visiting our friends there again, we met one very threatening person, whom I could not regard as good company, but whom ashram members could not really avoid. There was no form of social duress whatever from the swami or his followers.

As the inward intensity of the whole experience continued to increase I wrote the swami a letter in which I frankly explained my doubts and asked a number of questions, the answers to which I privately decided would be crucial to deciding on any future commitment. This I did not enter into lightly. Never had I done such deep soul-searching before. Much hinged on whether he accepted my right to question what my critical powers might require of me. The letter was such that any answer to it must show whether he could (or chose to) understand me or not.

The answer to my letter I could take only as a rejection, though it was characteristically ambiguous and most peculiar in several ways. He gave me the advice that I should always remember Sai Baba, or else I could go mad. One or two of my questions were half-answered, the replies trailing off into incomprehensibility, quite possibly on purpose. It was upsetting, but all in all it left no doubt that the swami was not for me. He no longer seemed as infallible as he had been made out to be.

Despite the brevity of my actual meetings with him, a number of other non-ordinary events took place. Their causes or the agency involved exceeds my understanding, so much so that I now regard the ultimate explanation of such things as simply being beyond the grasp of mind. There exist a wide range of philosophical and scientific views on causation and agency—both modern and ancient views, West and East—yet none of these are adequate to account for all that I certainly experienced. No variant of modern psychological theory, whether clinical, Freudian, Jungian, or any of many more recent approaches has proved adequate in penetrating the inner meaning of these matters.

For instance, the swami was frequently present in my dreams with symbolic or even direct messages. Mental questions I put to him or thoughts I had concerning him were sometimes "answered" immediately in mysterious ways. Once, for example, a warning clap of thunder issued from a clear blue sky that immediately interrupted some thoughts about whether the swami wasn't actually a womanizer! It rather shook me. I should also add, though, that this sort of "paranormal occurrence" (as physically-minded scientists like to classify them) had become more and more frequent for me, and surprisingly unusual in character, without their being related to the swami.

Some time after the denouement of our relationship I took down my photocopy picture of the swami and stowed it away on a top shelf in my library. Well over a year later, having forgotten it, I took down a pile of books and papers and in doing so uncovered the picture as it lay on my desk. As I saw it I thought, "How I wish I really knew whether the swami ever did have the highest of spiritual experiences!" At the very moment I thought this, a folded sheet of yellowing paper fell onto the picture from the top shelf—right onto the center of his forehead. "Oh, no!" I thought. "Here we go again!" The folded paper had come from the back of a book about the *kundalini* power, in which I had kept it unwittingly for about ten years! It was two pages that I had copied by hand from a book in a shop, listing and describing dozens of different phases of consciousness, from deepest sleep up to the highest of all realizations (*nirvikalpa samadhi*)!

Without a doubt, the swami knew somehow right from our very first meeting that I was already somehow connected with Sai Baba. That he dubbed me "Baba" highlights this. Whether he knew that I would become a follower of Sathya Sai, rather than just Shirdi Sai, I do not know. Even so, a skeptic might argue that being given the name would itself be a stimulus to following a guru of that name.

In fact, the swami had given spiritual names to all of his closer followers, who regarded themselves virtually as his disciple-servants, the ideal of selfless service to God being exemplified, among other ways, through supporting and obeying one's guru. Giving me a name, however, did not keep me in the fold as a blind follower, even though that is not generally the reason for having spiritual names.

The philosopher Hegel, pointed out that he who is able to name someone else is his master; the named one becomes the servant. The relationship of master-and-servant (*Herren-Knecht*) is determined and maintained through the one who is in a position to name or classify the other. Thus when the one who gave you the very name or title by which you are known to all withdraws or is gone, your very sense of identity can suffer disruption and change.[2] It's true that I was wary of losing my autonomy, which can mean risking personal security and whatever may be cherished as one's own.

---

[2] G. W. F. Hegel, *Phenomenology of Spirit*, A. N. Miller, trans. (London: Oxford University Press, 1972), pp. 115ff.

In modern Western societies, a master-servant relationship is now looked down on, not without good historical reason, and it even generates resentment and revolution. However, the best sort of spiritual guru-follower relationship refers to an inward relationship rather than outward subservience. Service then takes the form of self-alteration in accordance with the master's guidance, rather than actual servanthood. But such a relationship presumes one can have complete faith in the master as having the requisite wisdom! This relationship can prove positive if the guru has the true qualities, and I was not confident that this swami was either faultless or infallible. I had much faith in his goodness, but not sufficient for the surrender of myself or my identity into his care alone.

Yet the swami's foresight in naming me proved very remarkable in this case—for can one think of a more infallible way of ensuring that one will never forget a name than by giving it to someone? For this and other reasons, he must have known that it was my inevitable destiny to become a follower of Sri Sathya Sai Baba. Looking back, I was still rather too much a victim of an attitude that is almost a hallmark of Westerners today—in regarding "individuality" as sacrosanct and as the very cause of initiative, enterprise, and all forms of freedom and progress. On this subject, one of those who has been close to Sai Baba for many years, the multi-talented Professor V. K. Gokak, puts it most succinctly:

> There is a notion current in certain circles that to be a disciple is to lose one's own individuality. The one possession which modern man values is his own personality. A person moulds his character, nourishes his intellect, refines his emotions and awakens his intuitions by experiencing deeply the beauty of Art, Life and Nature. He is intensely aware of his own unicity in the scale of creation. To surrender to another man what one has fashioned for oneself with so much labour and to be ironed with others the disciple of this individual or that is worse than primitiv' imal sacrifice, for what is sacrificed is infinitely more pre´ be a master's echo is to be a gramophone record.
>
> But persons arguing in this fashion hardly l￵ side of the medal. It is true that in some cases lead to mental dependence and lack of origi ty to a known discipline may be better tha and eccentricity or originality without subs

a true disciple is not a mere shrub growing under the shadow of a banyan tree. He is himself a banyan sapling. He grows and fulfils himself in his own way. Sri Ramakrishna did not swallow up Vivekananda. On the other hand, Sri Ramakrishna enabled Vivekananda to be himself, more truly and nobly than he would otherwise have been. A true disciple accepts the teachings of his master, not because of intellectual servitude or his own capacity to think but because he finds in those teachings a philosophy towards which he himself has been spontaneously evolving. He does not surrender his personality to his master. On the other hand, he finds that his own personality is essentially like that of his master. The only difference lies in the fact that, in the master, it is raised to the nth degree. What the disciple is striving after is what the master has already achieved.[3]

The self-same Sathya Sai Baba to whom the swami first "introduced" me repeatedly warns against relying on gurus in these times, for none who proclaim themselves teachers today actually master all aspects of spirituality, and many who pretend to do so are themselves selfish and impure. From what I know of the swami, I certainly would not fault him there. He demonstrated much selfless love and care for his followers and was surrounded at all times by an atmosphere of spiritual intensity and even sanctity. At the time, he did exercise considerable influence on my view of life, of myself, and of the nature of divinity. Above all, perhaps, he prepared me in various ways for approaching Sathya Sai Baba, by sweeping away a number of my mistaken conceptions and acclimating me to a more authentic spirituality.

My first introduction to the actual teachings of Sathya Sai came in 1979 through two books: *The Holy Man and the Psychiatrist,* by the American psychiatrist Dr. Samuel Sandweiss, and *Sai Baba, Man of Miracles,* by the Australian writer Howard Murphet. I was fascinated by them and was, through knowing the swami, able to consider many things that Sai Baba allegedly had done as possible. Though I was of course unable to judge the authenticity of their more amazing reports, I was much taken by the appealing teachings, at once deeply philosophic and poetic, yet strikingly simply

Gokak, *Narahari: Prophet of New India,* Somaiya Publications, N.
Quoted in V. K. Gokak, *Bhagavan Sri Sathya Sai Baba (An Interv)* New Delhi, 1983, p. 45.

stated. They struck many a harmonious chord in me. Their range and penetration was extraordinary, and I felt that at last I had come across in Sai Baba a spiritual authority who not only reinforced many of my own convictions and hard-won insights, but who also filled in gaps in my understanding as no one and nothing else throughout world philosophy, science, or literature had done before. Above all, here was a great living teacher and master of many paranormal and other powers who was still available to seekers. I also became as convinced by the impressive reported evidence, as far as reasonable evaluation could allow, of the identity of Sathya Sai Baba as a reincarnation of Shirdi Sai Baba. Sathya Sai's discourses also supported my feelings about relationships with gurus.

A true guru, according to frequent warnings from Sai Baba, is recognized only by his actions, not his words—and is then only found with much difficulty. Genuine gurus, he also says, cannot easily be found today, for they never advertize themselves. The best a teacher can do is limited to the guidance of pointing out the correct way, Sai Baba assures us. Though such knowledge is priceless, all the rest is up to ourselves: it is we who must actually walk the path, step by step. This requires self-reliance and that authentic self-confidence that stems from the recognition, in one form or another, of one's own inner divine origin and potential. This must be why Sai Baba has frequently said that he is not a personal guru in the traditional sense, and also why he usually does not give clear and specific personal directives about particular events or choices with which a person is faced:

> Avatars seldom give advice directly. What they wish to convey, they give indirectly. The reason is: there is divinity present in each human being, and it is by making man realize it that he should be enabled to correct himself. If the correctives are applied directly, man will never try to realize his divinity.[4]

This I find to be consistent with Baba's teaching of the need for individuals to each find their own way and to have at least sufficient free will to be able to choose between right or wrong. I believe that this process of individuation generates the self-confidence that alone will lead to eventual self-realization.

---

[4] Sathya Sai Baba, Discourse Brindavan Summer Course, May 26, 1990. *Sanathana Sarathi*, Aug. 1990, p. 207.

5

SAI ANSWERS A CALL

Sathya Sai Baba made his presence in my life definitively known to me through the miraculous visitation to and healing of my mother, Mrs. Jane Priddy. Her life was one of hardship and deprivation, hard work, and many serious illnesses, some of which necessitated major surgery (for duodenal ulcer, twice for breast cancer, and also after a serious auto accident). Amid all this she had to find her way back to working life to provide for herself and me, after many years as a housewife. She never remarried after my father died when I was 15. She bore all this with brave determination and a constant sense of humor, but without the consolation of any religious belief. As far as I know, she never came to believe in God. She always held that we must be like other creatures that live and die, that being the end of it all.

Since first settling in Oslo, Norway back in 1959, I had traveled to England to visit my mother regularly for over two decades on a yearly basis and more frequently in the later years. Being tied to Norway through family and work, I was often very worried about her and upset at being able to visit so seldom and help so little.

During her last ten years she suffered progressive loss of memory and, on top of everything else, a major fall down the stairs that crushed a vertabra in the lower spine, causing a lump that was later judged to be about the size of half a tennis ball. Due to her doctor's fixed idea that she was suffering from "old-age depression," this lump went unexamined for six weeks while she was in agony, until a chance visit from a surgeon who had replaced her hip joint led to a medical examination. Because my mother had been a staff nurse in psychiatric hospitals much of her adult life, her doctor let her use many types of painkillers at her own discretion. These gave only brief partial relief during the next six chair-ridden years. Being very independent, she insisted on living alone. Only when she became partially sightless from cataracts in both eyes did she allow my uncle to move in to care for her.

During my visits after her spinal injury, I always saw how constant was the suffering it caused her. She used a hot water bottle all the time for relief and was using more painkillers than seemed right.

She had suffered nearly six years of constant back pain by the time she was 81, when I arrived there in January 1983 to find she was now taking no painkillers at all. When I asked her why, she replied: "What pain?" and she couldn't even remember having had the accident that had caused it! Even though her memory was much impaired, I found the absence of pain almost incredible. My uncle confirmed that she had taken no pain killers for months. I later told people, "It's a miracle," not imagining at all *how* directly miraculous it really was. For ten days or so I observed to my pleasure that my mother evidenced no signs of pain whatever. Yet the inexplicable fact simply wouldn't quite sink in. It was a relief to me, nontheless.

After that, it was seven months before I was able to fly over to visit her again. By then her memory had deteriorated so much that she could not even remember who I was. She even asked me if she had been married and to whom. Once a very talkative person, she was now quite silent and accepting of everything. Although I knew she was still very much herself, in some remarkable way she was very far away, too.

One evening, asking me to sit beside her on the sofa to talk, she asked if I knew who the person was who had visited her in the clinic. It soon became clear that someone she felt was very special had come to see her while she was being examined by a team of doctors at a clinic where she was under regular observation for perplexing new symptoms. "He was really *so* nice—wonderfully charming!" was what she said, more or less. She thought he was either an African or an Indian. He had smiled very beautifully at her, she said, but the strange thing was that before he departed he had uttered the words: "You will have no more pain!" I asked her if her pain had stopped thereafter, and she couldn't even remember having had much pain! But she was most eager to find out who it had been!

I thought only of the swami, who still lived in England, for he had spoken to me of my mother. I also knew that he had once unexpectedly appeared at the bedside of a devotee in hospital to instruct her and her doctors very strictly that to perform a cesarean operation would be wrong, adding that the child would be born the following morning without complications, which did indeed occur as he had predicted.

The swami was over six feet tall, was bald on top, and sometimes wore a saffron orange shirt. In trying to establish if it were him, I asked my mother about all these points. She insisted he was short, hardly taller than her own shoulder height. Nor was he balding, no, he had lots of hair—really a lot of it, and she gestured firmly to illustrate what amounted to full Afro-style hair. Finally, he was wearing the same color as the doctors on either side of him, white. I asked if they had said who he was, or if they had spoken to him, but she said they had not. He had just walked up into a space between them where they stood around her, and he had been *so* nice, so *very* nice. This she repeated, still wanting to know who it could have been. I had to say that I did not know!

How it was that I did not consider Sathya Sai Baba, I simply cannot understand! His picture, which of course shows his Afro-style hair and in which he wears a long white robe, had been central on our shrine for about five years. I had also read that Sai Baba is very short in physical stature. The thought that it might have been him had once flashed through my mind, but I had also rejected this notion in a flash. I felt it was completely improbable in our case, for I had already long since begun to consider him with awe and virtually as an unattainable person for one such as I.

Less than a week later I returned to Oslo and, after entering our house, greeted the picture of Sai on the shrine as usual. Not until that moment did I remember: I had stood at that very spot sometime the previous autumn in great sadness and cried out to Sai Baba to help my mother because of all her suffering! I recalled that my plea had been: "No more pain! No more pain!" Also, I had prayed that she might soon die peacefully, as she had long wished herself.

My intense cry of anguish for her sake had come straight out of me and, once uttered, had simply left my thoughts until this very moment, about one year later!

The realization that such a great figure as Sai Baba must actually have appeared to my mother, for all intents and purposes materializing himself for her, was stunning, and it took time for this to sink in properly. In short, at this one stroke, Sai Baba became the definitive focus of my seeking and the *sadguru* supreme for me. He gently stepped into the foreground of my life, into the place in which the swami had stood. The subtlety of the miracle in all its intricate ramifications took days, weeks, and even months to become clear to me. For example, it is just as amazing to me even now that my mother should have been able to recall the incident so well, or to think to ask me who it was, considering that she hardly mentioned a thing else during the whole visit. It proves to me what a wonderful impression Baba made on her. I am quite certain that I had never shown her a picture of him because she had been disturbed by my previous connection with the swami in England. The chances that she had seen Baba's form pictured in any other connection were absolutely minimal.

About ten days later I was still wondering how to explain to her who it had been and how to convey to her the huge significance of being visited by an incarnation of God from India. Then I received the news that she had died peacefully in the hospital, on October 2, 1983, without suffering, after a period of unconsciousness. So the other part of that "prayer" had thus also been answered. Telling her that it was Sai Baba and sending her his picture was not to be—but she would not have understood much about it anyway, and might not have been able to remember who I was on the telephone. Since my talk about gurus had usually disturbed her, I might even have spoiled some of the beauty of the experience for her if I had phoned and told her who I was coming to realize Sathya Sai Baba truly to be. In her life, spent largely in nursing, doctors had been her only gurus, which surely explains why Sai Baba chose to appear to her in a clinic dressed in white.

There is no way that I can express fully how much that miracle meant to me. Along with the inner certainties it brought about, it also lifted from my heart the sadness about my mother that I had carried for so many years! Since then I have had no sense of loss or any of the grief I had often felt at my helplessness previously, for I felt the conviction that she had achieved her life's purpose. These events bear out the guarantee given by Sai Baba in his words:

> He is there, ready to respond to the call from the heart. Call on Me and I am always by your side.[1]

The nature of the impact that this visitation by Sai Baba made on my life should be evident from this book.

By the time my mother died, I had already gone through over two years of increasingly debilitating back and neck problems, which would respond to no treatment. These problems were serious enough to put a stop to many of my plans for the future, but their cause was uncertain. They were the cause of suffering and naturally also of anxiety. I had begun what proved to be a long search for a sound diagnosis. Yet none of the varied opinions, whether traditional or alternative, were either decisive or able to prescribe the cure. Almost everyone who examined or treated me was hugely optimistic about the effects their own efforts would have, but few gave me any relief at all. All I knew was that I was feeling the combined effect of four chronic shifts in the spinal column caused by various accidents that had occurred from early years onward.

On top of all this, my wife and I were going through the most critical phase in our relationship since our first meeting ten years before. It had come to the point of separation; we had lived apart for some months. Though neither of us felt the other was to blame, the problems of life together had come to seem insuperable. Our ways seemed to demand that we part, for both of us had let our desires wander elsewhere, each toward our country, our way of life and future livelihood, and even toward possible other partners. My wish to live in England again had also been frustrated by my illness. It was a time of extremely painful feelings and much depressing desperation.

Just at this crucial time, we came to hear of a talk about Sai Baba to be held in Oslo, which we agreed to attend together. Here we first heard accounts by an eyewitness of wonders experienced in the physical presence of Sai Baba. The talk was given by a Swedish visitor, Conny Larsson, who showed some of the extraordinary films

---

[1] Sathya Sai Baba, Discourse Hyderabad, April, 1973, *Sathya Sai Speaks*, vol. VIII (Prashanthi Nilayam: Sri Sathya Sai Books & Publications Trust, n.d.), p. 233.

about Sai Baba by Richard Bock, as well as some of his own. Some weeks later Conny also led a weekend seminar arranged in Oslo and attended by a few dozen people.

This gathering proved to provide the setting for the decisive turning point in our marriage, for we went out to a café where it was settled "once and for all" that we would remain together for better or worse! I cannot recount the details of those turbulent times nor quite how or why it was that things were resolved there and then, but I have no hesitation in affirming that Sai Baba's hand was helping us in some unseen way that caused our feelings to still like oil on troubled waters from that day onward. From my viewpoint at least, the change-over was dramatically undramatic, and the troubles of our past were suddenly gone.

Reidun had a dream of Sai Baba during that decisive weekend, and from then on, he also began to appear in my dreams in a friendly way. I had read various accounts in which he had assured that *any* dream of him was actually a visit from him. In one of these I was standing on a sandy space, like the one in front of the main temple at Prashanthi Nilayam, where Sai Baba usually resides. He showed me a human figure, which I knew was myself and, using a finger that somehow "wrote" in white light, realigned the spinal column by drawing the Sanskrit symbol for "Om" through it. This he repeated twenty times. When I awoke, I realized that this dream was a visual demonstration of the Norwegian phrase *å gjøre deg om,* meaning "to make you otherwise" or "to remake you." The sacred sound "Om," known as the *Pranava,* is held by the scriptures to be that of the original creative urge itself. Baba maintains that it is the mantric summation of the teachings of the holy *Vedas.*

Since my first visits to the Radha Krishna Temple in London over a decade earlier, I had enjoyed occasionally chanting the sacred Om (pronounced more like A-U-M) and singing Indian chants, which contain names of various forms of God. I knew such songs from *kirtans* with the swami in England. Baba also lays great weight upon the chanting of Om and the singing of *bhajans* (a type of devotional song) as being the easiest way, for many, of approaching the realization of divinity, at least at first. He affirms the Indian tradition that such devotion *(bhakti)* is the main path to God in this very long and dark age known as the *Kali Yuga,* in which success on the spiritual path by other means is nearly impossible, due not least to the absence in our time of fully enlightened and wholly pure gurus and religious teachers.

As a result of the Sai Baba gathering in Oslo, a small group was formed to meet twice monthly, as it has done more or less ever since. A film projector and films had been made available by Connie Larsson. We viewed one of these often, alternating this with a study circle along the lines that Baba recommends, and we held a *bhajan* singing session afterward, learning these group songs in Sanskrit from cassette recordings. Whatever the reasons, people seemed to have other priorities than organized Sai activities, so our regular group was eventually reduced to four people, who were its nucleus for about ten years.

I took the opportunity of sending a letter to Baba with a friend who was going to see him. In it I thanked Baba for what he had done for my mother, and I also asked that my wife and I might one day be able to see him in this earthly incarnation. When the friend arrived at Puttaparthi, he was told that Baba was away in Madras. He decided to attend the temple *bhajans* as usual. On an impulse he also took along the letter. No sooner had he sat down than Sai Baba arrived, having just returned the several hundreds of miles by car. Soon he walked over and reached forth for the letter. This friend returned from India with two large pictures signed by Baba, one for the Oslo circle and one for the group where he lived, further to the south in Norway.

At this time I obtained more books on the life of Sathya Sai Baba, especially the four biographical volumes titled *Sathyam, Sivam, Sundaram,* by Professor N. Kasturi. I was already convinced that Sai Baba must be the greatest embodied spirit of our time. Deeper reading filled me with joy so many times and in a way that no story or book had ever done before. It seemed to me then, as now, that no author, living or dead, has ever been able to conceive of a life as marvelously pure, moving, miraculous, and wise. There is nothing so perfected or richly-woven in mysterious, heart-moving events, or constructed with such an architecture of fathomless meaning, as the mission described in this literature. This biography contains the assertion that the major avatar of this current machine age, all as predicted in the *Bhagavatha Purana,* is Sai Baba. This claim is backed up by some of the most extraordinary historical evidence and the deepest theological philosophy I have come across, all of which I found more and more convincing as my understanding progressed.

PREPARING FOR THE PILGRIMAGE

Traveling to India to visit Sai Baba is not usually undertaken light-ly. To anyone who has, as I had, already begun to feel that Baba may well be the embodiment of God in its highest potential, the decision whether or not to visit him was unlike any other. To accept that God is everywhere and in everyone, however well-concealed by the ego, as Sai Baba teaches, does not have quite the implications as standing face-to-face with a person in whom this capacity is com-pletely realized. The question for me was whether we *could* visit, whether I was sufficiently prepared both inside myself and in the eyes of Sai Baba!

I seriously had to review myself more thoroughly than ever and prepare myself for an eventual visit to him as best I could, by try-ing to absorb his teachings and practicing them as much as I could. One morning I awoke from a translucent dream in which I heard a voice that sounded to me to be my own—and yet it was in some way "more" than mine—saying, in a most self-evident tone: "You will go to Puttaparthi under unusual circumstances."

Before my relations with the swami in England had cooled, he had one day suddenly said, "Don't go to India!" Like all else he said, this had made a strong impression on me. I knew that this swami sometimes warned people about things and that the conse-quences of non-observance had been negative, even very dire.

I had often wished to go to India, but had chosen to wait until I was sure that it was right or necessary in some way. I thought it wrong to break with one's various duties and then to hope for spiritual fruits and experiences. Admittedly though, the idea was very tempting at times. Yet those who spoke as realized masters have always held that one can find everything within oneself. Sai Baba affirms this and also points out that he is easily able to come to anyone, anywhere, anyhow, depending merely upon the degree of their readiness and the particular need! I even had my own proof of this, in the case of his appearance to my mother. So what need to actually visit him?

A further brake on India plans was whether I could manage the physical demands of such a journey and stay there in my poor condition. Doubts arose as to whether it was Sai Baba's will for us to visit, whether we would actually manage to see him, or whether we might have to come away disappointed. This was really a question of self-evaluation or self-confidence, after all: I wanted to be ready for getting the fullest benefit from such a boon as seeing the avatar himself.

Sai Baba's teachings, as available through books, struck me as deep and all-encompassing. Yet they did not seem at all easy for me to follow and especially not with the degree of rigor he prescribes! His proclamation, "My life is my message," together with the example he is in all things, from the smallest to the greatest, set the highest possible standard of thought, word, and deed. It was all too easy to see that I fell far short of this shining model of perfect love in tireless action. Though it may seem contradictory, this realistic evaluation of my own shortcomings also gave me the basis of a greater confidence in myself, too.

I read and heard how Sai Baba inspired many people to entirely selfless work. There were also many accounts of the infallible and unique ways in which he gradually teaches people and cuts their egos down to size, without alienating them. On the contrary, the change of heart that Baba facilitates usually brings them back sooner or later for more inspiration and whatever deflation they might need, so fruitful is the progress achieved and experienced by them. However, in wishing to know that I had done something to follow Sathya Sai's teachings before going to India, I did make various conscious efforts to improve myself in thought, word, and deed during that year.

Having heard how spartan the conditions were for most visitors to Baba's ashram, I had also to see whether I was physically fit enough, so we decided to go on a camping tour in France for the summer vacation of that year.

During our visit to Normandy, I had a dream in which we were awakening in a tent outside a building, a temple or sanctuary of some sort, in which ecstatic singing by many people was well underway in Sai Baba's presence, and I was wishing that I had gotten in there already.

On our brief tour of the coast of Normandy, I made a major life decision, after much painful regret, that I would thereafter completely give up what finally seemed to me to be the vain pursuit of music-making and get rid of my musical instruments. I played music for thirty-five years and had tried to make a living at it twice during different phases of my life. Music eventually became only a hobby, albeit one that I really loved. As it was, never had the circumstances—whether practical, social, or artistic—been right for me to be a musician. Other musicians had always been very happy to have my help and support, both musical and practical, which I gave quite freely, though none seemed to understand what I wanted to express and everyone always seemed to let me down. It was a steel-studded and well-founded case of "no-more-fool-I" and "poor-old-me."

As I was approaching my 50th birthday, I reached what for me was the inevitable but saddening conclusion that I had only been challenging the hand of fate in this matter, which was evidently dead against me. I told Reidun my vow, which would save me from all similar disappointments in future: I would definitely cease playing from then on! Though it made her sad, she understood my feelings and the good reasons. Seldom had I made a vow, never one of such absoluteness.

Then it was, while encamped at Yport in Normandy, I was awakened one Thursday morning just before dawn by the tolling of the clearest church bell I have ever heard. Its tone was exquisite. I had just had a crystal clear and very inspiring dream, which I recorded as follows:

Dream of Aug. 9, 1984: Reidun and I were sitting cross-legged in the front row of a lot of people in a room where there was a very expectant air. All at once Sai Baba came in and very smoothly and quickly came straight before me and greeted me with a namaskar gesture. He beamed a beautiful warming love energy while conveying this traditional form of greeting to the true and pure divine self within. He communicated various things to me, which I do not recall exactly, and told me, "Now you will make music!" He also distinctly said, "Yes. I am going to . . . " and indicated something that I very dearly wished with my deeper being. I was about to burst into tears, but he somehow surprised me into saying, "That's incredibly nice, sir." He then turned his attention to three young men who were present. Before he left us, he said he would be putting me in touch with someone whose name I recalled as "Mr. Cadeau," and he gave me a very knowing and amused look and said, "Then we'll see!"

Within one month various unanticipated events made it possible for me to obtain a 16-track recording studio. I was able to fulfill all my long-thwarted musical yearnings, under my own conditions, at home, and to my own full satisfaction in the following years. Some years later, Baba gave his blessing to the products of this music-making by touching a cassette compilation offered to him at Prashanthi Nilayam.

Two years later, the real meaning of "Mr. Cadeau" (literally, *cadeau* means "gift") was revealed when Baba gave me a wonderful present.

By the autumn of 1984 the worsening of my spinal and neck problems and the inability of anyone to improve them had brought my spirits so low that I felt the only hope was to visit Sai Baba. My wife was able to ease the tensions somewhat by intensive, deep massage of the muscles. Still, up to thirty hours of sitting on planes and at airports, followed by 140 miles in a jolting taxi was a very daunting prospect. Many accounts of exceptional circumstances surrounding journeys there had convinced me that those Baba allows to visit him are under his special care from the very beginning of their trip to the end.

My work permitted absence from mid-December to the end of January, but the imagined prospect of a mass of Christians at Prashanthi Nilayam for Christmas was very off-putting to us both. Though I knew that many Westerners there would be non-sectarian, I presumed—mistakenly, I was later relieved to learn—that we would also encounter more than enough of the doctrinaire, the tiresome evangelical, or even the fixedly-smiling pietistic sort, of which we have a dread. So we arranged to travel and arrive for the New Year instead.

Although I had been around in poor Eastern countries many years before and we were somewhat prepared for conditions in India, we were both still quite shaken by the real-life shock of Bombay. Literally *everything* was foreign, from a glass of water to the color of the sunset, from the dust to the taste of any food or drink. Even at the airport nothing looked safe to eat, let alone palatable. The famous stench was worse than literature ever conveys, the begging children more pitiable. The airport porters wrested our baggage from us for a five-yard stretch and then tried to charge us ten times the normal fee. Even the maneuvers of the mosquitoes were foreign. Whenever we bought anything to drink, no one would give us change for our paper money, claiming that small change was in too short supply. Almost all the young men we saw were thinner than garden rakes, coughing and spitting like sick men.

We had unfortunately just heard from a foreign resident of India that taxi drivers in Bombay might drive you to a deserted place, rob you, and leave you to your fate. Also, seeing the extreme filth and poverty of all the shanty slums along the roads awakened as much anxiety as pity in us, as we imagined how our rickety bus might break down, leaving us amid them. Even though my neck was noticeably much less troublesome than it had been for months, despite the strain of the very long journey, we were both in a shattered mood, feeling ourselves lost aliens in a most unhealthy and inhospitable environment. Perhaps Baba had not intended us to visit after all, we thought!

Just then we were approached by a nice Indian lady at the airport who, it turned out, had herself been to visit Sai Baba. She gave us useful information and looked after our luggage so that we could move about more freely. This was the first reassuring sign that things would work out for the best.

After two days of recovery in a poor but passable hotel in Bangalore, we at last found a taxi (charging only twice the going rate!) to take us the four-hour journey to Puttaparthi from Bangalore. That mad ride—for drivers in India seemed to care for nothing but the clout of a bigger vehicle, such as a train or truck—wildly blared its way on through the most varied pastoral scenes, teeming with human, animal, and plant exotica.

The unpaved road to Puttaparthi was lined with great and ancient shady trees, chiefly mango trees planted long ago, I was told, by the famous ruler, Tipu Sultan, so that the poor would be provided for. The whole environment exuded the impression of being hoary with age, and it was easy to imagine these rustic highways as having been trod by yogis and *sadhus* since time immemorial. The red-earthed landscape, with its occasional, peculiar gray granite outcroppings that Rama supposedly once beheld, was already there entire ages before Arizona's Grand Canyon was carved down to the bedrock (which, incidentally, is known to geologists as "Vishnu gneiss"). The road crossed large areas of semi-arid scrubland. Enormous rounded boulders, sometimes the size of churches, perched on the very topmost points of ridges and heights in a quite inexplicable manner that certainly seemed to defy the possibility of having been produced through mere wind erosion. Nor, evidently, could known or available human methods have placed them there either. Many signs of the religiosity of India are seen inscribed on the landscape—from rock temples in boulders on top of the hills to gaily painted temples in groves of trees. These temples are of many shapes and sizes; some of them are the size of a dolls-house made around decorated stones. Much of the landscape in the area is certainly very ancient-looking.

Tears came to our eyes when, still many miles from our goal, we passed under a decorative arch across the country road, inscribed, "Welcome to the Kingdom of Sathya Sai." The road wound into the broad Chitravati valley, enclosed by distant hills, and on this day it was as if everything here was energized, because the sky was rolling in huge, magnificent clouds and the greenery was freshly wet from a shower.

Our dust-ridden weariness and strains from the entire journey simply dissipated, before we even caught sight of the breathtaking vistas of Prashanthi Nilayam itself, with its uniquely-shaped college, school, hostel, hospital, and many other buildings in heavenly pink, blue, and yellow pastels—the same colors as regularly blend together in the sky during the exquisite tropical sunsets there.

Only a few people could be seen inside the ashram gates, and we were soon shown to the temple compound, where everyone was seated cross-legged on the sand or in the *mandir* (temple) itself, awaiting the afternoon *darshan* of Sai Baba ("darshan" means the blessing of seeing a holy person). As I saw these expectant thousands amassed together in perfect silence, all watching for the orange-robed figure to appear, I felt very moved and thanked Baba inwardly that he had helped me to make it there, among these spiritual brothers and sisters.

Never before had I witnessed so peaceful and light an atmosphere with so many people together. We waited a long while, maybe 40 minutes, without any sense of restlessness among the three or four thousand people present. It was New Year's Eve and sundown was imminent. After so many years, the moment had come. Just as Sai Baba has said: "Most of you have come here on a pilgramage, fulfilling the dream of a life time."[1]

Sathya Sai Baba moved gently into view from the recesses of the porch, very slowly making his way toward us all, with pauses here and there, each of unpredictable duration. He came out onto the sand while everyone watched him in an atmosphere of quiet expectation, his gaze unruffled and spacious, his presence all-encompassing yet completely natural before that great assembly. Inward sobs of emotion rose up in me and filled my eyes with tears. Quietly and very slowly, he walked around the whole compound, stopping here and there without going very close to anyone.

Flocks of beautiful white cranes began to fly past above the temple, and the evening chorus of other birds reached a climax. This made me remember that we had been told how birds would come to sing along with the *bhajans*. A bit of romantic hyperbole, that, for it was naturally evening song time for the birds, too. We had also heard that Baba had waved his arm to stop a monsoon downpour so as to make his rounds at darshan, then restarted the rain directly with another wave as he went under the shelter of the porch roof. I had wished that I might someday witness this incredible feat. Sathya Sai continued his round of the assembly and gradually moved back toward the porch. As he neared its cover a very fine rain began to fall. The moment he came under cover, the rainfall increased so that, within less than a minute, everyone fled from the considerable shower!

I began thinking that Sai Baba's keeping out of the rain might have been no more than a case of good timing, for I felt it presumptuous of me to think he would have demonstrated this particularly for my benefit. Yet the few people I asked had not paid any attention to his natural-seeming timing. The next morning he again carried out his full round, as he had done the first time, and unhurriedly arrived under the porch just as the Scotch mist was turning to real rain! He had not looked my way once during either of these darshans, and had not come closer than twenty yards. Again

[1] Sathya Sai Baba, Discourse Badrinath Temple, June 17, 1961, *Sathya Sai Speaks*, vol. II (n.d.), p. 52. New Indian edition ISBN 81-7208-118-9: vol. 2, p. 39.

I did not come across anyone who had noticed his having managed to arrive under the veranda roof at the very moment the rain began. I began to realize that he must have, after all, arranged for me to see this.

7

AT PRASHANTHI NILAYAM

Our first darshan was like a brief call at an oasis amid a fairly tortuous desert journey. Its direct effect on us was benevolent, but it was all too short-lived. Intense pains in my thighs, midriff, and neck had begun at night in the hotel in Bangalore. These grew worse on our first night. In the family hall where we had to live for about a week, there were no chairs or beds, and everything had to be done at floor level, which was causing me continual physical strain.

Though I had genuinely not come there with expectations of special treatment in any way, it upset me that we experienced wholly unprovoked unpleasantness from a few of the ashram staff. I was unprepared for the ways of many of the people, especially mindless pushing and forcible line-jumping. I was also put out to hear the words "Sai Ram" used as an all-purpose cliché, especially either pitifully or aggressively by the many beggars outside the ashram, but also by elderly staff ladies, when hissing us angrily away from places that they seemed to wish to clear us out from only when the whim took them.

Even making all allowances for the obvious fact that most things are done differently abroad, the negative sides of life here stood out glaringly for us during our first days. Undoubtedly, one reason for our lack of mental preparation was the many books we had read describing life at Prashanthi Nilayam in nothing but glowing terms.

Though it is quite natural not to dwell on the bad side when thinking of Sai Baba and his ashram, many writers tend to gloss over the problems of being there, which must raise to unrealistic levels the expectations of many potential visitors. On the one hand people are excited about the overall circumstances of being in the presence of Sai Baba and the final fruitfulness of such a visit, while on the other, they are disappointed when they meet the nitty-gritty of daily existence there. Few, if any, of the accounts we had read had laid due weight on what Sai Baba himself says: that wherever the good is, there one will necessarily find the bad nearby also.

We knew we had to sleep in the large concrete-floored and tin-roofed hall. We had to line up outside for none-too-clean washing and toilet facilities. In the family shed there were many disturbances, like crying children, noisy adults, and armies of tiny ants. As the doors were not constantly guarded in those days, sudden thefts of anything edible were perpetrated by sick and ghastly-looking mangy dogs, baggage-bearers, or washerwomen. Yet these were comparatively minor worries for me compared to my back and neck problem.

Looking on the bright side seemed highly unfeasible. Apart from a young couple from Frankfurt who were friendly and helpful, hardly anyone seemed capable, bright, efficient, or even particularly intelligent. I saw only what seemed to me then to be neutral, apparently semi-lifeless devotees of the hazy, helpless sort often found in guru-dominated spiritual movements.

Up to that point I had seen hardly a sign of dynamic, joyous, freely helpful people eagerly putting Sai Baba's teachings into practice at every opportunity, as I had simply assumed would be the rule rather than the exception. We kept getting aggravated by thoughtless, selfish, and undisciplined people around us. Sai Baba has said that people approach him for a variety of reasons. There are those who want some worldly goods of him, those who are sick, suffering, and in need, those who are spiritual seekers, and those who are already realized and wish to have his darshan. Sai Baba made it clear that the last group is by far the smallest, the first the largest. But I had still looked forward to encountering mostly spiritual people, courteous and bright-minded, soft-spoken and happy.

Here I was, feeling reduced to a helpless and needy suppliant myself, down at heart and inequably wavering in spirit at the sort of difficulties that were surely less dramatic than much of what I could observe of others suffering near me. My whole attention was focused on poor old me, and I no longer had much interest or care for others.

There was some small trial to face practically every hour. It is said that Sai Baba knows precisely what each individual goes through and moreover sees to it that each learns exactly the lessons he or she needs, so as to be able to gain maximum benefit from the stay. At that time I had too little experience of ashram life to judge how to take such an assertion. Though I hoped I might eventually receive some sort of attention from Baba, my realistic self managed to keep my expectations of that at a very low level.

By the time of the fourth darshan I received my first general glance from Baba, and it was a look that I was not very keen about. I had seen a similar glance before on the face of the swami in London; an indescribable sort of look, somehow impersonally angry. I was feeling more and more that the visit might be a vast mistake after all, that the conditions facing me were beyond the threshold of what I could stand. Even the lowest minimum of my hopes seemed unfounded. It felt like a real test situation where I was being tried and stretched to my limits.

All optimism, happiness, love, and hope were drained away. In the previous days I had seen others with enormous sufferings all around outside the gates of the ashram—general intense poverty and malnutrition, all sorts of ghastly deformities: a woman whose flesh hung in dozens of awful long clusters like grapes, and wretches dragging what remained of themselves through filth and garbage. From my viewpoint, the Earth seemed generally to be a dreadful place. Nothing, I felt, could ever justify those sorts of scenes, even if one somehow "understood" the horrors of it. That my own illness had rapidly become worse became all the heavier to bear, and seeing others' evidently much worse fates failed to alleviate mine. Despite this, these feelings did not cause me to doubt Sai Baba's divinity.

Faced with the human misery around and within me, I decided that I had had enough of it all and that I wanted to leave. Reidun felt we must wait and see. This calmed and helped me a bit, but then the sense of having to be, as it were, on public display in the family shed with all my physical and mental bad feelings became too much for me. Despite all my self-preparations for the possibility of having to spend a spell in Sai Baba's famous "spiritual repair workshop," there I was indeed, no longer able to see or hear good anywhere—and unwilling to see or hear anything good, as well!

I had already read a good deal about Sai Baba's ways of remolding people in his crucible:

> I must say that I accept certain things, before giving you that
> Grace; I demand and take Sathya, Dharma, Shanti, and Prema.
> I seek the gifts of truth, virtue, peace, and love. I draw you to
> me and then reform and reshape you. I am a kind of smith who
> repairs broken, leaky, damaged hardware. I repair broken hearts
> and fragile minds, warped intellects, feeble resolutions, and fad-
> ing faith.[1]

These repairs appear to require primarily that the broken parts first
become visible to the individual concerned, who must then attempt
to mend his ways.

My antipathy grew, and as if by some vicious circle of fate, everything around me gradually worsened too—or perhaps it only
seemed so. For example, when we were walking past the canteen an
Indian stroller had given us a few green grapes that he said had been
blessed by Baba. However, they were sour-tasting. This seemed to
say to me: "Only sour grapes for you!" As people had begun leaving the ashram in numbers with the New Year over, we heard there
were plenty of room vacancies. Several of our neighbors had moved
into rooms already. We had already gone twice to ask for a room but
had been rejected brusquely and without any attempt at civility. The
injustice of this and all else included, I determined, was too much;
I would not even go to darshan. I only wanted to withdraw from all
these people and lick my wounds, but the problem was where to go.

To get away I walked through waste ground at the rear of the
ashram and up into the scrub-clad hills. Finding a spot where I was
not visible to anyone working in the fields—itself no easy task—I sat
on the ground for about an hour trying to decide what to do. The
loss of my equanimity and my complaints at God for creating a
world of such suffering brought me to tears of final despair. Despite
the dictates of my own reason, I felt like blaming God for the very
existence of the ills and sufferings of this vale of tears. There was no
way out, nowhere else for me to turn from my pain—physical or
emotional. I was brought up against my complete inability to draw
on any further resource within myself, it seemed, and up against a
deep-lying and stubborn distrust and aversion to life, in me some-

---

[1] Sathya Sai Baba, Discourse Prashanthi Nilayam, Oct. 10, 1961, *Sathya
Sai Speaks,* vol. 2 (n.d.), p. 86. New Indian edition ISBN 81-7208-150-
2: vol. 2, p. 77.

where, that throve on frustration. Strangely, I had never really encountered this in myself before. At the time, I had no idea that my having to discover and face up to this was itself the turning point in the permanent cure of it!

Sooner or later I had to move. I went on to get further away, finding a tiny brook and some flat patches of greenery amid the rock and scrub. Beside one of these was a small shrine with a Shiva *lingam* and some fresh tagetes flowers. I mentally asked Sai Baba if he could not at least arrange a room in which I would then do my best to recover some equanimity and start afresh, whatever my illness was like. In this, one could say, I turned to him. The result was very soon forthcoming.

After some time I felt well enough to make my way slowly back in the direction of the ashram. As I was crossing the wall I was hailed from about 100 yards off with the usual "Sai Ram" by one of a group of about eight bullock-cart drivers carrying bricks and mud to the site of yet another ashram building. This was still too much for me to acknowledge, so I ignored it. Other drivers took up the cry, so I eventually raised my hand in greeting. This only loosed a chorus of many excited shouts of "Sai Ram! SAI RAM!" which they kept up until I had moved beyond their line of vision. This incident is as mysterious to me now as it was provocative or disturbing then. I have often observed the drivers of these bullock carts since then and have never seen them behave in such a way.

I had a good long siesta on my own in the empty shed. As soon as I saw Reidun she came to tell me that she had been to the accommodations office and that we had been given the key to a room of our own. This marked a turning point. Thereafter my experiences improved gradually through the remainder of our stay. That night, having recovered somewhat from the crisis, I had a very meaningful dream which implied that Sai Baba was carrying out an operation to reopen my irregular heart where it had suffered, due largely to two traumas in childhood. This is an example of the special and spiritual "open-heart surgery" Sai Baba has effected on many who have visited him.

As if to prove the validity of the adage that what is inside is also outside, the surrounding environment began to improve in my eyes, not least because I began to encounter people and reactions quite different from those that had dogged our first days at Prashanthi Nilayam. Some of those who had seemed a naive and sorry-looking lot, short on initiative, now appeared in quite a different, positive light, as unassuming, unambitious persons practicing spiritual self-discipline, keeping to themselves unless called for, and observing silence rather than chattering away. What was more important to me was that Sai Baba began to look my way without sternness. Though I had not seen him smile so far, I at last heard his voice.

Characteristically, the "thought for the day," which quotes Baba and is written on a blackboard outside the main offices daily, seemed to me to be a fitting comment on the trouble I had just come through:

> The most precious possession is mental equanimity, and it is the one thing you cannot give to another even if you have it. Each has acquired it the hard way. It cannot be earned through a higher standard of life or riches or power or authority or physical strength or scholarship.

I began disciplining myself more in regard to my talkativeness and laziness in not getting up. I tried to sit silently at darshan (or in my case perhaps "less talkatively than usual") until Sai Baba came in our direction. Next day, I saw for the first time that he was standing firmly to make those passes with the hand that I had seen him do on film when materializing holy ash, but my view became obscured at the crucial moment. Silently I asked, "Oh, please do it again. Go on!" He came directly opposite where I was sitting some rows back and produced *vibhuti* in my full view, handing it out to several people in the front row.

So far I had not seen Baba smile once. Having read and heard so much about his overflowing love and relatively little about how stern and overpoweringly impersonal he could appear, I was disoriented as to which accounts to trust and which were over-imaginative. Judging by the glorious reception many authors had been able to report, I began to think that perhaps I was so objectionable as to not even merit seeing the avatar smile. I began to ask him mentally for at least a smile.

One afternoon I was sitting behind a tree with a forked trunk when he approached, smiling. As the tree came between myself and him, I craned and caught sight of him framed alone in the space between the fork. It was like a long "still" picture of him, in which an uneven upper tooth he has was in fact an added charm. He was bending forward toward some devotee and giving that fortunate

person, whoever it may have been, a long, long smile of such penetrating beauty and love as I had ever imagined.
I can still clearly see this inner cameo at will. At the same time
he radiated a brilliance, like a light but not physical light, that struck
me as a truly glorious sheen, a glossy translucence giving a definite
physical impression of whiteness and purity. There is nothing with
which to compare it, unless it was what painters may have seen and
tried to depict as a halo. It was different from the golden "double
halo" I later read about in Dr. Hislop's *My Baba and I*.[2]
About two years later on I came across a very exact description
of the phenomenon, an effulgent and shiny "halo" shape seen by a
devotee and quoted in Sri Ganapati's biography *Baba, Sathya Sai*.[3]
In the official biography by Prof. N. Kasturi, Baba is quoted as having said that "thousands have seen the halo."[4]
All hindrances to our being able to thrive in the ashram had not
been removed, yet I was learning that the lesson was to stand steady
amid all the ups and downs that assailed our feelings, particularly
where our reactions to Sai Baba's attention, or comparative lack of
it, were involved.
I began to feel generally better than before, in body and spirits.
I noticed that Sai Baba was coming physically a bit closer to me at
each darshan. The next day he made *vibhuti* very close by me, and
at last I heard him talk—very gently in a low voice to some men
near me. He came yet closer and stayed about a minute on the next
day. By then he was giving me the odd, quick glance—just as if
making sure I was there, or rather, letting *me* know that he was actually looking for me. I now know that he has often done this with
new arrivals in just the same manner.
While lining up with the many people waiting to enter the compound for darshan, I learned that one is not allowed to take camer-
as in there any longer. As it was too late to deposit mine anywhere,
I had to watch from outside the perimeter wall. So I decided to
make use of my son's old Kodak Instamatic from there, setting it up
to "catch" Sai Baba when he should appear on the porch. It was a

---

[2] J. S. Hislop, *My Baba and I* (San Diego: Birth Day, 1985), pp. 37–39.
[3] Sri Ganapati, *Baba, Sathya Sai* (Madras: Satya Jyoti and Sai Raj, 1984–
1985).
[4] N. Kasturi, *Sathyam, Sivam, Sundaram: The Life of Sathya Sai Baba*, vol.
IV (Prashanthi Nilayam: Sri Sathya Sai Books & Publications Trust,
1980), p. 193.

long wait for the single shot I planned. When the moment came, I snapped, then Baba moved a bit in my direction. I thought saucily to myself, "Come straight on this way, Baba—just climb that intervening fence!" Directly, he moved toward the fence as if to go through it, then simply walked around the edge of it and slowly approached me, making a bee-line toward me. I had not ever seen him take this unusual route at darshan before. In my confusion, I managed one picture but was too taken aback to snap any others when he came straight up into really close range.

We had spoken to a member of a Scandinavian group that met daily under a neem tree for mutual aid, advice, and preparation for any possible group interview to which they might be called. Sai Baba had said, "Yes, yes," to their request for an interview for twenty persons, but it had not come about thus far. We were invited to join, too, which immediately made the lone wolf bristles along my neck twitch in warning, so to speak. In my individualism I had become very wary of all organized groups. So I held back lingeringly before making a trial attendance. However, at the second meeting I went to, one of the members gave each of us a pinch of *vibhuti* that Baba had materialized for him that morning. After all, I thought, groups and rules are sometimes necessary for the great me, too.

Professor N. Kasturi, the long-standing devotee and official biographer of Sai Baba, held some charming noon lectures for overseas devotees. With his unique self-irony he claimed that, though already ailing physically at 86 years of age, thanks to Sai Baba he had entered not his dotage but his "anecdotage." Here we heard firsthand accounts of some of the many major miracles of Baba back as far as the late 1940s, all illumined by Kasturi's glimmering sense of fun and the most expressive of gestures from his exceptionally long, graceful, and very bendy fingers, as well as by his learned depth and practical insights into Sai Baba's teachings. Those lectures, more like heart-to-heart talks, were a genuine inspiration and help to the spirit. I was pleased that we were at last encountering some "ups" to compensate for the "downs."

8

THE LANGUAGE OF SILENCE

Around midday one day, as I was coming from our rooms, a passing devotee made me aware that Sai Baba was nearby, just behind our block, where he was blessing the foundations of a new accommodation roundhouse that was being built. It was already too late to get there, as his car was preparing to take him elsewhere. The car began to approach where I stood. Something prompted me to cross to the other side of its path. I stood quite alone, with no one within a hundred yards. Then it came alongside me close by at a slow pace. His small figure on the back seat all at once looked imposingly huge! How this was possible I cannot say, but many others report having had the same impression at times. He did not look my way but instead angled his head to look up at a spot outside the ashram, and I could see his expression. He was clearly putting off giving me any direct attention, and I felt convinced it was because he was dissatisfied with something I had done. The great problem was exactly what?

It took me a long time to realize clearly what it had been. Not until after we left India did I feel sure I understood. The fact was, he had cast his gaze toward the spot to which I had gone on the day of my crisis, as if to say, "That was a poor show, no equanimity. So now you must wait!" Had I not crossed over the path of the oncoming car, I could not have noticed his looking that way, for I would have only looked at him. I had felt rather silly, crossing before the car, even though it was still at a very safe distance. I couldn't imagine why I had done it!

A similar incident took place one day when Baba walked in a semicircle around where I was sitting, as if pointedly demonstrating avoidance of me and evident dissatisfaction with something I had been feeling. I knew what he meant intuitively, and it was only in later years that I heard of him making the very same, perfect semicircular avoidance at times of a number of other people.

On Sunday, January 13, exactly two weeks after our arrival, hearing that Baba might be leaving Puttaparthi on a journey, I felt that the time had come to make an extra effort and take a chance on praying for healing. During the last two weeks my back and neck tensions had reduced somewhat so that I could just manage to sit cross-legged without too much cramping. While waiting for Sai Baba each day I tried to contemplate some relevant spiritual thought or prayer.

As if in answer to my wish at last to ask for help, I found for the first time that the row I was seated in was selected as the first, front row. I had no definite idea in what manner Sai Baba might answer such a prayer, yet I had previously thought that a definitive way that Baba uses in some cases is to materialize *vibhuti* for the sick person to eat.

I formulated my prayer in words, including just what *sadhana* or spiritual practices I would promise to carry out in the future if my condition should allow it. On this I concentrated as deeply as I could, in silence and with closed eyes, for perhaps 30 minutes.

When I felt it time to open them and look, there was Baba, twenty-five yards off, instantly turning on his heel and hurrying over toward me. Coming close, he fixed me with one sympathetic brown eye as if to say, "Agreed then?" and he stopped to stand firmly and wave his right hand. A dozen hands shot out eagerly from all around me. He beckoned me to put mine out and then his own easily found a space through the jumble of outstretched hands as if they were simply not there. The very fine-grained *vibhuti* fell down exactly into my palm. Sai Baba flicked his thumb, and I saw it send a large speck onto the hand of a tall Swedish boy beside me, with whom I had become acquainted during our stay there. I could not see that so much as a grain was spilled!

Someone I knew had once tried to explain how perfect every movement of Sai Baba's is, and what incredible control he has of every grain of *vibhuti* he makes. However, I have also since often observed him flicking his first two fingers so that a puff of vibhuti is carried on the air like a tiny cloud, usually toward someone or other. So at last I saw what had been meant. Similarly, at her very first darshan, Reidun had seen Baba throw a large pink rose through the air to land right in the hands of a lady devotee several yards away at the rear, in a way that eluded all the hands that reached up.

After having eaten most of the *vibhuti*, I noticed as the day went on that the aches and pains that always came on toward the evening were absent. That night I meditated for half an hour without a hint of neck trouble, which had not happened for years. The next morning was a new year festival (Pongal day or *Sankranti*). Sai Baba gave me what I could see was a brief "check-up" glance as he passed by. I was still feeling fine and was becoming convinced that it was proving to be a cure! That night I dreamed that Shirdi Sai Baba came and gave Reidun and me two large ripe orange-colored papayas.

Some of my old spinal troubles did, however, recur for a day or so, making sitting erect for meditation very trying indeed. Nonetheless, I was quite better.

Baba explains the reason for his healing some who come to him as follows:

> Many of you come to me with problems of health and mental worry of one sort and another. They are mere baits by which you have been brought here. But the main purpose is that you may have grace and strengthen your faith in the divine. Problems and worries are really to be welcomed because they teach you the lessons of humility and reverence. Running after external things produces all this discontent. That type of desire has no end.[1]

Sai Baba said not a word to me during the whole three weeks we were in his presence. I took this to mean that talk is unnecessary, all the more so in my case—my predilection for talking being something I had to work to counteract. At a lecture for foreigners, I also learned that Baba says that too much talking leads to premature loss of memory. (My mother was a great talker who began to lose her memory in her 70s, while her mother was the same and lost hers almost completely in her mid-60s).

---

[1] Sathya Sai Baba, Discourse Prashanthi Nilayam, March 3, 1965, *Sathya Sai Speaks*, vol. IV (n.d.), p. 303. New Indian edition ISBN 81-7208-1153-7: vol. V, p. 70.

At the entrance to the temple compound, people often bow and make the Indian *namaskar* greeting with clasped hands, along the line made through the temple by its two main doors. I had also begun regularly to do this as a reminder and a self-discipline for trying to develop humility and faith, mentally directing the greeting to divinity and toward Baba. One morning, seeing that Sai Baba was unexpectedly visible in the compound, I hurried to the men's gate and on the way had to pass the temple's central entrance. As I did so, I clasped my hands in greeting and, to my surprise, saw that Baba was actually standing right in the line of my greeting, under the roof of the porch some thirty yards away. He was standing sideways to me and talking to a man, but his head turned instantly in response to my *namaskar* and he regarded me for some moments. It was very unexpected and, not knowing why, I moved a little and repeated my greeting. Again he turned immediately and looked at me—a striking instance of his extraordinary awareness and wordless communication.

From then until the afternoon I wondered about this response of his. The gestures of recognition had been most welcome, of course. Yet it awoke various difficult feelings in me, evoking how I had as a boy made exactly the same bow and greeting to the Holy Spirit when crossing the line of the nave in church, as I had been taught to do. This perturbed me, in case Baba might be suggesting I could benefit by becoming a churchgoer again—a very far from attractive idea to me! I was repelled by the thought of ever having to sit through misguided interpretations at sermons about often ill-translated texts which, among other failings, imply the inferiority of other religions and ways to God. Finding a quote from one of Baba's discourses eventually saved the day for me, namely, "It is good to be born in a church, but it is not good to die in it." [2]

Later I also realized that this episode actually helped me to recover more of my own inner boyhood faith, as if renewing it by separating it from the circumstances and feelings that had weakened it at the time. I even enjoyed recalling one charming and joyous old vicar who had really been both naturally himself and also enlightening to listen to, but whom I had never thought of since, until that day. What a relief he had been, to me, compared with the unctuously-serious, boring repetitiveness of most of the clergy.

---

[2] Sathya Sai Baba, Discourse Prashanthi Nilayam, July 29, 1969, *Sathya Sai Speaks*, vol. VII (n.d.), p. 85. New Indian edition ISBN 81-7208-157-X: vol. 9, p. 79.

Meanwhile, I was still uncertain about all this at afternoon darshan and was hoping for some sign to confirm that I need not bother about church services. I saw a smile flicker across Sai Baba's face as he passed me. After a brief round of the compound, he was soon hidden from my view by the pillars of the crowded porch. I thought to myself, "He must be standing there just about where he was when he acknowledged my greetings." Just then, his torso popped into view, bent forward at a right angle, and he looked right toward me. This made me let out a loud peal of laughter that momentarily felt quite out of place amid the silence of the thousand or more devotees who evidently saw no funny side to it. Such is Sai Baba's incomparable brand of humor, hand-tailored as if to personal taste or need, in this case answering my questions. And I had always felt that if God lacked a sense of humor, I would surely choose to go in some other direction! The odd posture Baba adopted surely came of his letting me see him while remaining standing on the same spot as that morning.

The next day I discovered that it was possible for Westerners to sit in the *mandir* (i.e., temple) during the singing of *bhajans*. While awaiting the start, I noticed Baba through a small lattice window beside me. He stood just a few yards off at exactly the same spot that he had stood to gesture to me twice before. I was placed so that I could see him through this window at an acute angle, while he was not visible to others inside the temple. I watched him talking with one of the chief ashram officials for all of ten minutes, and his expression and manner toward this man were very severe all the time. It was surprising to see this, and it answered some of my private musings as well as showed how demanding it surely is for those who live close to him and hold responsible positions. I felt sure that Baba knew he was letting me watch him for so long at such close quarters. Right since first seeing him, he had been coming nearer gradually, "step by step," as it were.

That day he also answered some questions of a very private nature, which I tried putting to him mentally as he sat on his chair keeping the beat for the music during the afternoon *bhajans* in the temple. With my background in logic and scientific skepticism, I was very loath to accept interpretations of meanings or significances that are not securely founded in the facts of a matter, and all the less so where vital personal matters are at stake! Still, I was already convinced that Sai Baba is telepathic, and the answers he gave each question, immediately, by looking straight at me with expressive and affirmative nods and one negative head-shake, were so unmistakably for me—even though I sat amid a hundred others—that I had to marvel at the ease and clarity of the communication. In fact, one of the questions about a spiritual goal sprang into my mind unannounced. This question was of a nature that I had never even contemplated before and came ready-worded in a symbolic way that was very unlike my way of thinking—yet I found I had already "asked" it of him unthinkingly (not my way at all!). His very definitive nod came a split second later. This left me surprised and befuddled, but also very grateful too! I am convinced that he actually put the idea into my mind and influenced me to ask it! Following the example and advice of close devotees, I keep to myself the content of interchanges that are close to the heart, as in this case.

Sai Baba left Prashanthi Nilayam on a tour to Madras and elsewhere in India. We stayed on about a week more, during which Reidun had a quite serious stomach infection. When she was on the way to recovery but still not feeling well enough to travel, I went on a quick two-day pilgrimage to Mysore, traveling by bus, train, autorickshaw, and horse-cart. This excursion proved as physically strenuous as anything I had been subjected to since well before my illness began. There were seven and a half hours squashed tight on a truly over-crowded bone-shaking bus, then four hours of walking carrying a very heavy shoulder bag, and five hours more sitting on the corridor floor of a second-class train compartment. Not one single pain or other symptom of illness did I feel!

The place I visited was a small temple and orphanage at Srirangapatnam, which had many most attractive photos of Sai Baba on which thick layers of *vibhuti* continuously formed; one was almost "snowed under." It stood almost vertically, and the ash was configured in a way very like the snow can be in the deepest frosts of winter in Norway. Only the facial features of Sai Baba were visible in a central clear patch.

Another picture, which had been wiped clear the night before, had a few small patches of ash forming around Sai Baba's heart. There was also a faded photograph on the wall of Shirdi Sai Baba— presumably one of the four extant photos, according to authorities on the subject. The temple keeper pointed out his father standing in the background of the snapshot. He told me that he had been a thief before Baba picked him out of a crowd and told him to start the orphanage. He also told me that his father had been granted a wish by Shirdi Sai Baba—that he would look after the son who stood before me! Quite evidently this wish had been granted very liberally.

In a glass jar were two small amulets of the sort one can buy in stalls in Puttaparthi, one bearing a colored picture of Sathya Sai and the other of Shirdi Sai. From these ran a slightly-yellowish-tinged liquid, or *amrit*, that tastes very sweet and has a heavenly flavor. The closest I can describe its taste is to combine the taste of South Indian runny honey with a tropical jasmine scent. Yet even this hardly does justice to its refined aroma. I was able to see how droplets slowly formed from each of these amulets—each no bigger than an undersized coin—while holding them on my hand. The jar was almost full and the temple-keeper already had drained off a supply, from which he gave me about a quarter of a liter. I had come there hoping to obtain some and to be able to bring some of this *amrit* back to Norway for others there.

The day before I left Puttaparthi on this excursion, Reidun and I had been looking at various stalls in the village, full of Sai trinkets and memorabilia, of which a wide variety of sorts and qualities exist. I had been very much taken by a small and very cheap amulet that had a picture of Sathya Sai on one side and Shirdi Baba on the other. Reidun thought it was an unnecessary purchase and bustled me on (usually when shopping our roles are the reverse). I insisted that I liked it and went back to the stall and bought it. The two amulets from which *amrit* was issuing at Srirangapatna were the same size and bore the identical pictures and framing, a typical though minor Baba synchronicity.

Baba is said to have produced this *amrit* (called "holy ambrosia" in the Christian tradition) in a variety of ways. At one of his lectures, Professor Kasturi had recently told me that, in 1945, when Baba had visited the sands of the Chitravati river with devotees on many evenings, *amrit* had sometimes begun to run from his hands while he clapped time to bhajans. Sometimes Baba simply let it run into people's mouths or palms, and once he had raised his hands to receive a conch "out of thin air" above him,[3] from which he poured

---

[3] The conch is sacred to Lord Vishnu, of whom all the major Indian avatars are incarnations. The primordial creative sound or word "OM" issued from a conch. Conches are essential to all Hindu rituals and are also blown on festive occasions.

amrit into a vessel. Kasturi said Baba had given it to people on many, many occasions, and once he had seen Baba materialize a small golden spoon to serve it to devotees. I have since also seen the continuous film sequence by Richard Bock of Baba serving *amrit* with such a spoon from a very small vessel to more than 2,000 devotees who received it from him in person at Prashanthi Nilayam during one sitting on the day (May 7th) that commemorates Baba's mother, Easwaramma day!

The temple keeper also showed me two *lingams* materialized by Sai Baba. These were the size and shape of an egg, looking as if they were made of stone, but apparently they were not; their material is an enigma. One was made by a wave of the hand, and the other had emerged from Baba's stomach through his mouth, in the dramatic and painful way in which Baba used to create lingams publicly in past years, during the annual Shivarathri festival. The form of Sai Baba was supposedly visible in markings on this Shivarathri *lingam*, although I could not discern it myself.

There was also a large, heavy silver medallion with the head of Sathya Sai Baba on one side and the elephant head of the divine form of Ganesha on the other. Outside the temple, under a sort of covered porch in a garden overlooking a river, was a raised altar-like plinth, on top of which was a carved representation of the feet of Shirdi Baba in jet black stone. From these feet issued ambrosia with a stronger scent than the other had had. The feet could be wiped dry with a handkerchief, upon which the liquid seeped forth again. The only handkerchief I had at the time was quite soiled, but the keeper of the shrine insisted that it made no difference and wiped the feet with my handkerchief, saying that this *amrit* was not for tasting, but for the scent only. (After about four years I noticed the formation of fungus on it, so I decided that the time had come to wash it and thus sacrifice the ambrosial scent. I washed it very thoroughly with a strong soap and then rinsed it well. When dry, it was clean but otherwise exactly as before! The ambrosial perfume is still just as pervasive as I write this, twelve years after wiping the feet with it.)

Before visiting the Srirangapatnam temple, I had already been given a few drops of the ambrosia and some *vibhuti* from one of the pictures. What was special about the *vibhuti* I received at the temple, however, was that it tasted very fragrant and was exactly the same as that which my wife and I had received through the swami on the occasion of our marriage, of which he had reportedly said, "It is from Sai"! I had not come across any other *vibhuti* with that particular fragrance before, though I have had a taste of quite a few different varieties of this holy ash of Sathya Sai's through the years. However, about nine years later I visited the house of a Sai Baba devotee in London, where large quantities of *vibhuti* had been forming continuously for five years on many pictures, in jars, and in vases. The *vibhuti* was of various sorts, one variety having exactly that distinct fragrance. Reidun and I had even inexplicably smelled just that fragrance in the air twice while going there on the train, even though we had no idea whatsoever that we were on the way to a place where such manifestations took place.

Sometime during this India visit, I attended a lecture for foreigners by Al Drucker, one of the earliest of American devotees to go to Baba. He related that when he had once gone to Srirangapatnam to get *amrit*, Baba had commented that he should seek only the *amrit* of Sai's presence instead. Then the bottle of *amrit* in his rucksack, though most carefully packed, had inexplicably broken, and all his effects had been soaked. Drucker added that Baba has said that anyone who tastes his *amrit* should never thereafter defile his tongue either with alcohol or untruth.

On a later visit to India, I asked Professor Kasturi about the story of the stone feet, for I had heard that he had brought them there himself. Baba had previously given instructions for the construction of the porch and plinth beside the river and had later sent Kasturi along with the feet, which had been ordered from a carver elsewhere. Baba then visited the place and the ambrosia began to flow. That was nearly twenty years previously, in 1967.

After discussing the manifestations described and other related incidents with Professor Kasturi, there seemed to be no doubt that these were all genuine Sai *leelas*. He told me that he had witnessed large-scale manifestations of *vibhuti* and *amrit* through the previous two decades at this place, although there had been a period when they had all temporarily ceased.

What I did not know before my visit there was that, as early as 1971, Sai Baba warned generally as follows:

> . . . there are some who distribute amrit, vibhuti, and other articles, announcing that they are showering from my pictures at their places; they do this free for some weeks, and later, they

start begging for money, like any common mendicant! This is sin, to ask so and also to give so. Devotees should keep far away from such places and persons.[4]

Again, in Febuary 1988, the official journal *Sanathana Sarathi*, published the following under the title *"The Warning, Again"*:

We have received enquiries from overseas devotees as to whether they can make donations to organisations in India carrying Sri Sathya Sai Baba's name and claiming to run orphanages at Srirangapatnam (in Karnataka) or educational institutions at Visakhapatnam (in Andhra Pradesh). Recognised Sathya Sai Service Organisations are not permitted to solicit donations from any source. Overseas devotees are hereby cautioned against making contributions to any institution seeking donations as a Sathya Sai Organisation.[5]

Unfortunately, it is therefore my duty to warn that the place I visited used the name "Sri Sathya Sai Baba" in collecting donations on false premises, for I later learned that it is definitely not authorized to do so. It is even against Indian law, not being a registered charity, and foreigners who donate can in fact even be prosecuted.

Especially during our last days at Prashanthi Nilayam, we became acquainted with some people from various parts of the world, nearly always hearing something well out of the ordinary from them. One evening we were sitting in a shrine room near to the flower-bedecked shrine of Mr. Walia, the gardener at Prashanthi Nilayam. We had been talking about an episode I had read about a lady who had not believed Sai Baba to be genuine until she saw a flower fall from his picture three times after she herself had fixed it back on securely with a rubber band. A lady from Sweden was present; she was most happily telling us that she felt as if she had found her true home there in Prashanthi—when suddenly she started up with a shriek. A flower had simply jumped out over two yards from the shrine, from a garland around a picture of Baba, and had landed on her hands in her lap! At first she had taken it to be a large insect.

---

[4] Sathya Sai Baba, *Sathya Sai Speaks*, vol. VII, p. 34.
[5] Sathya Sai Baba, *Sanathana Sarathi*, Feb. 1988.

I knew that I would regret it if, before we left, I did not manage one proper meditation under the tree that Sai Baba had planted for this purpose many years back. At the planting in 1959 he had reportedly materialized a thick copper plate, about 15 by 10 inches in size, covered in mystic symbols and letters in many known and unknown alphabets. This was buried under the roots of the *bodhi* tree, which is the same sort of tree under which the Buddha sat and attained the ultimate realization. This plate, Sai Baba had told those present, would energize the spot spiritually and aid those who would come there to meditate from all parts of the world, for a very long time to come.

It was a warm sunny evening that my wife, a lady friend, and I went to the *bodhi* tree. Ever since my neck problems had begun, with their effect on spatial awareness, I could no longer sense within me the location of the center of my forehead, and meditation had become a trial.

After about ten minutes under the *bodhi* tree, I felt a drop of something fall on my forehead, near to the middle. In contrast to those Himalayan monks over whom one can pour buckets of iced water without disturbing their meditation, *I* had to see what this drop was! It seemed to be water, though its effect on the sense of touch was more vital. I continued to try to meditate. Sure enough, as I had begun to wish for, another drop fell, marking what I then knew was exactly the center of the forehead. It almost burned its way into the skin, yet it was pleasant, too. It was not long before I got up to examine the leaves of the tree above where I sat. They were bone dry. I checked with my wife and friend as to whether they had felt raindrops, perhaps, but they had not, and the sky was completely clear.

9

LEELAS AND PEACE OF MIND

Some of the *leelas* attributed to Sai Baba are what some would perhaps call "extraordinary coincidences," even though they are too extraordinary to be chance happenings. Moreover, many of them bear the clear signature of Baba. He says of them that they are "divine play," or sport on the playground of the cosmos. They include various forms of creation, protection, and healing but also sometimes cause loss, too, such as the removal of unnecessary burdens, unfruitful desires, or bad traits in a person.

Through such *leelas*, we are undoubtedly drawn closer to divinity. William Temple, former Archbishop of Canterbury, once remarked that what was miraculous to him but seemed to be only coincidence to others, stopped happening to him only when he didn't pray. No one, to my knowledge, can predict the *leelas* of Sai Baba or why and when he performs them for anyone. Yet they seem mostly to occur where or when there is some intensity of genuine need, faith, inward worship, or selfless service activity.

We had heard several firsthand accounts of journeys to and from Sai Baba on which remarkable *leelas* had occurred, making things smooth and unproblematical. A Danish engineer we met, who was in India for a development agency, and who was highly skeptical of spiritual teachers, was traveling from Bombay to Frankfurt at the same time as we were, but via an expensive airline. We all left Bombay around midnight, very tired from journeying since the crack of dawn. My wife and I traveled by Air India and found we had a whole row of five vacant seats each to stretch out on and sleep

all the way. Arriving at Frankfurt we met the exhausted Dane waiting for his connection. His plane had been full up to the very last
seat. Though this may have been mere chance, the regularity with
which similar strokes of good fortune occur to Sai Baba pilgrims
shows that very special circumstances must be at work. One often
hears such people report that an empty seat was beside them on the
plane, often the only remaining vacancy. Baba has on occasion referred to the extra "empty" seat as his seat. In later years, Reidun
and I also experienced the famous empty seat beside us more than
once, also in an otherwise fully-packed airbus.

When aboard the plane on the last leg toward Scandinavia, we
realized too late that we had not asked for vegetarian food at the
check-in counter. This presented us with a dilemma, because we had
been following Sai Baba's declared wish and advice to spiritual aspirants, to eat only vegetarian food.

Though we had both been vegetarians for many years, we had
lapsed occasionally in the previous year or two. I had long hated the
maltreatment of animals on the vast scale that the whole meat industry involves. I had also realized that the effects of uric acid on
health and the human body, which cannot eliminate it sufficiently,
are only among the most obvious ills of meat consumption. Further,
the lessons Georg Borgstrøm gave the world on the enormous pro-
tein-wastefulness of producing meat, instead of utilizing crops directly, are enough to make any rational person wish to see
vegetarianism become universal in the future. Despite all this, I had
found no fully-valid grounds for not sometimes eating meat. So, in
the unrepentant Norwegian meat-eating society, which made no allowances for vegetarians, we had continued eating some fish and
eggs.

Besides, neither the short-term nor long-term effects of all the
many micro-chemical components of a carnivorous diet on the
largely unknown and impenetrable electrochemistry of the human
brain and subsequently even on urges, thoughts, feelings, and the
more subtle aspects of the psyche remains a closed book to modern
science, for all its amazing techniques. In addition to such considerations, too, are Sai Baba's frequent explanations of the unrecog-
nized, subtle, and long-term karmic consequences of eating animals
that are kept and killed for human consumption (in all those societies, that is, where living from hunting is not a natural necessity).
After visiting Baba and keeping to a non-animal diet while at his

ashram, according to his rule, we felt we wanted to be as complete vegetarians as possible.

The stewardess said she had no vegetarian meals for those who had not ordered them, and only two persons on that flight had. She then gave us two "normal" cartons, which contained slices of boiled egg, meat, and smoked fish. She even showed us those two vegetarian meals while passing us, so, as she said, we might know what they looked like for the next time we flew, and she apologized that they were not for us.

We did not immediately break the plastic on our food packs, and five minutes later the stewardess came back to us, clearly flustered and actually blushing as if she had made an error. Were we *sure* we hadn't ordered vegetarian after all? She checked our tickets and seats, but we had not. Yet she said that she had asked throughout the aircraft and no one else had ordered vegetarian meals. So she exchanged our packs for the vegetarian meals anyhow! We both felt strongly that this was a sign, probably a Sai *leela*, and the message was to stick strictly to vegetarian food.

Having provided ourselves with a big load of books about Sai Baba, including the series of spiritual teachings that were penned by him in earlier years for publication in the journal *Sanathana Sarathi*, we studied the teachings more thoroughly still. The wide range of accounts of people who have come to him, each under unique circumstances, and each to experience a whole range of instances of his nature as indicative of omniscience, omnipotence, omnipresence, and "omnifelicity," were a great inspiration. We reveled in this ever-expanding marvel, always thirsty for more of its inspiring spirit. However, since much reading in fact gets one nowhere at all unless practical consequences follow from it—as Baba emphasizes again and again—I was determined to improve my spiritual practice, if only I could. Baba has often made it very clear that, in order to get closer to the sphere of the avatar himself and to progress toward the goal of realization, there must be yearning, effort, and *sadhana* (spiritual practice).

As a result of this India trip, I discovered in a deeper way how we in the West see problems in a host of circumstances that must seem preposterous to a poor Indian. India brought home to me again and again that there actually are people who do live happily and unselfishly under conditions that most of us could not envisage ever tolerating. During our visit there we came across a woman beggar who had only half a body and sat on the dusty and garbage-filled street, literally radiating love to us! There was definitively no "sales pitch" about her demeanor; it was something beyond anything I have experienced anywhere else in the world, and she was not the only such person we encountered among the very poor. I definitely do not think that we should condone poverty or consider material destitution a blessing in any sense. At the same time, never having seen anything remotely like the same felicity and brightness of spirit among the beggars and paupers of Europe, I recognized that in the case of a few such Indians, I was seeing demonstrated the spiritual adage that "only one who has nothing can truly possess everything". "Having nothing" can also be taken in the sense of being totally detached from a sense of ownership or selfishness toward whatever one happens to own.

I can think of nothing harder than the task of eliminating all dependencies, self-centeredness, and egoism. Baba teaches, however, that there is in fact nothing easier than life without any of them, for they create intolerable burdens that destroy peace of mind and cause endless types of sorrow! If one suffers from none of them, one might surely congratulate oneself on being nothing but a blissful saint in all things—except that self-congratulation itself is a form of egoism.

At various times I have viewed the causes of the troubles I have experienced as stemming from the demands and shortcomings of relatives, the fickleness of friends, the ills of the social system, the mediocrity of people in various professions, authorities, and so on. Who hasn't, in the thoughtless and cruel world? Yet even though I have certainly often had good reason for such complaints, the only way to surmount the problems at long last proved to be to change myself. The alterations needed have already been many, both in mental attitude and in practical action. Non-attachment or selflessness is not just an attitude one can adopt and realize at the mere drop of a hat, of course. It comes as a result of gradual self-discipline to counteract self-centeredness and control the impulses of body and mind. Yet I feel that the need for furthering this self-renunciation at an adult level, which arose as the only means to further spiritual growth, was made evident and the task was made possible only after the arrival of Baba in the forefront of my life.

As can well be imagined, it was something of a letdown to have to return to my university work again, but at least I was not suffering from neck problems. When I arrived at my office, a letter was waiting for me with a sudden and quite unexpectedly large sum of money in back-pay. During my absence, a long-standing claim for seniority increments for teachers in my category had been approved. The sum that I was able to collect, after tax deductions and so on, was N.Kr. 20,134 (Norwegian Kroner). Now it so happens that I have not kept up any clear or accurate record of my expenditures for years. But the evening before returning to work, I had actually calculated how much money we had spent on the entire India visit. I had rounded the result to the quite accurate sum of twenty thousand Norwegian Kroner! Of course, the tally between this and the back-pay could be thought a coincidence, were it not for the fact that there are many reports of the same type of unexpected "refunds" of travel expenses on Sai Baba visits, on other journeys following him, or in going to events connected with his organization, in the literature by people from around the world. I had not expected it to happen in my case, not least because we felt the visit to have been quite affordable to us at the time. Since then I have met several people for whom money for the visit has come in very dramatic and completely unexpected ways, when they had no money, and with some typical Baba hallmark involved in each case.

As the weeks went by, I began to feel the very gradual return of tensions in my neck and back. Though it began ever so slowly, the realization that I was not permanently cured, as I had assumed I was, came as quite a shock. I did not lose faith in Baba, though, for my experiences had by then been such that I felt quite secure in that faith.

A few days after having had to admit that I really was slowly relapsing into very much the same condition as before, I happened to be reading the delightful two-volume book by Sri Ra Ganapati, *Baba: Sathya Sai*, which noted that, while many of Baba's cures by *vibhuti* are permanent, some visitors to Sai Baba are cured only temporarily, often so that they can get settled in with some new *sadhana*, such as service or meditation. In fact, one of the chief reasons I had specifically wanted the cure from Baba was so that I could regularly manage to do the meditation he recommends.

Naturally enough, I wondered much about the return of my ailments, for they increased more and more until, five months after our visit, I was actually physically unable to continue my lecturing and examination work any longer.

From Ganapati's book I learned that the duration of Sai Baba's cures can sometimes vary for reasons that no one knows. No reliable rules can be drawn up about the great variety of the cures he can effect, whether partial or whole, temporary or permanent. However, I had to begin another series of self-examinations.

I could not at first realize how Baba helped me most. It had more to do with a new faith and considerable peace of mind than with relief from pain. It is often hard for persons who have not had an undiagnosable illness that becomes chronic to understand what effect this can have on one's life. Uncertainty as to the future becomes the law of each day. My physical sufferings belonged to the category of the medically unknown, which I am aware is still a much larger category than most of the medical profession either know or wish to admit. From my visits to many types of experts and therapists—both orthodox and alternative—and wanderings along the corridors of the medical powers-that-be, I learned that most spinal and muscular problems are hardly understood and that "human error" is at its peak among doctors. The discovery of the arrogant fallibility of professionals, the continuous sending of difficult cases from pillar to post and all that this involved, caused me more worry, even, than thoughts about how the illness itself would develop.

After my return from India, these matters became very much easier for me to handle, both mentally and practically. I was in increasingly good spirits. Since then I have not suffered from the low spirits that would occur from time to time throughout my adult life, and I have had notably improved overall equanimity and patience.

I would not presume to generalize on how Baba confers real and lasting peace of mind, yet I seem to derive it both from a combination of adult maturity, with faith inspired by his *leelas*, and the experience of having been in his presence. The richness and rightness of his teachings, never far from my thoughts, dispel most otherwise disturbing ideas and worries. The sense of his omnipresence is also intensified by his continued regular visits to me in dreams.

10

DREAMS FROM THE SOURCE

Sathya Sai Baba has frequently said that no person can dream of him unless he himself desires it.[1] That Sai Baba comes in dreams is certainly a great inspiration and is often an aid, even if—as sometimes in my experience—there is a message in them that can be hard to understand or accept. Baba has often told devotees that he comes to them in dreams, and that when anyone dreams of him, it really is a visit from him. A young Danish friend of mine had some dreams of Baba and was in doubt as to whether they were to be fully relied on. At a private interview, Baba confirmed that he had actually been present with him, and that every dream of Baba amounts to the same as having his darshan.

Many people have regular dream darshans, and Sai Baba uses the dream scenario both to "visit," instruct, and correct, as well as to amaze, enthuse, and convey moods of love, peace, and exquisite joy. It seems beyond doubt that Baba's grace is entirely unrestricted by any quantitative physical conditions such as the number of dreams and people he visits, the duration of the dream, or the extent of what it can effect.

Such clear visits or visitations in dreams and the subsequent proofs of their validity appear to be so uncommon elsewhere in world culture that many find this hard to give credence to. The

---

[1] E. B. Fanibunda, *Vision of the Divine* (Bombay: Sri Sathya Sai Books & Publications, 1976), p. 99.

Yoga Sutras of Patanjali[2] state that an aspirant gets guidance through dreams, but it does not state that God can appear "in person" or set up the entire dreaming scenario, as Baba clearly often does.

In reporting some of the instances learned during decades of meeting those drawn to Baba from India and abroad, Professor Kasturi has written that it is beyond doubt that Baba plans, designs, and structures the dreams through which he initiates or deepens his impact on people.[3]

The nature of the scenarios and the range of subtle and direct connections of Baba's words, hints, or symbolic types of instruction, with what later occurs in "waking reality," are a form of "self-exhibiting evidence." Their content demonstrates the influence of the divine agency beyond normal or natural limitations. I, therefore, relate here some of the many dreams that I have been fortunate enough to experience, that have come "from the source."

The understanding of dreams has for ages been a portal to self-inquiry and thus spiritual improvement. Always having been an enthusiastic sleeper, and all too frequently an over-sleeper as well I'm afraid, I have had at least my fair share of dreams. Very seldom do I awaken without remembering some dream, and quite often long and intense ones. Why this is so in my case I do not really know, but the dreams have often been quite awe-inspiring, both nightmarish and paradisiacal.

I learned how one can recall dreams in considerable detail by retracing them before becoming fully awake and then writing them down shortly after getting up. I did not fall into the mistake of interpreting them according to any one theory, largely due to a book that I came across in the early 1960s titled *Dreams: Mirror of Conscience,* by Werner Wolff, which favored a many-sided approach to all such symbols and dream theories that have been held through-

---

[2] Swami Prabhavananda and C. Isherwood, *Yoga Aphorisms: The Yoga Sutras of Patanjali* (London, 1953). This classical Indian yoga source is from A.D. 300, and has been commented on by India's greatest thinkers since, such as Vyasa and Adi Shankara. Trevor Leggett's translation of Shankara's newly-discovered commentaries and the sutras to which they refer is perhaps the most illuminating English source. See Trevor Leggett, *Sankara on the Yoga Sutras* (Delhi: Motilal Banarsidas, 1990).

[3] N. Kasturi, *Sathyam, Sivam, Sundaram,* vol. IV (Prashanthi Nilayam: Sri Sathya Sai Books & Publications, 1st ed., 1980), pp. 85ff.

out the world. It is well-known that dreams can have symbolic functions, bringing into consciousness, in a variety of subtle and strange ways, impulses, emotions, and notions that have been excluded from the individual's awareness for all kinds of different reasons.

With interpretations based on any theory, one must often go to absurd lengths to twist and turn dream materials into some sort of meaning. I soon discovered the futility of efforts to drag meaning from every dream or image. The Freudian theory that all dreams express at least some elements of wish-fulfillment, has occasional validity, but is obviously far too narrow an idea to apply to all dreams. The approach of C. G. Jung is much deeper and mostly non-doctrinal, supported by his archetype theory. Yet it seems that even his ideas do not do justice to the full scope of possible dreams.

It is a common experience among those who receive Sai Baba's help and guidance through dreams and visions (and this occurs in normal interviews, too) that the experience often has concealed significance that takes a considerable time to discover and understand. When the time is ripe and they do yield insights, these are very clear, with the correct interpretation seen as self-evident, as in seeing all the pieces of a jigsaw puzzle fit into place. Of course, some dreams speak directly for themselves at once, especially certain vivid and strongly moving dreams.

One example of the latter occurred during my university studies and I now know it to have been an early intimation that the spiritual search would not prove to be wasted effort and that unseen help was also coming from somewhere to help me keep my worldly footings and induce me to continue with the studies that often bored me dreadfully. As part of my M.A. work I spent a year and a half studying the history of ideas at Oslo University. The aging professor who reigned at that institute had apparently simply been adding everything to the syllabus that he had found important since his original appointment, so that the reading material had become extremely voluminous, with far too many thousands of pages of obligatory reading ranging throughout the classics of European philosophy, history, literature, and religion. I got through most of this somehow, but when the marathon eight-hour examinations came, it was a matter of chance what to review.

The night prior to the most crucial exam, I had a very extensive and vivid dream, in which I took Dante's place, being met by Virgil and given a detailed guided tour down to hell! Fortunately for me it did not end there! I was likewise conducted through the devil's jaws into purgatory and finally even up into paradise, where I had a wonderful glimpse of the celestial spheres. The dream was so remarkable because it followed the entire course of Dante's wanderings in his work *The Divine Comedy* that, though somewhat incredulous at the idea that it might be a premonitory dream, I nonetheless used the last half hour or so before the exam reviewing my notes on it. Sure enough, the obligatory set question was to give an account of one central idea of Dante, showing its development through his poem *The Divine Comedy*. It was with some awe that I set about this task, accounting for his idea of the "eternal soul" and its development through the various spheres. I could hardly believe my good fortune, nor the exam results that later appeared. (To a spiritual seeker, academic studies surely often bore like hell and feel like purgatory.)

Even after I met the swami in England, it took years before I was able to realize that not only gurus, but also God, himself, can and really does communicate directly with the dreamer, assuming whatever form is appropriate in order to instruct. As the following summaries show, I was gradually taught in dreams, through explicit language or verbal hints from Baba, through non-verbal demonstration, distinct symbolism, precognition of events, and by other means.

Years before Sai Baba became the focus of my life, I had dreams that heralded his approach. Although I had read books about him, he was then still a distant figure of speculation rather than one of substance to me. The following are some examples of the variety of ways in which Baba may communicate in dreams and directly steer one's surrounding events, from both great physical distance and temporal remove.

I had the following dream long before I came to Baba:

> I was peacefully sharing a large natural garden with many birds and animals, where I pointed out a magnificent golden eagle to Reidun. A voice announced, as if to prepare us, "Here comes God!" The animals all turned towards an approaching white-robed figure and joined his entourage as he passed. He was most kind and fatherly and we were awe-inspired at his presence. We bowed our heads to the earth until he was almost past us. He was old and white-haired.

Though Sai Baba is younger and has black hair, I now recognize this white-robed figure as just another outward form of the same Holy Spirit that I was led to discover later.

Two months before my last meeting with my mother, shortly before I knew of the joyous event of Sai Baba's miraculous visit to her in the clinic, I had two dreams that I can now see were also heralding his arrival. The first reflects his dramatic entry into my life, so to speak.

> *Dream of June 20, 1983:* I was at home looking out onto the beauty of our local nature when a tremendously powerful shock of a crash occurred, and instantaneously an enormous head of a bull splintered its way through the wall beside me. Reidun was frightened, but I felt only great joy and said, "It's Shiva!" She then recognized this too. I said that he made the sun shine, the wind blow, the grass sway, and he even sends the mail. The wind blew to prove it, and several letters and a postcard came addressed to me from Shiva. I saw many natural events and that they were due to his agency, including a holy *lingam*[4] that came through the wall, too.

---

[4] The slightly elongated but wholly symmetrical oval *lingam* is, above all, the symbol of creation, and its form is that of creation or the universe, according to scriptures and to Sathya Sai Baba, who has produced many such *lingams* in the course of his advent, some having curative properties, some being of different colors and of unidentifiable materials, and some shining mysteriously with a light from within (*jyothi lingam*). The method of production varies, but on the holy Maha-Shivarathri or great night of Shiva, which falls on the new moon in late February or early March each year, Baba used to produce them from his stomach through his mouth, as if regurgitating them. This was witnessed yearly each Maha-Shivarathri day by hundreds of thousands of people until the late 1960s, when the crowds became too enormous. The event and production of the *lingam* was even filmed by the late Richard Bock of Hollywood. According to Sai Baba, the ovoid *lingam* has the form most approximate to the concept of the formless, attributeless Absolute. It has no beginning or end and is thus a symbol of infinity. The term *lingam* is used both to refer to these nearly egg-shaped (but symmetrical) ellipsoid objects, of which there are various types (with names such as *Shivalingam, Brahmanandalingam,* etc.) and also to the more well-known cylindrical objects found in countless shrines and Shiva temples, interpreted by Western observers, on

At that time I had forgotten what I had once learned of the symbolism of the *lingam* from my Indian seaman friend, Hari. Also, I looked up Shiva in an encyclopedia to see what connection there was to a bull. God is Shiva, who rides on the bull (his motive power) Nandi, a symbolism that is very ancient in India. Though I had doubtless read of it once, I had certainly forgotten about it long before. It long perplexed me that such an intense dream gave me so much joy when I could not understand the reason. It was about six years later that I came across a quotation in a book about India that surprised me. Unfortunately, the source was not given, but the quote was, "Shiv, who poured the harvest and made the winds to blow"! That concurred so well with my dream that it could hardly be a mere coincidence.

> *Dream of November 30, 1983*: I wandered into a bazaar. A dark, Eastern-clad person had a huge amber-colored egg ornament that was set up on a gold pedestal. It was on sale at a price I could afford. I thought I might buy it as a present for Reidun. The man said the price did not include the frame, and I did not buy it. Later in the dream I wandered back that way, and the same man was still there with the *lingam*, but I left without approaching the stall again.

Comment: Sometimes, Baba also appears in dreams in different guises, frequently having a symbolic meaning, yet one which may tax all one's resources to discover. Among other things, I think this referred to my unreadiness to "buy" the teaching that then seemed in some ways incomplete to me from someone of whose authenticity I was as yet not fully convinced.

After our first visit to Prashanthi Nilayam, we both had dreams about Sai Baba regularly. Some of these were followed by, or were otherwise connected to, dramatic *leelas* that "explained" them, sometimes the next day or week and sometimes not until over a year later. A few of these are reproduced here, just as I noted them at the time, along with comments that there added at various times:

---

4 con't. the basis of Puranic texts, rather too one-sidedly as the symbol of a phallus and male fertility. To regard the *lingam* as other than a holy and entirely nonsexual object of veneration is repugnant and offensive to most Hindus. The cylindrical form is derived from the ovoid one, and both usually stand vertically and rest on horizontal square bases (*peetha* or *pir*).

Dream of late April 1985: I was in a glass-windowed pavilion room where many devotees were sleeping, including Reidun and a lady from Cincinnati we had met during our first visit to Prashanthi Nilayam. It was set in a summery park with trees and grass. I saw Sai Baba in his orange robe walking over to the window, which he tapped from outside asking, "Priddy?" I was a bit awed that I was being called, uncertain if he could mean me. Thinking the morning air might be chilly, I pulled my jersey on over my cotton sleeping outfit and hurried out. In the hall on the way out, where attendants were standing, Baba was approaching. He came very close to me and was conversational. He said, "Bob. There is some foreign problem?" I didn't quite understand this, but he went on. "Do you have a driver's license?" "Yes sir!" I said. "What about the car then?" he asked. The meeting was over.

Comment: I felt silly calling Sai Baba "Sir" and couldn't think why. This also happened in several other dreams. Not until over a year later did I learn to my surprise that he now and again addresses various people as "sir," sometimes even ladies, too.

The "foreign problem" had two distinct meanings. First, we had an old Morris van that we had brought to Norway for its last trip. To get rid of it, however, required that it be imported formally. The impossible regulations required that a large duty be paid even though the van was valueless. All this must be done just to be allowed to deliver the vehicle to a wrecking yard! The van now stood rusting away, its tires deflated, on a neighbor's property, where someone had pushed it off the road. It was a real headache, so I had conveniently forgotten it, though Reidun was concerned that we should solve the matter, not least for the sake of good neighborliness.

After the dream we began to consider what to do, and therefore noticed in a local information paper we get, that our council was making an extra clean-up effort in the area. Against all probability, and contrary to the regulations that everyone else has to comply with, they just agreed to take our van free of charge and our problem simply disappeared!

As to the driver's license, the dream caused me to check it, and I found to my surprise that it was missing. Some weeks before, my wallet had been stolen, but I had not realized that my driver's license had been in it. This caused me to replace my license, even though I had decided never to drive a car again. After several incidents and not least my wife's fear-backed opinion, I had submitted to her judgment that I was an unreliable driver, a danger to the public highways. Yet if Sai Baba wanted me to have a license, then I would.

It was not until nearly one year later that I understood why. During Easter 1986, a Sathya Sai Organization convocation took place in Norway, with visitors from four countries. When all were to return it was found that, due to a misunderstanding, there was no transport for some devotees from the Netherlands to reach their plane unless one of the hosts drove them in a minibus. This person's car, however, could not just be left up at the mountain hotel, so a driver was necessary. The only remaining candidate for the job was myself! Thus does Sai Baba, even long in advance, set right the details for the events held by his organization.

> *Dream of August 23, 1985*: I was fitting on some ice skates to skate on a small, exquisite rink where one "couldn't go wrong" when I noticed, through a window dividing the rink from an office, that Sai Baba was sitting there at work. He was in orange, but with aquamarine blue near his neck. I looked no more, so as not to pry. He came to me and showed me into a room saying, "Come in. This is my school." He was serious then, saying, "I need some help with English. But it's some time since you taught it?" "Yes, Baba, but I could always brush it up. However, your English is perfect, Sai Baba." He looked at me and said, "Perhaps you'll find it's not so good." I said, "Whatever you say, Baba." He repeated, "You have not worked with English for some time now?" He looked into my eyes, and his were covered by a grayish film, like a cataract. Then I was in a school hostel with young Indian men—students and maybe teachers, too. One smart youth drew me to a room, proudly pointing out an oscilloscope displayed on the way there. The room was upholstered in emerald green. There was room for two people "for one year," he said. Some young Indians sat about conversing and looking at us.

Comment: Months later I read to my surprise that Prashanthi Nilayam has a "green room" that is actually green, where Sai Baba trains students for drama productions. The expression "green room" in English means a room—originally painted green—where actors and actresses go when not wanted on stage. I was then finishing the writing and recording of a musical drama called *Land of Light*, partly based on the novel of the same name that I had written. I was fairly certain that I had received divine help in obtaining my home recording studio for fulfilling this work. (In other dreams, Baba has told me that I should continue working with music, and in one he even discussed this play with me—referring to it also as a "film"—and performed a "dream materialization" of a marzipan-like sweet that is eaten in the drama by the main actor. This dream provided the needed inspiration to complete the recording work.) Events took place during our next visit to Sai Baba that further clarified this dream.

> *Dream of October 10, 1985*: Baba and I walked off, leaving the others, across a wide lawn surrounded by woods and garden. We came to an old mansion with a broad flight of stone steps leading up to a large veranda or porch. I followed him into the drawing room, which was very large with a grand piano, antique furniture, and much else. There was also an area with settees where a thick wide curtain closed off the adjoining room or space.
>
> Baba asked me to wait. He went through the curtain, soon returning with one of the small vermilion heart-shaped candle tins of the sort I have kept his *vibhuti* in. It was open and full to overflowing with *vibhuti*, which even fell onto the floor from it. He gave it to me, and I cried tears of joy, saying, "Oh, Sai Baba— you give us everything." So saying, I leaned my head against his (I was standing on his right, as usual). He shed some tears, too.

Comment: The little heart-shaped tin was the twin of the one I gave to the swami in England and received back full of *vibhuti* from the shrine of Shirdi Baba, when he performed our spiritual marriage ceremony. I had chosen it quite intentionally to symbolize a private prayer, which Baba evidently refers back to in the dream.

> *Dream of November 11, 1985*: I saw Sai Baba in his orange robe sitting between Nancy Reagan and Raisa Gorbachev. I believe their husbands were there peripherally, too. He nodded or gestured to me that I should observe this fact.

Comment: When the Geneva summit of 1985 was first proposed quite early that year, and it was announced that the date would not be fixed until later, I immediately felt sure it would turn out to be close to, or somehow connected with, Sai Baba's 60th birthday celebration on and around November 23, 1985. I also thought that the wives of the two leaders must have a lot of potential influence on the whole situation, even a crucial role. The 60th birthday was anticipated with enormous interest by Sathya Sai followers, not least because of the great importance of this age for all realized saints and avatars in the Indian tradition. The Geneva Summit did in fact take place just days before Sai Baba's birthday, and I later read that the two wives had met successfully.

Not until 1988 did I learn of Donald Regan's writings and other White House officials' views that Nancy Reagan virtually ran her husband's itinerary (basing a lot on a lady astrologer friend's interpretations!) and was the decisive influence on many of his actions, including the positive outcome of the Geneva meeting. Much the same is true of Raisa Gorbachev, as was shown by her husband's words to the U.S. media, which he was unable to say openly in Russia due to the prevalent male-chauvinistic attitudes there! This was also confirmed later by the loud public complaints against the influence of Raisa Gorbachev, begun by Boris Yeltsin in 1987.

It was years after the famous Reagan-Gorbachev "fireside-chat" summit in Geneva, November 1985, that those great public pessimists—the world news media and the political intellectuals—in general gradually began to catch up with facts and recognize "peace breaking out all over the world." Not until 1990 did I discover definitely that Raisa Gorbachev has known about and been very interested in Sai Baba for a long time. This I learned from a young Russian living in Copenhagen whose family knew the Gorbachevs from the 1960s onward and have photos proving it.

One may wonder, as did I, why Baba should have given me such information, for it could have no practical consequences and I could surely not have publicized it in any fruitful way, even if I had wished to do so. It was inspiring to me, revealing yet a little more of his omniscience relating to world events (and also concerning my various thoughts). It further endeared Swami to me that he would bother to confide such a thing to such a really insignificant player in the drama of the world as myself, just for the sake of the pleasure it gave. It also further confirmed my faith in Sai Baba's predictions made to Dr. John Hislop at the height of the Cold War and other increasingly ominous world troubles, about the great era of peace that was "much closer than you think." I can only think that it was an act of his to enthuse me and share a tiny bit of his mystery.

Dream of January 14, 1986: People were gathered around a mansion with lawns in a beautiful tree-lined park. I was telling some of them how Baba had come to me and singled me out, to my great surprise, to give me a packet of *vibhuti.* I could see it all again in my mind's eye.

Comment: This day I found, on awakening, was the anniversary of Sai Baba materializing *vibhuti* for me during our previous visit at Puttaparthi!

Dream of January 19, 1986: Reidun and I were in an old square, black 1950-type car. I was in the back seat when a friend opened the right-hand rear door and said with a great smile of pleasure and surprise, "You'll never guess who is here!" I looked out of the rear window and could see Sai Baba in his orange robe on top of a vehicle like a hay cart. I called out through the open door, "Love, Baba!" Then I saw him come to the rear window and peer in at me from outside. There was a haze on the window and his eyes were hazed over, too, but I saw him clearly, and the haze cleared up as he bent forward and looked into my eyes. He nodded as if satisfied and gave me a knowing and friendly smile.

Comment: My eyes had become very sore indeed over the previous months. I had begun to use reading glasses and had not bothered to get my eyes checked further. This partly aggravated my other muscular problems in the neck, which I did not connect with weakened vision. The strange dream effect of my misted sight paradoxically combined with a clarity of vision of Baba was due to the presence of window-glass between him and me. This suggested my actual need for glasses, a fact I did not appreciate for many months—not until just before I next traveled to a North European Sathya Sai Organization gathering that was being held in Norway. Sure enough, that was the first day I wore my new glasses, which gave me great relief and made my participation at the meetings much easier than would otherwise have been the case.

Dream of early February 1986: Sai Baba was saying or singing the last words of my song "Move On," part of which I had just rewritten in two alternative versions.

Comment: The versions were either, "The day, still on its way, not far away, with a song to be sung," or else, "The day yet to be is on its way, with a dream to be done." Though I didn't quite get which of the versions he said or sang, I had prayed the day before that he would ensure I got the right one. Later, I chose the second, though I feel he indicated that both were satisfactory. Subsequent events were to occur at Puttaparthi, a "day on its way not far away," where both a song would be sung and a dream come true, perfectly illustrating the truth of "my" song text that Baba made his own.

Dream of March 2, 1986: I was seated on the ground amid a crowd waiting for darshan. The place was not Prashanthi Nilayam, but like it. Sai Baba in his orange robe appeared and went amid the gathering some way off. Then I was inside a building with unglazed windows, and rows of Westerners were also waiting there. Baba entered at the door on my right and came toward us, talking to and looking at people on either side of me, but not at me. I made the *namaskar* greeting to him. He spoke in a pure Swedish accent to someone on my left who was mourning the recent assassination of the much-loved Swedish Prime Minister, Olaf Palme. He passed me by without a glance, but suddenly and most mischievously spun about to look at me and, smiling, briefly touched the "third eye" part of my forehead. I had to laugh. He gave me a mock frown that fooled me at first; then he smiled sweetly and touched my "third eye" again, very gently.

Comment: This scene's reference to a real event tragedy is followed by fun and laughter. This is not untypical of Sathya Sai, who many witnesses report seems quite unmoved—if anything more blissful—when death occurs in his vicinity, although he will often show much compassion in various ways to the bereaved. He has reportedly said to some persons on whom he has touched "the third eye" or applied *vibhuti* thereon, that this signifies the fact of ephemerality and death.

Dream of late September 1986: Sai Baba in an orange robe was giving darshan to a great crowd. I was in a hut with several Indians where I was staying. I saw Reidun receiving darshan in the front line. Sai Baba took one of her paintings and looked at it intently for a long while. Then he looked over toward me and smiled with great bliss, having taken her features onto his face.

Comment: A reminder of Baba's central teaching that divinity, represented by himself, is also present in all others, specifically here in my wife and her interests.

The above selection of a few dreams shows the exceptional clarity of detail and subtlety of connections between events that occur in many dreams of Baba. These cannot convey the intensity of feeling of some types of dream that I have not included. In one sort, Sathya Sai shows himself in indescribably blissful visions, often in connection with flows of fragrant *vibhuti*, flowers, or sweet food offerings (*prasad*). In another sort, Sai Baba has influenced the course of an illness I suffer from, sometimes improving my health by most unusual methods, sometimes preparing me for physical problems yet to come. Such dreams bore a range of different significances for me that are too involved to detail here.

Sai Baba has given very thorough and penetrating accounts of the relationships that pertain between deep sleep, dream states, waking consciousness, and various forms of higher awareness, both in writings and discourses. Even though we only remember (or deduce) the absence of consciousness during the deepest sleep, we are even then unified with the divine being, he informs us:

> Your real "I" exists in all the stages of waking, dream and deep sleep. But in the dream and deep sleep states you are not conscious of your body. The entity that exists in all the three states undergoes no change. You must try to understand the nature of this "I".[5]

When we go to sleep, the mind plays awhile with itself through dreaming at various levels before returning to the Universal Spirit or *Atma*, according to Baba. The dreaming mind dwells upon illusory objects, he tells us. The objects of the waking mind when it relies on sensory data seem real to us by comparison, yet even these

---

[5] Sathya Sai Baba, Discourse, Feb. 16, 1988, *Sanathana Sarathi*, March 1988, p. 60.

are ultimately insubstantial. The mind itself is the product of a network of desires, these being projected onto and stimulated by the sensory objects of the world. Ultimately, even these objects are illusory. The mind is subject to change, as are its changing objects of desire. When mind is subtracted from all this, only *Atma* remains: the Witness, also called Brahman.

As far as I understand it, the *Atma* is non-temporally omnipresent, being a supreme awareness beyond the worldly-oriented form of consciousness that we call "mind". By virtue of this being everywhere at all times (omnipresence), the *Atma* can impinge upon the dreaming mind. This being so, there is no reason why it should not impress the waking mind by the same measure, too, and also adopt any form that is convenient to the circumstances, the culture, and the individual concerned. This possibly accounts for how people without any known psychic abilities or mediumistic powers have waking visions of Sai Baba, whereby they are sometimes able to converse with and literally touch him, just as in normal experience.

THE RAT IN THE DRUM

Nearly seven months after our first visit to India, I had a dramatic dream of Sai Baba. Toward the end of it he gave me some enigmatic advice, which did not become clear until much later on. The relevant portion of the dream, duly noted at the time, was:

> *Dream of August 18, 1985*: I was in our living room with Reidun and my son Kai when I saw Sai Baba in his orange robe looking at our vegetable garden and herb patch from the path. I told them and Baba came in. He spoke to them, whereupon they withdrew into another room. Then he came up to me where I sat praying, and I said, "Thank you so much Sai Baba for what you have done for me!" He said, "I am sending you something that will be good for you—a calendar. But don't use it until I tell you to, for I don't want any harm to come to you!"

I naturally wondered about the meaning of such an odd promise as to send me a calendar, not thinking that an actual calendar would turn up. But arrive it did three months later! Bente, a friend of ours, had gone to the huge 60th birthday celebrations at Prashanthi Nilayam. On her return, to my great surprise, she brought a large Sai Baba calendar as a present for each person in our little group. I had told no one but my wife and son anything about the dream.

Because of the definitive nature and seriousness of Baba's warning, I thought far and wide in the attempt to figure out what his advice not to *use* the calendar could refer to. Convinced from experience that Baba's words always bear meaning, I literally racked my brains and ransacked all sorts of literary and other sources in hoping to find a significance that would ring a bell. Somehow I could just not see any sensible explanation, however much I mulled over it.

For the sake of completeness, I must admit to an embarrassing fact. At the end of our visit to Prashanthi I had taken with me an old, out-dated calendar with a picture of a radiant Sai Baba in a white gown, from the wall of a room in which we had been staying. At the time, my desire to have just that picture of him, surrounded as it was by photos of his schools, colleges, and the university buildings, overwhelmed my sense of right and wrong. I rationalized that this was not theft, for the year was past, the room was to be painted, and the porters or the painters who were to work in the room the next day would probably just tear it down.

Besides, that calendar was one of those cheap sorts given away by firms in India each year, ran my guilty reasoning. Now I see how convenient that idea was for myself, for most residents of Prashanthi Nilayam treasure any pictures of Sai Baba. It may have belonged to the owner of the room, even though those rooms are used continuously by others in the owner's absence.

After the dream, however, the matter of those calendars began to worry me. I realized that I had in fact stolen what was probably someone else's property, and in Sai Baba's own ashram! Need I say that Sai Baba is not exactly in favor of theft! In any case, I really did have to ransack my conscience much, as a result of all that. Sai Baba's promise to send me a calendar was surely a gentle way of showing that he knew how much I had coveted that calendar.

Not until about one year after the dream did I realize what the specific meaning definitely must be. Though I had, so to speak, "misused" the calendars I took, the only time I had actually *used* a calendar in the previous years was once, when I had put a ring around the day we saw Sai Baba for the first time. It was on the very calendar I had taken, the ringed date being the last day of 1984! At last I understood the meaning: I must not travel to see Sai Baba until he told me to!

* * * *

The following selections of certain dreams seem, when viewed in hindsight and looked at "on paper," to all point toward a future visit to see Baba. At that time, however, I was still not clear about the meanings they conveyed, apart from Baba's obvious intention to give happiness through his darshans. Only what actually came to pass clarified many of the details involved.

> *Dream of June 12, 1986:* I was in the darshan line at Puttaparthi, receiving love, which was flowing in and out of my heart area.

Comment: Sai Baba has said that every dream of him is his actual darshan. Therefore I did not see this one as the premonition it later proved to have been.

> *Dream on or about June 20, 1986:* Someone from the information office at Prashanthi Nilayam was looking for me. He said I was wanted by Baba for an interview.

Comment: Upon awakening, it was inspiring to think this might be a premonition. But then I began to think that it was probably just a wish-fulfillment dream. In any case, I would just have to "wait and see"! On second thoughts, it was so promising that we decided to try to go to India.

We soon booked a flight to Bangalore for the following month and were assured by the Indian Embassy in Oslo that visas could be ready in a few days without problem. However, when the time drew near and we did apply, we were blandly informed that it would take at the very least six weeks to arrange! This *force majeure* made us rethink our plans: since our flight would have to be postponed, it would probably be best to wait until Bente in our group was also free to travel, we thought, even though that would not be before the end of the year.

Though we knew that our efforts to follow Sai Baba's teachings could have been greater, the longing for a closer acquaintance and its spiritual benefits outweighed our uncertainty. That, at least, was how we saw it when we booked our flight. However, once the visa problem arose and the journey seemed impossible, we had to consider what to do instead. Straight away we became aware of various tasks at home that we really wanted to get done but which we had been setting aside. We were disappointed, but it was as if Baba was helping us to know our own minds. The dreams continued to be positive, too.

> *Dream of July 6, 1986*: Standing in a wide crescent of persons in some space near a temple in Bombay (probably the Dharmakshetra building where Baba lives during his brief visits to Bombay), I turned out to be in the center and Sai Baba, clothed in orange, came and stood opposite me. He was wearing an orange ring (one my wife in fact has). He told me to meditate on it.

> *Dream on or about July 28, 1986*: Sai Baba stood amid the clouds, like Zeus in heaven, magnificently powerful. He said, "You can know yourself if you come south." Then he let off a great thunderclap beside me, one that made me really jump yet did not threaten my being in any way. "But you can never know me!" he said, and began to send off yet more huge bursts of energy, like storms and thunder.

Comment: Sai Baba has said: "It is not possible for you to understand the Divine and gauge Its potential or know the significance of Its manifestation."[1] Again, in the famous long letter (of May 25, 1947) to his elder brother, Baba also wrote: "No one can comprehend My Glory, whoever he is, whatever his method of enquiry, however long his attempt."[2] Furthermore, in *Sathya Sai Speaks*, we read yet further: "In truth, you cannot understand the nature of my reality either today, or even after a thousand years of steady austerity or ardent enquiry, even if all mankind joins in the effort."[3]

> *Dream in July 1986*: Sai Baba was giving darshan to a lot of people filing past him where he stood at the main entrance to the temple *(mandir)*. On my right beside the interview room door stood either Sri Kasturi or another close devotee of the same age, observing me as I came up for Baba's darshan. I think I was last

---

[1] E. B. Fanibunda, *Vision of the Divine* (Bombay, India: Sri Sathya Sai Books & Publications, 1976), p. 55.

[2] Sathya Sai Baba, in letter dated May 25, 1947 to his elder brother Seshamaraju, quoted in N. Kasturi's *Sathyam, Sivam, Sundaram: The Life of Sathya Sai Baba*, vol. II (Prashanthi Nilayam, India: Sri Sathya Sai Books & Publications Trust, 1973; 2nd American printing, 1984), p. 11.

[3] Sathya Sai Baba, Discourse at Bombay, May 17, 1968, *Sathya Sai Speaks*, vol. VI (Prashanthi Nilayam, India: Sri Sathya Sai Books & Publications Trust, n.d.), p. 225ff. New Indian edition ISBN 81-7208-156-1: vol. 8, p. 99.

in the line. Sai Baba briefly handed me an oblong piece of paper, on which it said, "The bridge that Bente is on leads to me." I also saw a photo of a bridge with a group of people on it, posing for the picture. Bente was among them. She also appeared to look at the photo now and recognized that such a snapshot had been taken while she was down in India (we were no longer there).

Comment: Bente had just returned from a visit to the Findhorn community and, I found out days later, had actually been on the same sort of a bridge with another Sai devotee she met there "by chance." It was a smallish arched stone bridge of the sort found over streams or small rivers, without parapets.

A lady we knew who had just been on a visit to England had met a Sai follower at a *bhajan* meeting in Central London who had just received a letter from the ashram office in reply to her request to visit for three weeks. The letter had stated she could stay for three months. Apparently she always wrote and would never visit without permission, addressing the letter to Sai Baba. So, together with Bente, we decided to do likewise and asked for permission to stay at Prashanthi Nilayam over Christmas.

Dream of September 11, 1986: Someone in front of the temple at Prashanthi Nilayam (maybe Sai Baba) handed me a letter of reply from Sai Baba, which looked like an orange envelope, strongly resembling the (orange-colored) journal, *Sanathana Sarathi*, that we get monthly from Prashanthi Nilayam, which contains Sai Baba's latest discourses.

When I tried to understand the dream, though, I was puzzled and even rather exasperated that it was unclear. How could a copy of a magazine be an answer to our letter? How would I know which part of which edition might be relevant? Yet another dream with something important in it—but of which I could make neither head nor tail! Previous experience had taught me that there probably was a definite meaning, but how frustrating it was to wait in ignorance like that! And there *was* a very clear message in it, which I could not possibly know at the time, as will soon become clear enough! On Thursday September 25, 1986, the day of my 50th birthday, Sai Baba sent me a peculiar present. In the morning I was thinking about my life and how it might appear to others. To what extent might it have been wasted? Or purposeful? I was toying with what I often suspected might be a megalomaniacal idea of reviewing some of it in an autobiography and pondering playfully over titles for such a book. I thought laconically of "Why I would never grow up?" and then of "Reach (for) the Source of Dream," a line from a lyric I once wrote in the 1960s.

Later that day, at about 2:30 to 3:00 P.M., I noticed that the sky, which was sunlit and an exceptionally deep blue, had the most marvelous array of high-flying clouds, apparently some variation of cirrocumulus. Not even in two years of flying, mostly above most clouds in the R.A.F. had I seen anything remotely like this. Countless tiny, fuzzy, wisps of cloud were spaced out regularly from horizon to horizon, making the hemisphere look enormously expansive and giving the sense of trmendous height. We watched this amazing phenomenon for about half an hour.

As Reidun and I took our lunch on the lawn, we noticed that the whole show, which was directly above us, formed a gigantic wedge-shaped mass that pointed and moved toward the southeast, like a gigantic arrow. Some distance above the horizon the clouds were simply vanishing into its tip, concentrating towards this point. I knew that Prashanthi Nilayam lies in that very direction, southeast of us from Oslo. It made me think of the words "Reach for the Source of Dream," which was the working title of the book I was considering writing. Clouds are like dreams, coming seemingly from nowhere and disappearing likewise. And at the unchanging source of dream itself, I realized, is Baba!

Unsurprisingly enough, the weatherman did not report on any such interesting phenomena on that day. Nor have I ever heard quite such an atmospheric freak reported anywhere. So Reidun and I were left to wonder at it on our own. However, I was convinced by its sheer scale and unique formation that it was nothing less than a *leela* as a birthday gift from Sai Baba. According to many accounts, he is known to have caused other such "natural" phenomena of the most unusual sort, such as a vertical rainbow for a skeptical Hollywood film director and a freak lightning show around the entire horizon for a lady staying at the ashram. Also, Sathya Sai often sends his blessing on important anniversaries in many various ways.

Another aspect of the matter was that each morning, when chanting the Gayatri mantra, which among other things praises the divine power in nature, I always first looked out at the day's sky as being a unique manifestation of the divine play with nature. More often than not, gulls or other birds would fly past, and without exception in the very direction of Puttaparthi! At last even the passing clouds were hastening that way, too, which somehow promised that we would be able to visit Puttaparthi again.

There is a tradition in India of making a long and decisive pilgrimage in one's 50th year. Though I knew that this somehow lay ahead of me, I went on wondering *when* I might travel "without harm coming to me." I thought that only a letter from the ashram could solve the issue. I was in a poor physical state, with awful tensions in the neck, complicated by increasing problems of the right hip and lower spinal area. I could not see how I could manage the difficult journey and subsequent stay under ashram conditions. By then I knew that Sai Baba helps those who make real efforts and put full faith in him, whatever the outcome. My only reservation was that I must have some definitive answer before I would actually go, because of his warning about not using the calendar "until I tell you to."

We decided to go ahead with our travel plans and made preliminary bookings for December, because our agent assured us we would not have to confirm them until one or two weeks before the actual departure date.

One's 50th year, I had read somewhere, is a time when one should look back on life and see what one has achieved, for one's main work is then already done. This seems a foolish defeatist view (or perhaps that of a younger man), not least since many truly great achievements are not made until after that age. Yet the half-century does seem to be a time for serious reflection on one's life. In the West today, a person is judged mostly by status, achievements, who one knows, material or literary products, name or fame, and so on—in short, for one's outward worldly doings. I had long dreaded any sort of celebratory function, though the danger of this was admittedly remote! Whatever I had or had not then done according to the "eyes of the world," I felt that it is the inner life that is decisive. Despite all the many serious mistakes I had made, I knew that I had not let striving for outward appearances and success become of much importance for me. What has real lasting value is in oneself, and I knew this to be ultimately hidden from the perusal and judgment of other persons. The marvelous heaven that was provided that afternoon was an eloquent discourse to me, one that went straight to my secret heart—though I am quite sure it is no secret to Baba.

The day came when our travel agent, premature to our previous agreement, suddenly insisted that we confirm our booking and pay for our tickets within 24 hours! I had still received no "higher confirmation" of the journey. By that time some other people had made plans to go with us, all dependent on us going together. This put me in quite a dilemma! If I withdrew, so would my wife, Bente, and another person. I felt responsibility, yet felt it would be wrong, and plain foolish, to decide without receiving Baba's go-ahead.

Three of us had applied to enroll in a teacher training course on Education in Human Values that was to be held at Prashanthi Nilayam between Christmas and the New Year. We realized that we did not have the required qualifications to join, having none of the necessary previous experience. If we were admitted, we thought, and if we *also* received confirmation of this from the Chairman of the Sathya Sai Organization for northern Europe, it might serve as a go-ahead, even though that would not amount to a definite instruction from Baba. But on that evening, before our decision had to be made, Bente got a telephone call from one of the organization's spokesmen in Europe about another matter, and then he also pointed out that we were not eligible to attend the course.

Bente told us that in her evening meditation she would therefore "send a mental telegram to Sai Baba" (using that very phrase), asking for an answer on whether or not to travel. Next morning she received a phone call from Thorbjørn Meyer. By chance he had heard what we had been told the day before by the other spokesman, and so had phoned straight away to correct this. He said that, because we would be the first people from Norway to attend any E.H.V. course, he had made an exception especially for us and had sent our names to India. Not having heard anything to the contrary, he assumed that this meant we were enrolled. Bente explained my problem to him and the fact that we had written. He said that nowadays no one to his knowledge received replies to such letters.

Despite all that, I was still uncertain as to whether I had gotten a proper go-ahead. I had read much about how exacting Sai Baba can be with those who do not follow his instructions quite perfectly, and I didn't want to make any mistake whatever. It was also a matter of faith: Baba had given a clear instruction, even though it was in the dreaming state.

That evening Bente got home to find a letter had arrived that morning for her from South Africa. It was from a lady she had met at Prashanthi Nilayam once before. It began by telling her not to worry about whether she should go to India, because this lady had just had a vision in which Bente and herself were standing together on the temple veranda beside Sai Baba, *who was waving a telegram!* This lady informed Bente of her planned stay at Prashanthi Nilayam, which concurred with our projected visit to include Christmas and New Year.

Amazing though this was, I still could not be certain that it included me, as Sai Baba had not actually told me. Praying to Baba for some solution, we ended up having to ring the travel agent. To our surprise there was "no problem," we could wait about "another week or so" before deciding about the booking!

The answer from Baba did indeed come, and the manner of its delivery was definitely unique. I can safely say that the whole episode goes to show how the drama was not of our own making, and in this act it was sheer comedy at our expense, too, but also to our lasting joy and benefit.

During the week previous to the travel agent's sudden demand, I had been awakened in the middle of the night by an awful sound. It was the sound of a rat scrabbling about inside something near to my head. I thought at first that I had dreamed this, for I used in the past to have occasional nightmarish dreams of rats. The sound was so horrid it made me jerk myself up on the edge of the bed.

I was sleeping in the studio room where I often stayed up to get the quiet of the night to record music undisturbed. Near my head was a bass drum that has a circular cutaway hole on one of its skins. The sound had come from inside it. I gave the shell of the drum a tap and, shockingly, I heard what indeed sounded just like a rat blundering back and forth inside! How I felt so sure it was a rat and no other creature, I cannot quite explain.

Without a second thought I ran through the house to awaken Reidun, raising the alarm like a prime fool by calling out, "Reidun!" and causing her too to spring upright in bed like a jack-in-the-box (I'm certainly not in the habit of waking her up so drastically). "Reidun! Quick! There's a rat in my drum. You must help me!" When she understood where she was and what I was saying, she scoffed at the sheer ridiculousness of it. I insisted plaintively that it was really so and that I couldn't face it.

She got up and went toward the studio, confident but perhaps a bit irritated. I warned her repeatedly in serious tones to take a broom or something. She did then actually get one and advanced into the dark studio. I put the lights on in the adjoining room,

where I awaited developments, standing at its door like some useless nincompoop. Nothing moved as she went near to the drum.
"There's nothing here!" she said in a confident tone. "There *is,*
there *is*!" I told her. She gave the drum a tap, which resulted in a
desperate scraping, amplified by the drum itself, which made her let
out a shriek and jump up on the bed.

I couldn't resist telling her, "I told you so!" She then wanted to
know what to do. "Get behind the drum and give it a bang!" I suggested. "Use the foot pedal!" Meanwhile I realized that, if I remained standing where I was, the rat or whatever else it might be,
despite all, would probably have to run right over my feet. There
was a chair beside me, so I stood on it, which gave me a fine view
with some security. Stan Laurel could hardly have done better, but
nothing like this occurred to me at the time; I felt simply that I was
acting quite sensibly!

Reidun gave a few good bangs on the rear of the drum and,
after some nasty scrambling sounds, I saw the creature emerge and
run past me. It was indeed a brownish rat! It fled across the carpet
and then lost its footing as it crossed a varnished copper fenderplate
that we have in front of our fireplace. It ran alongside the fireplace
and disappeared behind the wood box that stands there. I told Reidun where it was. There was only one possible way out, through
which it also must have come in—a small cat door that we have
beside our main door. The rat had not crossed to the exit at all, as
I had a clear view of the space, which was several yards in length.
Reidun came, broomstick in hand, to dislodge this unwelcome
night lodger finally. However, it was nowhere to be found! I came
to the natural conclusion that it must somehow have gone out nevertheless, but I was in doubt indeed, for I had not seen or heard it
do so, and I had watched very carefully all the time. Yet by sheer
force of habit, my mind insisted that it must have gone out anyhow.

Our tomcat had been drowsing through all this on a sofa close
to where the rat had scuttled past. He got up, streched himself at
leisure, and strolled out to the kitchen to examine his empty food
dish as if nothing had occurred at all. Meanwhile we were quite
perplexed about the rat; why it had come into the studio where
there was no scrap of anything edible, and why it had "nested" in
my drum (in which I happened to keep a small cushion for damp-
ening the high frequency sounds). It was all quite inexplicable.

During the following week I told various friends, including
Bente, about the strange episode, and asked them if they had ever

heard of "a rat in a drum" before, using exactly that phrase to them. All agreed it was most peculiar. Exactly *how* peculiar it was, none of us had any inkling then.

Before I tell the solution to this conundrum, I must add that I had begun to doubt that I really could manage the journey at all, due to the continually worsening condition of my hip, lower back, and neck muscles and joints. I felt that the necessary walking for any India visit could cause "harm to come to me," as Sai Baba had warned. Amid all this I had toyed with the idea that, in the event of receiving no answer about going to see Sai Baba, I might at least be able to make it to England, instead, where perhaps I should as a consolation try to see the swami with whom I had not had any contact for several years and who had after all once been my guru in one way or another.

As the last day for deciding about the air tickets approached, Bente arrived at our house with the October 1986 issue of Sai Baba's magazine *Sanathana Sarathi* (which means, incidentally, the "Timeless Charioteer," with reference to Krishna, who was Arjuna's chariot driver as related in the *Bhagavad Gita*). She proclaimed that I had now received an answer without doubt! On the back of the magazine was a quote from one of Sai Baba's discourses from a previous year, as follows:

> The secret of liberation lies, not in the mystic formula that is whispered in the ear and rotated on the rosary; it lies in the stepping out into action, the walking forward in practice the pious pilgrim route, and the triumphant reaching of the Goal. The best Guru is the Divine in you; yearn for hearing His Voice, His Upadesh. If you seek wordly[4] Gurus, you will have to run from one to another, like a rat caught inside a drum, which flees to the right when the drummer beats on the left and to the left when he beats on the right![5]

---

[4] The original has this spelling, though it was corrected to "worldly" in the second edition of *Sathya Sai Speaks,* vol. VII. That this misspelling is reproduced time and again wherever it is quoted in publications must be due to the Indian love of word play and puns, such as Sai Baba often employs when he brings home a spiritual point in English.

[5] *Sanathana Sarathi,* October, 1986, back cover. The words were first printed in *Sathya Sai Speaks,* vol. VIIA, p. 26.

When I say that I was still not immediately convinced that this was a message for me, some people will probably conclude that I am just dull-witted. Others may think I was only being careful and scientifically skeptical until all the facts were known. Still, in my defense, I ask who can be so quick-witted as to grasp all the facts where Sai Baba's playfulness is involved? Only gradually did I recall the dream in which I had received from Baba a letter of reply to our request to visit. It had come in the form of a copy of the orange-covered journal, *Sanathana Sarathi*. Only then did I know that this *was* an answer giving me the go-ahead. Now I felt confidence at last that I, too, might, so to speak, "walk forward on the pilgrim route and reach the goal." I was reassured that the walking I would have to do would not harm me, and I could therefore visit India and Baba.

Later on, I realized the significance of the spot where I last had seen the rat beside the fireplace, just below a mantelpiece shrine on which we have pictures of Sai Baba and other incarnations. I wondered about the symbolism of rats, and though I knew them to be held as holy in India and to appear on some religious pictures, I saw no special significance in this. Ganesha, I understood, rode on a mouse, symbolizing the greatest and the smallest together. However, much later on I read, in the discourses of Sai Baba:

> The rat whose presence every one abhors, becomes an object of worship when Ganesha Puja is done, for the rat is traditionally the Divine Vehicle of Ganesha.[6]

On that shrine, before which we meditate, worship, and sing *bhajans*, we have long kept a small soapstone carving of Ganesha, the elephant God. The elephant's intelligence and ability to stride through the jungle regardless of obstructions are a symbol of the confidence and strength to overcome obstacles, whether physical or spiritual, which qualities are therefore symbolized by Ganesha. Sai Baba did at that time give me the physical relief I needed to visit Prashanthi Nilayam, for I found out on the journey there that I could walk some distance without it causing the excessive tensions in the back and neck that it had come to do. The manner in which

---

[6] Sathya Sai Baba, *Sathya Sai Speaks*, vol. X (Prashanthi Nilayam: Sri Sathya Sai Books & Publications Trust, 1988), p. 200. (Note: In some later editions of this book, this passage has been omitted.)

this curative improvement itself was effected by Baba took seven months for me to discover, but that is another matter—another episode in the continuing saga of my bodily ailments, which sounds like one long patient's waiting-room complaint, compounded by a catalogue of imponderable riddles.

Ten months previous to all this, in January, I had dreamed one night of sitting before the central picture of Sai Baba in our little shrine room. The flower offerings swirled about and dissolved, rematerializing as the living form of Baba. He was wearing the usual orange and, looking straight at me, smiled and said, "I am coming to fetch you."

I was unable to make any sense at all of that dream. The only possiblity of meaning I could extract was that it could refer to death. Sai Baba is ever reminding us of our mortality and the day we shall have to go without even packing up our bags. He is known to appear to some of his followers just prior to the moment of death, and he often says to the bereaved that he has taken the deceased to himself. The atmosphere of the dream had been natural and harmonious, not ominous—but "what else could the meaning possibly be?" I thought. It just goes to show how inscrutable Baba's messages are, what a play of mystery with which he surrounds his motives, and what joyful wonder the solutions bring at last. I do not doubt at all that Baba, who has been seen by certain devotees of earlier days in the form of Ganesh, actually fetched me through the rat.

About two days before we were to leave for India at last, our much beloved black tomcat came up to us and began staggering about in an awful way. One-half of his body appeared to be paralyzed, so he could only half-drag himself to us.

In spontaneous sympathy I called out to Sai Baba straight away, and after some minutes of watching this truly sorry spectacle, I thought of trying *vibhuti* on him. Previously he had always avoided any attempt to give him this ash, but I did not recall this and immediately took a pinch of it from the mantelpiece shrine and went up to him. Before I could apply it, a tiny speck of it dropped from my fingers by mistake and landed right on his nose! He leaped up as if an electric current had gone through him and shook his whole body.

Immediately, all signs of paralysis were gone, and he circled around a bit before making off on an excursion through his little door as if nothing had happened! He never did get the rest of the *vibhuti* applied. The tiniest speck was clearly sufficient. Had our cat not been cured, we would hardly have been able to leave for India two days later, or certainly not without much sadness.

12

"UNUSUAL CIRCUMSTANCES"

One of the last noteworthy dreams I had before we left for India on our second visit seemed happily portentous. In the first week of November, I dreamed that I was in India in a hotel room with yellowish walls. An elderly Indian man, a very kindly and firm character who looked rather African, was attending me there. He said, "So you are with two lady friends. That must be fun?" and he smiled a bit mischievously, "Oh no!" I didn't want to be misunderstood. "She is a religious friend." He showed that he knew this and said, "Don't worry. I'll get you an interview with Sai Baba."

When I awoke I was uncertain whether the "African-looking man" had been Sai Baba incognito and also could not be sure whether he had meant one or two lady friends besides my wife. It puzzled me, but I knew we were traveling with only one lady friend, Bente. By the time we left, one month after the dream, a second lady friend of Reidun and I, Diney from London, had actually decided to join us. Well after our tickets and visas were all in order, she phoned to find out whether she could join our party. I told her that judging by our experience I thought it highly unlikely that she would get a booking at such short notice, but I also added my belief that Baba could arrange it if he would.

She had gotten her plane ticket from London by what seemed sheer luck, for an Indian couple in front of her had been turned away due to the news that everything by Air India to Bombay and Bangalore was fully booked up during the relevant period. Despondent at overhearing all this, Diney had been about to give up the attempt, when something had made her wait at the counter nonetheless. To her surprise, the clerk immediately told her that there were vacant seats on another airline one day before our flight! Moreover, her visa had taken less than a day to arrange and cost nothing, compared with weeks of waiting and a large fee for ours at the Indian Embassy in Oslo.

On the journey itself, altogether three of our fellow travelers experienced very fortunate "coincidences." First, Bente and Göran had been waiting for a train that they must catch in order to reach the airport on time, when they found it had been canceled that day! Fortunately for them, Bente's father had waited in his car outside the station, a thing he never usually did when dropping her there. He didn't really know why he had waited, but because of it he had been there to drive them in the emergency and to reach the airport in good time. The plane of a third person, traveling from North Norway, arrived in Frankfurt about two hours late. The plane for Bombay, the one for which we were waiting, was about an hour late in leaving for Bombay, so he made it with just a minute to spare! It later proved that his baggage had been less fortunate than himself, which fact caused us all a long baggage ritual, dancing slowly around the Bombay airport offices. The baggage failed to materialize.

Giving it up at last, we decided to leave and walked through a gate, above which we read in rear-lit green lettering, "*IF YOU HAVE NOTHING TO DECLARE PLEASE WALK STRAIGHT THROUGH.*" An official came running angrily, as if he had caught us red-handed, almost shouting, "No! No! No!" He looked at us much as if we were either plain fools or criminals. "Nobody can go through there!" Such delightful scenarios keep you on your toes and well amused, too, if you can keep the right attitude of nonattachment!

In Bangalore we went to the hotel where we had agreed to meet Diney, who had arrived the day before. As that hotel was full and she was out, we left a message. At the Rama Hotel, due to limited vacancies, rooms had to be shared. Reidun and I decided to share a room with Bente, while the single men shared another room. We were still installing ourselves when Diney walked in to see us. I recognized the situation from my dream: here we were in an Indian hotel room with jaded, yellowed walls, with my wife and *two* of our lady friends! I related the dream to them, including the man's promise to "get you an interview." It was all an open question still as to who might be included in such an interview, if it all *was* to do with Sai Baba in the first place. We decided not to lay too much store by it. Still, it did bring a delicious air of expectancy to us. We all felt full of energy, and my back and neck were no worse, for the 36 hours of continuous journey, than if I had been resting at home, which was very unusual for me!

After a long "wait" of nearly two years, we eventually arrived at the Prashanthi Nilayam ashram again. Though I did not think of it at the time, due not least to the extra-extraordinary rat in the drum, I had already "come to Puttaparthi under unusual circumstances," as a voice like my own and yet also like Sai Baba's had assured me just before I had awakened from one of the earliest dreams I had of Sai Baba. That had been in December 1983, three years previously and prior even to my first visit!

Reidun wanted me to get a new set of "whites," as she thought my old ones shabby. In fact, the white cotton trousers I was wearing, made for me the last time we were in Puttaparthi, had turned out unfortunately. In the interest of friendly entertainment, I had explained to the tailor, who seemed to know some English, how readymade trousers in Europe often turned out to be too short in the leg for me. I had demonstrated this by pulling up my trouser legs ridiculously high. Next day, the two pairs the tailor solemnly brought hung a good four inches above my ankles. That was another lesson about opening my mouth too often!

One thing I dislike is going clothes shopping, especially to tailors, with whom one almost unavoidably has to haggle. I put it off or simply forgot it until it all became quite a problem. When I did get moving, sure enough, I ran into problems with a tailor out in the village—over-pricing, this time! One of the ashram residents, a very sweet gentleman in his 60s, when he heard about the difficulties I was having with the tailor, insisted on accompanying me to get the proper service and price at another tailor's shop.

Reidun had been lingering nearby among the ladies to see whether I would actually remember to turn up, as I had already forgotten one previous appointment. One of Sai Baba's very close attendants, who tidies the interview room and often walks behind Sai Baba during darshan, was also apparently waiting to see that I came. Following ashram etiquette, she did not talk to these gentlemen. She soon had the satisfaction of seeing me, a fully grown man in too-short pants being shepherded away in the direction of the tailor's to be made respectable-looking. It was later arranged that I should get the best quality cotton cloth from the ashram shop, which is entirely non-profit and sells at low Third World prices. However, I was given a "special 10 percent discount" that had been decided on for me "by someone," even though I tried to pay the usual rate and felt rather ashamed to be receiving a discount on so low a price.

As we waited for the tailor to return from lunch, my helper kindly told me something of the miraculous way he had been brought by Sai Baba to stay at his ashram, but which I do not feel at liberty to repeat. As a young man, however, he had taken employment on the Indian railways because he had thought it would enable him to travel about and thus better to seek God. I was able to marvel with him over his indubitable success!

Where else but in India would anyone take such an initiative? Kipling describes this same sort of devotional faith in *Kim*, and the quest for divinity has been made by countless millions of Indians since the earliest days of civilization. The answer must now be, however, that people who want God are at last coming from every nation of the world.

This gentleman was so good as to order my new outfit for me, explain all the details, and see that I was measured for them. I was glad of this, but I was also perplexed as to why this new brother of mine was fussing for me to get two sets, and also why he was anxious I should collect them early the next morning, whereas I wanted only one and preferred to wait until noon the next day to collect it. However, my helpful friend insisted on my collecting it before darshan. He was a bit awkward about his own insistence, so after a while he let me know that Sai Baba's attendant, who had come to see me go to the tailor, had said that I should be ready in case we were called in to an interview the next morning! He also pulled a packet of *vibhuti* from his pocket, two of which he had received from Sai Baba's hand, and he said, "Ah! This one must obviously have been for you, I see now!"

Reidun was relieved that I was less of a sartorial discredit to her, having had to be figuratively frog-marched to the tailor by the aid of two men. We were naturally most excited at the prospect of an interview, but since nothing can be taken for granted where Sai Baba is involved, we did not rely on it or mention it to anyone. We even had to wonder whether perhaps I was not being shaped up to be a bit more respectable by the Tailor of Men Himself, from behind the scenes. (God knows, too, I ruefully admit, how I have never been averse to any discount, whether by special grace or not!)

At the first darshan, the afternoon of our arrival, Sai Baba had glanced at me, as if letting me see him noting that I was there. He looked at me at least once more at almost every darshan during the first week and also gave his "Wait" sign with his hand before me on two occasions, just after I was finally kitted out. One day I concentrated on asking him mentally if he would let us get close to him, and added that if he would give me the answer there and then, all he need do was to say some words in English within my hearing when he came by. As he was speaking to someone in the row exactly in front of where I sat at the rear, some dozen lines back, he said in loud and clear tones and without looking up, "Come on!"—the very words to answer my private question!

One evening the *bhajans* went on into the dusk. Baba came out and walked along about ten yards away from my place at the rear of those seated on the sand. As he came opposite me, though it was too dark to see his eyes at that distance, I sensed that he was looking straight at me, and as if in confirmation of that fact, I saw two pinpricks of light shining in his eyes! It was a striking "physical impossibility," and even would have been so had there been artificial lighting around, yet there was not, and I definitely saw these pinpoints fixed on me! In retrospect, I marvel how, with that *leela*, the tailor episode, and several other subtle but unmistakable signs, he was evidently ensuring that my expectations were to reach a maximum buildup.

Long before this visit, Reidun and I had decided that we wanted to be a part of a group. A question then arose about which group to be in. Three of us were already associated with the Danish Sathya Sai organization, whose large and very well-disciplined group of about twenty-five people we had originally been invited to join on this visit. As this would have left our friend Diney on her own, we decided to remain together in the group of six fellow travelers, which also included our Swedish friend, Göran. It soon seemed to be the right decision. One person who withdrew happened unknowingly to have chosen to sit under the very neem tree where the rest of us came, having decided on that new spot for our group meeting! Some moments later we saw Sai Baba, driven right past us in a car, on his way to some function. He looked over at us in the few moments the group were within his field of (physical) vision. This decided us to remain as the one small group.

However, on the seventh day after our arrival, Thorbjørn Meyer, then the leader of the Sathya Sai Organization in Northern Europe, from his place on the temple veranda, asked Baba for an interview for the Danish group and had received the reply that there should be just one Scandinavian group. This caused the people from Norway to join the daily Danish group meetings. Such a message was itself an inspiration, and though it led to Diney (from England) having to be without a group, that could not be helped. She felt it best for herself, too. Later events showed that Sai Baba had not forgotten her and knew of her not being in any group.

In March of 1975, Sathya Sai said that for two years he had not been granting interviews to people who came from the Western countries as single individuals. Baba has made it clear that he prefers groups that have not just "ganged up" in the hope of an interview, for he calls that "not a group but a gang." We have learned that Baba likes people who submit to group discipline, especially those already working actively together where they have come from. He has also said that, "just because there are four or five persons who are bad and whose behavior is not acceptable at Prashanthi Nilayam . . . they are ruining the opportunities which the whole group can have and wishes to have."[1]

At the big group meeting at dusk on the steps of one of the accommodation roundhouses, Thorbjørn told us he felt sure Sai Baba would grant an interview the next morning. The sense of anticipation and pending fulfillment of years of yearning was made bearable by the joyful spiritual intensity of the atmosphere created by the buildup of all manner of signs and promising portents through dozens of dreams and *leelas*. I seemed hardly to have any pains or muscular tensions, and we slept very lightly and briefly.

---

[1] See *Preparations for the Presence*, a booklet containing directives for visitors to his ashrams, issued by Sai Baba in a Discourse at Brindavan, March 28, 1975.

13

THE INNER SANCTUM

The next morning the men in our Scandinavian group found that they had drawn number "1" from the bag full of numbered chits for the thirty-six or so rows of visitors waiting to enter the temple compound. This meant that we would sit in the front line on the sand where Baba comes out to give his darshan.

Sai Baba first went around to the ladies' side of the compound. When he arrived in front of us, he stopped and stood firmly on the sand while waving his right hand to produce *vibhuti* for someone, as we had seen a dozen times since we arrived. Then he told one person in our group that we should all come to an interview.

At long last we were truly going to enter that hallowed sanctum where so many long to be and which frequently seemed to be beyond my reach. We filed up onto the spacious veranda of the temple, between the pillars and lines of students and servitors, and sat waiting cross-legged on the cool marble floor. An atmosphere of peacefulness enveloped me, tinged through and through by quiet yet enthralling anticipation, just as others have often described the magic of that moment. The ladies of our group assembled, as is the custom, on the opposite side of the veranda. Altogether there were thirty-one of us, I knew, for we had daily checked the number in case Swami asked any of us his usual question, "How many?"

After ten minutes or so, having concluded his ever-unhurried round, Baba arrived and stood before us, looking quite unapproachably majestic. After some moments he invited us to go into the interview room. We sat closely packed on the floor of this small room, men on the right side of the room as seen from Swami's chair, ladies in front on the left side. Sathya Sai came in and leaned over the men to turn on the light and the fan himself, now as familiar as a mother or any close family member. The door was then shut, and Swami stood before the ladies and waved his hand to produce *vibhuti*, with which he went around to let a portion fall into the hands of each of them in turn. I became clearly aware of what has been called "a rare sanctity of the divine presence in the air."[1]

Baba seated himself on his high-backed chair, which stands on a slightly raised dais so that all can see him properly. He began to talk about love being the way to God and other of his teachings. There was a real surprise for me at once.

His whole manner was suddenly *exactly* like some pseudo-spiritual Indian I knew, pretending to be a guru and speaking in very broken English. I felt my heart sink—literally a sinking feeling! "No! He can't be like *that*—" I thought, confused and put off by this. However, the small voice of sanity in me said, "There *must* be some explanation. Don't panic. Wait!"

As it went on, though, I could not free myself from a sense of disappointment. After everything—the long, long critical searching and the final marvelous discovery of the avatar, could this really be just a hoaxer? I recoiled at the thought, but it would not leave me. Then, remembering the way Baba had made fun with me in dreams and had even performed practical jokes on me in them, I told myself there must be some explanation and time would bring it. (I did not recall at the time a dream in which I had said that his English was perfect, to which he had replied, "Perhaps you'll not find it so good"!) After a minute or so of this unpleasantness I was relieved to feel that he was behaving much more as I had expected. The illusion of being like a quasi-guru was gone.

Thinking it over some days later, I realized that this had been mostly a taste of my own medicine, for I sometimes talked with an exaggerated Indian accent for fun. Yet the main point of the joke did not occur to me fully, though, until *two whole years* later, when I recalled how I had once—about fifteen years previously at a dinner party—dressed up in an ornate one-piece Eastern priest's gown someone had given me, bared my feet and given an imitation of

---

[1] Ra Ganapati, *Baba: Sathya Sai*, vol. 2 (Madras: Satya Jyoti, 1984), p. 295.

some young Indian quasi-guru I had heard give a confused "spiritual talk," in broken English full of parroted clichés.

One young lady had been provoked to interrupt angrily that she didn't believe in these spiritual things, but I had put on a big, falsely magnanimous smile, in character, and preached on with Indian-style hand gestures about how one should not criticize anyone, but only love everyone. To my genuine surprise and amusement, I later realized that one Norwegian diner had actually taken my whole satire as if it were meant to be the real thing, and even asked to touch my feet—all of which made me a bit ashamed. It was not done in ill-will, however, but to entertain by satirizing gurus of the most dubious sort who were lording it around Western countries in those days.

Sai Baba certainly turned the tables on me, anyhow, when he easily took me in by his play, showing me both how he knew of my predilection for taking people in for a bit of fun and also how it feels to be on the receiving end! I have since laughed and marveled greatly over that bit of divine mischief. Another consolation for those nervous minutes is that I can perhaps boast of having the world record for slowness in appreciation of a joke.

At some point during the interview, while Baba was greeting various people and asking the seated ladies to move closer, I saw him meanwhile open a letter that had been handed to him. He took out the contents—I think it was one of two enclosures—and quickly threw this onto the floor beside him with a very brief but most intense and powerful expression of disgust. The incident was over in a second and seemed to go generally unnoticed while the ladies were getting comfortable.

Baba spoke about practicing the *SOHAM* breathing meditation, which he demonstrated for us with a deep and slow intake and outlet of breath. He said that we have (an average of) 21,600 breath cycles per day. The body is a sensory phenomenon that is *conscious*. The mind has *conscience*. By continuous practice of breathing and listening to *SO* (intake of breath) and *HAM* (exhalation of breath), we can rise above the sensory phenomena of the body and above the mind to experience *Consciousness* itself, the bliss of the *Atma*. "I keep telling you this but none of you are practicing it," he said, and his meaningful glance caught me in passing.

One young man beside me had a silver ring that he had told me Sai Baba had materialized on a previous occasion. It was inset with a colored enamel picture of Sathya Sai Baba's head and shoulders. It had received a disfiguring white scratch across the face. Suddenly Swami simply asked its owner, who was sitting about three yards from him, whether his ring was not scratched and asked if he wanted it repaired. The answer was affirmative! Sai Baba sent the ring around for several of us to examine and see the scratch, meanwhile instructing the young man about some personal matter. He then took the ring and said he would repair it. "My helpers are very quick. *Very* quick!" he said, and closing his hand over it in full view, he blew into his fist once before opening it. Before Swami returned the ring to the owner, it was sent around again so that we could observe that it was the same ring as before, apart from its return to a perfect, unscratched condition!

Baba then made much fuss of a young man from Sweden, whom I knew from our first visit there, and who had since received numerous interviews before this one. He was invited to sit close beside Baba, receiving lots of friendly slaps on the shoulder and playful cuffs. Eventually Baba asked the young man what he wanted. The answer was nothing, except for Swami himself. He was even asked if he would like a wife. Swami compared him with those who ask for all sorts of things: "But you see, this boy is not full of desires. He wants nothing at all for himself!" He made it clear that this is exemplary behavior and that putting a limit on desires is required if one wants God. Despite further protests by the young man to the repeated question, "What do you want?" Sai Baba waved his right hand a few times, and out of it came a beautiful bracelet consisting of a thick silver chain and plaque engraved with the *Pranava* or "Aum" symbol.

It was evident that Sai Baba's person was the sole focus of interest the whole time for everyone in that room. If he had not been the one to speak or question anyone, I wondered how anyone would have said or done anything in his presence but sit there and wait for his initiative. One Danish man did eventually answer Sai Baba's invitation to put some question about God. The answer was on familiar lines, that everyone is God but they are not fully aware of the fact: "You are also God!" The Dane couldn't believe or accept this, whereupon Sai Baba said again, "You are God. You *are* God." It was certainly said intensely and in a most convincing manner!

A lady asked why twins occur, to which Sai Baba answered, "It is a private matter in the family. Something you cannot understand."

Sai Baba made us all laugh now and again by the subtlest of mimicry and comments, and he asked questions to various people in such a way that there was often some teaching for all of us in it.

I was of course wondering whether Baba would say anything to me, and though I had several matters I had decided I would like to have information or else guidance about, I did not have very high expectations. Just then he asked whether anyone was sick. No one spoke. He asked again. After some moments I held up a hand and he turned to me. He immediately put his hand to the right side of his neck and said, "Pain here?" Because no pain was noticeable at the time, I said it was not pain but strong tensions. "Nerves are pinched here," he said. I had settled on this as the most likely cause soon after I fell ill, but medical and other "experts" had been of a dozen different opinions, so that I had virtually lost sight of this basic fact amid all the theories.

He turned his attention away from me and toward a lady at the rear of the room to tell her of a skin complaint she was suffering. She was clearly astonished and said there and then that she had not told *anyone* about it. Sai Baba waved his right hand around a few times and closed it momentarily. Turning it palm up we saw a *lingam* shaped like a small egg, brownish on one half and whitish on the other. It was handed first to Thorbjørn Meyer, of whom Sai Baba asked what it was. Thorbjørn asked if it were not a *Shivalingam* representing *rajas* and *tamas*.[2] "Correct!" said Sai Baba, and giving the lady the *lingam*, he told her to put it in about a liter of water overnight and take a teaspoonful daily. No more was needed. The water could also be used by others for healing purposes.

---

[2] According to Sankhya philosophy there are three "qualities": *tamas*, *rajas*, and *sattva* (from lowest to highest), representing 1) inertial energies (*tamas*), or sluggish, low, and dark aspects; 2) active energies (*rajas*), the outgoing, aggressive, and vital aspects; and 3) peaceful energies (*sattva*), the refined, high-minded, peaceful, balanced, and inward aspects. These qualities are compounded in various proportions in all things that exist, including the human being. The two lower qualities have to be overcome in human life by reducing them to the absolute minimum and becoming as *sattvic* as possible in one's lifestyle. One can only guess at the possible significances of a *lingam* representing two of these qualities, but it probably implies a strengthening of the *sattvic* qualities, for these are closely related to healing properties.

Before he began to take twos and threes into the small adjoining room for brief private interviews, Sai Baba also materialized a silver medallion locket for an elderly Danish lady who sat at the rear of the room. With complete ease, and without visibly taking aim, he cast it several yards right into her lap.

The young man whose luggage was lost on the journey from Norway was carrying all he still had with him in two small shoulder bags slung crosswise on his chest, bandolier fashion, one on each shoulder. As he went to the private interview room, one of these snagged on the door handle and shook the door heftily. Immediately, Baba peeked mischievously out of the doors after him and commented cheerfully to us, "Too much luggage!" (The luggage did eventually arrive some weeks later, but not until the very morning he was leaving! Afterward the fellow could make neither head nor tail of this comment, and none of us felt able to explain to him that it probably referred to the fact that he was carrying too much "mental luggage" in the form of weird ideas, strong aversions, and so on. That young man is no longer with us, having died in a car accident some years later.) In the private interview, Baba had said to him, "I will bless you!"

Another person hurrying into the private room misjudged the opening between the double doors, setting the fastened one rattling loudly. Baba told him not to worry or hurry; he would get in all right without having to break the door down!

Sai Baba came out from a private session and turned to me, to my surprise. "Yes sir," he said, pointing toward the other room. "Yes. You next. Where is your wife?" I was certain that he must know the answer, just as without being told he knew I had a wife. I pointed her out. "First?" he quickly asked. I couldn't make out what he meant at all. "Pardon me, Swami?" I queried. "Is it your first wife?" He paused a moment. "No. Second wife. I know!" Before she went in, Sai Baba said, "Your wife is angry with you sometimes, isn't she?" I said, "Not so bad, Swami," to which he immediately retorted, "Not so good!" to the evident amusement of the others.

This comment puzzled me a lot, and Reidun, too, for she was seldom angry, though she had been very angry for a brief while on account of some comment of mine on the taxi journey to Prashanthi about ten days previously. Otherwise we never could quite see how this could describe the state of affairs between us, even though it had been the case years previously. However, it served to make me more aware that all was perhaps not as well as I liked to think. By then I had come to know that Reidun had sometimes been extremely unassuming about imposing her own wants or feelings on anyone—or even showing them when thwarted—so I had to try to discover what caused this "not so good" comment. (In a recent dream, Baba said he knew that she and I now only disagree about unimportant things.)

Inside the inner room we remained standing. Baba came before us, and though I knew he was short in stature, I was most surprised to note how much shorter he was than my wife. As he spoke to us, he held me by the arm. He let us know some essentials concerning each of us, also for the benefit of each other. He told us things that both surprised us and moved us both very much. We both found ourselves asking things we had never imagined we would, nor had even thought of before. These impulses Baba seemed to draw from deep within us, where we had not even known they existed. One thing that I asked almost despite myself had surprising consequences and led to a series of events and Baba *leelas*, which also held several rather trying lessons for me to groan on and grow upon, but I do not feel at liberty to go into any details. As others who have had private interviews feel or know, it is not right to divulge everything that passes between him and oneself. Some matters can be so personal and wonderful that one wishes to keep them pure in one's heart to oneself.

One surprise can be told, however. Sai Baba said he would give us another interview the next day, not the group, but just us two. He took my right hand and looked at my silver and gold ring with its filigree of hearts round it. "That is your wedding ring, is it not?" I said it was. "Tomorrow I will make you another ring." I could hardly believe this and reminded myself of what I had learned from others: not everything Sai Baba says will come tomorrow actually comes the next day. He said that he had little time, seeing that so many people were at this interview, but added that there would be more time the next day.

Reidun had just gone out through the door when Swami stopped her and asked, "What do you want?" She said, "I want to know God in my heart." He looked at her intensely some moments, then looked down. She took that as a sign to continue to her place, but he put up a hand saying, "Look!" His right hand made passes through the air in the by-now familiar manner. He produced a silver medallion with a finely-wrought relief of his own head and face, which he held out to her. (Later, when I examined it, it appeared just as if it had been freshly minted, the silver not yet polished as bright as it became later through wear, with tiny extra fragments still attached, like one may see on metal work just out of a mold. Moreover, such medallions are actually hung close to the heart.)

After that I sat, dazed and "very happy" as Sai Baba took in others. Only few details of the remainder of the interview could I recall afterward. Before we rose to leave, Sai Baba reached for his *vibhuti* bag, which was a simple red plastic carrier basket of a sort commonly used in India for shopping. He gave a large handful of from thirty to forty packets of *vibhuti* to each of those present.

While he was signing a photo or two prior to ending the interview, I recalled that during the past two years since our previous visit there was one thing I had really decided to ask for, which was to touch his feet (*padnamaskar*). Of this, he has explained that it can bring together the complementary energies of the individual person and the divine source, always with beneficial results. The nature or strength of the effect depends upon the *sadhana* (spiritual practice) of the individual. I did not ask for this out loud, but sent a mental question only. As soon as I had thought it, he turned toward me, still talking all the while to another, and came straight across the intervening couple of yards to press one of his feet, the left, so gently against me where I sat. I took *padnamaskar*. There was no obviously noticeable physical effect, but there was the keenly peaceful and joyful sense of fulfillment in having for the first time reached the feet of the Master and of the Eternal Friend.

Baba left the interview room. I happened to be almost the last person out. As I came to the threshold I was struck by a very strong and most evocative scent that I knew from somewhere. It was the delightful scented nectar (*amrit*) that Baba can produce from his hands or that he sometimes lets flow from pictures, amulets, stone idols, and so forth. Looking around, I could see no possible source of it. Shortly afterward I asked those who had been beside me about it, but they had noticed no scent at all. That, I later learned, is the usual manner of Baba's scent *leelas*; one person will be almost overpowered by the fragrance of *vibhuti* or *amrit*, while others close by can detect nothing!

14

BE READY! BE READY!

As so many people coming from their first interview have reported before me, we could have been walking on clouds. The feeling of peace and inner happiness felt as if it could not be shaken by any incident or difficulty that we might have encountered. What might previously have seemed a bothersome duty or a trouble would only have awakened care and commitment. I was able to feel a deeper and more embracing sympathy than usual for everyone, such as for those who still awaited a first interview.

During the rest of that day I was often arrested by most poignant scents, yet I could not discover their origin, nor could people beside me detect them.

Apart from a bad cold that became a dreadfully painful throat and chest infection, which grew worse and worse daily, my chronic neck pains and muscular tensions had almost disappeared. I had even been able to sit on the floor of the interview room without more discomfort than one might expect. My energy had been increasing ever since my arrival, and I had become active in the cleaning work that foreigners were doing in the "Westerner's" canteen building and also in long and physically grueling sessions for the Christmas choir, sitting cramped up on a concrete floor. This was in strong contrast to how I had been living and feeling during most of the previous year.

That afternoon, at a choir practice for Westerners who were hoping to sing before Sathya Sai, the atmosphere created by a massed choir of over 1,000 singers was just too moving for words.

After about an hour, when the singing was reaching a special peak of emotion, the small orange figure of Sathya Sai quite unexpectedly appeared at the door, and he walked into the hall through the great crowd. That was a moment of tremendous beauty. The choir simply soared in a way that I had never heard before.

Baba stayed for several minutes, moving slowly between various sections of the choir. As he retraced his way to the door, the choir leader hastily started a new song, but people were unprepared and a discordant sound soon arose. Baba scorned this effort with an expressive and most amusing arm movement, making everyone laugh.

That afternoon our group chose the row that drew the number "1" tile from the bag, so that we were again able to sit in the front line inside the compound. It transpired that, during those days, we were in either the first or second row several times consecutively. The statistical chances against this occurring are very great, yet I have since seen this sort of bank-breaking run happen time and again with groups for whom the time was ripe.

Once again Sathya Sai gave a long and delightful darshan, and members of our group received attention and friendly glances. About an hour afterward, there was the usual half-hour of *bhajan* singing, during which I sat well to the rear at a spot where I could rest my back against a pillar. Sai Baba came out again and went around while thousands of voices sang divine praises. When he came opposite me, he beckoned to me several times before I felt confident that he meant I should come forth. I picked my way through the packed lines of singers on the sand, while he stood and waited. As I approached he was saying something to me, but all I heard was ". . . o'clock tomorrow." He waited, beckoning me closer, then said, "Interview tomorrow. Be ready!"

"At what time, Swami?" I asked. He said, ". . . in the morning," in a tone and with a gesture that made the exact time seem irrelevant, for one is nearly always called during darshan anyhow. I had heard the word "o'clock" most clearly, however, so this puzzled me. (The explanation came later the next day when a member of the Danish group, who had been sitting in the front line at Swami's feet when he spoke to me, told me that Baba had said, "Interview at six-thirty o'clock tomorrow." It so happened that Sai Baba called for me to go to the interview at *precisely* six-thirty, because the moment he did so the Dane looked at his watch to check this!)

At the time it did not seem quite credible that we should have another interview the next day. I had heard from reliable people that

Baba sometimes lets a person understand such a thing and then either ignores what he'd said or perhaps changes his mind according to that person's subsequent behavior, so I took nothing for granted. I put the idea of a ring out of my mind, not least because, if indeed I was worthy of anything, I really wanted something other than a material thing from the Master of Maya.

The night was very hot, and so was the air in the hall where we were staying. I did not feel like sleeping for a long time, not least because of the marvelous scents like a variety of the purest incenses wafting past, which in fact only I was able to smell. I even got up and snooped around to see if anyone was burning incense on the sly outside the hall windows! Though I had read of people experiencing the same after an interview, it took some time for me to reach the conclusion that it was actually occurring for me, too!

Just as I was waking up, a voice within me told me with full natural conviction of major life events that would take place for me before I die. This voice had the sound of my own voice, yet it was somehow also supra-personal in its confidence and its origin. It was the same voice that once before had said what already had truly happened: that I had "come to Puttaparthi under unusual circumstances."

Baba called me at precisely 6:30 A.M., as well as two Africans and a small group of Indians, including the family of a professor at the Institute of Higher Learning at Prashanthi Nilayam. We were about a dozen people altogether.

After materializing *vibhuti* and giving it personally to each of the six or eight ladies, Baba was most lively indeed, engaging in rapid interchanges with the Indian family and others all at once. It was quite unlike the more serious and quiet Scandinavian interview of the day before. Several of the Indians talked eagerly at the same time, while Baba kept conversations going with all of them, responding rapidly in turn to each with the greatest of good humor. I might have been witnessing a somewhat unruly family breakfast table.

Baba spoke English occasionally, but mostly in Telugu or Hindi. He called me "sir," as in my dreams, which form of address he seems to use quite often. Motioning to the gentleman beside me, Baba introduced him as a professor of history.

Baba looked at me closely: "What do you do where you come from, wasn't it philosophy you taught?" I said that it was. "What is that subject like there?" I felt quite free to voice my true opinion of it: "Not very good, Swami!" At this the professor broke in and urged me rather to say something positive about philosophy being the love of wisdom and so forth. Sai Baba ignored this and pursued my opinion: "So what do you say?" I told him that our philosophy is "all theory and no practice." He gazed thoughtfully for a second and said, "Practice is very important!"

We saw Baba wave his hand several times in large circular movements, almost as if he were taking hold of some elusive moving object. A very large necklace simply materialized from it all in the same movement, swinging around in the air with his hand. He put it around the neck of an Indian lady who sat before him, and explained that it was a rosary *japamala* made of 108 crystal beads separated by smaller golden beads.

After a while Baba invited us in to a private interview. As I was following him in through the door, he turned and stopped me, saying, "Wait." He waved his hand in the now-familiar manner and produced a ring. It appeared to be a brilliant white diamond in a gold setting. "See if you can get it on this finger," he said, putting it on the end of my ring finger.

Something told me straight away that this ring would not fit, reminding me of what I had read in a book about Baba purposely making a ring that was too small for someone. "It won't fit," I said. "Never mind, just *try* to get it on. Go on!" he encouraged. I squeezed it up to my knuckle, but in no way would it fit over it. "Try, try!" said Baba again. With that sort of urging I got involved in trying to press it over my large knuckle. At last he took my hand and himself tried to fit the ring on my finger before saying, "No. It's too small!" and raised a good laugh all around by slipping the ring off and away with a funny movement. With that he took us into the small room and asked us to sit down.

One of the surprises that Baba gave me in there was to ask, "What is your plan?" Since I had read about him saying we should not worry about the future, I had been trying to rid myself of plans! This question was thus quite unexpected, not least as one thing I had wanted to know was what plan *he* had for me, if any. In a very clear dream the previous year, Baba himself had set quite a definite possibility before me—of teaching English for one year in his school—and it had been difficult for me to adjust to the idea at all.

Not knowing when or how it might come about, I had partially prepared myself for teaching English, so I said, "I thought about teaching . . . " Before I finished, he said in an almost gruff manner, " *Not* teaching!" At first this felt like a rebuff. When I later was able to reflect over it, I realized that Baba had lifted from my shoulders the feeling that I, who have been privileged in receiving a university education and so forth, had a duty somehow or other to go on working as a teacher, despite my illness and my tiredness at the relative futility (that is, philosophy in the Western university context, at least). Besides, my spinal problems had returned after the temporary cure Baba gave me on my first visit, and my continuing teaching work was doubtless at least part of the cause. Baba seemed to be making me realize again that it is wrong to go on doing what one's heart is not in.

Instead, Baba made clear that he was expecting my further ideas about another matter, one that had arisen at the private interview the previous day and about which I had hardly even thought since. Nonetheless, an unexpected and quite dramatic answer came out of me, and it was certainly no less unexpected by Reidun! I mention this—without going into the actual subject we discussed, which should remain unpublicized—so as to show how Sathya Sai can evidently either simply put ideas and decisions into one's mind or else drag forth entirely unthought-of possibilities from one's soul in his presence. The immediate result of it was that I was in a state of joy!

Though we had visas for three months, and I had hoped we might stay that long, Reidun felt that, due to living conditions, one month was all that was tolerable and that six weeks was the limit. When Baba was on his way to the door again, Reidun fell to her knees before him as if to block his way and actually pleaded, "Swami, can we please stay here for three months!" I was flabbergasted at this sudden change in her view, too. "Yes. Very happy. Very happy. I shall arrange accommodation for you!" he said, and ushered us out of the private interview room.

With the private session over, my state was such that I couldn't even estimate how many minutes it had lasted. We came out and sat in the places we had occupied earlier. Sai sat on his tall-backed red velvet chair and looked at me. "Look," he said, and opened his right hand to show the very ring I had been "trying" on. "What about this?" I was lost for words, not least as I had completely forgotten all about the ring. "What do you want?" he asked.

That is the very question he often puts and to which both Reidun and I had carefully considered possible answers for years, just in case we should ever be asked it. Thinking about how to answer that question has the effect of genuine self-inquiry, a marvelously concentrating effect. One must think what really counts in life, what to ask for when that chance comes, a chance that might be the single opportunity of this lifetime. I knew what my answer was well enough but, as Baba looked into my eyes, the words were simply blocked—the succinct little formula I had memorized by heart just failed to come out. His eyes were still expectantly on me, but I only managed to get out a halting, "I don't . . . know, Swami!"

Some intangible impression that I could not grasp in those instants must nevertheless have been burned into the depths of my soul. I must jump ahead in time briefly here, because nearly four years later, a young Sai friend of ours asked for liberation in answer to the same famous "What do you want?" question. He had his wish granted and then actually fulfilled some weeks later, when we were with him at Prashanthi Nilayam! Not until that time did I realize more about the enormous possible consequences of such a reply. Then, too, I could recall clearly the look in Sathya Sai's eyes. Through one deep look, Baba had somehow intimated what such a request could involve, perhaps had even warned me that I was not ready for such a fulfillment! But more of this subject later on.

Sathya Sai handed the ring to a middle-aged Indian lady and asked her, "What is it? Tell what it is!" She held it up and examined it, then said, "It's a diamond ring, Swami." He nodded and asked, "What else?" "The ring is gold with a golden lotus-shaped setting for the stone." "That's correct," he went on, "Now pass it on for others to see it." After a short while he asked for it back.

He looked at me as he held it on his open right palm. "I will make you a better ring. Watch!" He simply closed his fingers over the ring and lifted it directly near to his mouth. He blew three times into the space between the thumb and first finger, looking at me meanwhile with a large and amused smile, like a father doing conjuring tricks for a child.

He quickly opened his hand and in the palm lay a different gold ring, set with a yet larger stone that was sparkling green. I heard one lady let out a big gasp in amazement. Sathya Sai stood up and took a few very lively steps over to me with a joyously benign expression. Taking my right hand, he slipped the ring straight onto the ring finger. As he did so he said "Perfect. Not more fit." But I first heard these words as, "Not Murphet," which meaning did not seem likely. I was still in two minds, for I did not think Baba would use the ungrammatical phrase "not more fit."

Baba took someone else in for a private interview, and I sat there, my mind entirely stunned by surprise and my heart overflowing at his loving kindness and at how great a good fortune had befallen me. In the interests of honesty, however, I must add that I had mixed feelings about the color of the stone.

As I was wondering exactly what Baba had said, I asked the professor beside whom I was sitting what the exact words had been. Without hesitation he said, "Perfect. Not more fate." Then he wondered if, after all, Baba had not said, "Not more fight." He thought it all amounted to much the same thing, saying that once anyone had received the grace of the avatar, it is like being reborn, so that one's life expands and expands more and more. He told me some of his experiences since Swami materialized for him the golden ring with three inset gems that he wore, saying that he understood that the green stone is for the development of inner vision. I only hoped he might be right! (See color photos between pp.182–183.)

As to what Baba had "actually" said, I can now accept that each of the four possible versions are meaningful. This is supported by other experiences. I have also heard of similar instances of his using one utterance to give different-sounding verbal messages to each of several people at the same time. The two interpretations of his cleverly-enunciated phrase that I "heard" have proven to have highly relevant meanings. The ring could not have fit better, being *smaller* than the knuckle over which he pushed it, so that I have never had it off once since then! My wedding ring is inside it, so I have been unable to remove that, too, not that I have intended to. The words "Not Murphet," however, remained a complete mystery to me for another six months.

A remarkable solution came from a book by Phyllis Krystal, a first copy of which she presented to Baba at another interview we attended some weeks later. Sathya Sai held it up for my attention as a book I should read. This book, *Sai Baba: The Ultimate Experience*, also contained information that was highly relevant to me regarding understanding the nature of my illness. In it she reports that one day Sai Baba gave her some betel for her indigestion saying, "Indigestion. Not Indra Devi." It had taken her years to find out the meaning of this. She came to realize that Baba was telling her that she should be more like Indra Devi, who is a very outgoing lady who lectures and teaches all around the world. Phyllis Krystal says she needed to overcome her tendency to withdraw from the limelight. It took six months for me to obtain the book, whereupon I soon realized the meaning of "Not Murphet." I, too, should be more like Murphet, who writes and publishes his experiences. I have written books that I have hardly even tried to publish. This present book is one of the main fruits of that *leela* of Sai Baba, for otherwise I would not have had the confidence to begin writing about such personal experiences.

Nevertheless, a year later there still remained a thin sliver of doubt in my mind about whether Sai Baba could actually have mentioned Murphet in this way. Imagine my surprise therefore when, just after darshan, in 1988, I was sitting on a chair beside a Sai follower from Decatur, Georgia, who told me of an incident he had once witnessed on the porch of the *mandir*. I had given no cues or clues; he simply chose to tell me this particular incident. Baba had come up to Howard Murphet, and patting his own stomach had said, "I'm perfect, not Murphet." This confirmed my interpretation of the words he had uttered when giving me the ring. It seems that this sort of oblique way of advising, through a jigsaw of highly coincidental events that keep hinting at something, is typical of the avatar. If Baba instead gave blunt directives, of course, it would virtually take away any real follower's freedom of self-discovery and strength to adopt personal responsibility.

When Sai re-entered the main interview room, he started to converse in Telugu with an Indian lady teacher from his Anantapur College for Women. Painful though it is for me to make the admission, I grew very irritated as Baba went on and on conversing. I had been hoping for some discussion myself but here was I being ignored! It seemed unfair. I tried to work up some sympathy for this keen lady questioner, thinking how, compared to myself, she doubtless worked truly hard and selflessly in the service of Swami's students, but for some minutes I could feel only a jealous impatience. Baba continued to concentrate fully on answering her ceaseless questions. (I later learned from the professor that the lady was a professor of Sanskrit and it had almost all concerned Sanskrit grammar.)

I was at the same time disturbed at the fact that this attitude should come over me there, right in the very interview room. It showed me something about a kind of vanity that I was compensating for by self-effacement (and vice-versa). How should the humble, reserved me of the day before, believing as I did that Baba is the God avatar, all of a sudden actually *expect* him to converse with me—he who can know all he wishes to know, even down to the most banal thought I might have (but only when or if he chooses to know it, I presume). My sudden rise in self-esteem lasted long enough to deflate me back down to size again, so to speak! I have since come to believe, due to further similar experiences, that Baba somehow induced those feelings in me, which otherwise might have remained subconscious. By experiencing them, I was able to learn more about myself.

A teenage Indian student from one of the Sathya Sai colleges was sitting a little to the left before me, only feet away from Baba's chair. Baba then turned toward this young man and began to talk lovingly to him, ask him questions, joke with him, and pretend to chide him a little.

I was able to watch Baba's expressions close up all the time over the boy's shoulder, yet not once did his eye wander to my face during the full ten minutes or so during which he drenched the youth in loving attention. I saw before me the very best friend a young man ever had or could have, a more mischievously playful bosom pal than I have ever dreamed of, and an intensely charming yet somehow completely natural companion in whom total trust could never be misplaced. Sai Baba became exactly as a boy himself, even his face and movements grew boyish while he coaxed and cajoled this tongue-tied youth into answering him and at length to bring out and hand over a letter he had written to him. All of this took place in Telugu, but for a few phrases in English here and there.

Sai Baba then sat back to peruse the letter. Directly he seemed transformed into a towering figure of great wisdom and fatherly implacability, but all of this still tempered with love. He took time over the reading, his expression changing as if mirroring the nature of the contents, as if it were most surprising, perhaps too difficult for him to grasp all at one time! I almost wanted to laugh but could not, seeing how seriously Baba was enacting this for the boy's benefit. As he came near to the end, Baba even mouthed a few words of its text here and there, looking as if he needed thought to grasp its depth. Only a lightning fast glance of warning, subtly directed beside me (not right at me), literally held me back from chuckling aloud.

This demonstrated to me what patient care one must exercise in playing one's role, so as to build self-confidence in others. It also reminded me of how the avatar Rama and his divine brothers, already knowing, even as children, all things that could ever be known, nonetheless sat for years at their guru's feet, pretending to learn from him out of respect for honored tradition and for the pleasure of that elderly devotee of God.

The boy watched, unmoving and devoutly, his hands folded as in prayer. Sai Baba spoke to him a while longer, then all at once held up his hand before us and began to wave it around. In a flash, a watch materialized, coming so fast from the raised palm that it was just suddenly there. Baba had caught the end of the linked wristlet so that it didn't fly right into the boy's lap. It rattled and bounced back and forth on its flexible metal chain-strap. Sai Baba looked at its face saying, "What time?"

He turned to look at the wall clock behind him and read, "Seven-forty. You see, perfect time!" I could see that the time on the watch was exactly 7:40. Baba gave it to the youth with the advice, "Don't waste time." The boy showed it to me: it was a digital model with the trade name "Seiko." (Some think this is a pun of the sort Indians are so given to, alluding here to "Sai Co." I now know that watches Sai Baba produces often bear this name, while some are Citizen, Casio, and other makes.)

Since I heard Baba say, "Don't waste time!" I took it as a reminder to myself not merely to pursue worldly pleasures and use time for fulfillment of ambitions that are merely personal and communally useless. I don't see it as advice to engage in ceaseless worldly activity—otherwise the Western tyranny of the clock and the idea that "time is money" would be acceptable.

After this, as if to gather everyone's attention, Baba held his hand up before him, at the level of his head, palm down and with his fingers partly curled. I could see through the hand from my side, and it was empty. Suddenly, in less than a trice, the fingers were pressed open by a mass of some yellow substance. He asked a lady before him to hold out her hands and he let the yellow sweets fall into them. "Tell what that is!" he asked her. "It's *prasad*, Swami," she said. "Yes. But tell what sort of sweet it is, and what is in it?" he insisted. "It's *laddu*, Swami, made from pulse, turmeric, and sugar."

He smiled at her, "You have forgotten something!" He waited a bit, then said, "Curds!" He motioned that each of us should extend a hand. He picked up most of the *laddu*, which was in broken pieces of various shapes and sizes, and distributed some to each of us. This he did with one swift movement for each hand while he walked around the room. I saw each extended hand holding pretty much the same amount—about the size of a mandarin orange each—despite the irregularity of the shapes. Baba gave this amount to every one of the dozen or so persons present, without appearing to manifest any more. Yet it was quite evident to me when I reflected on it that one hand could certainly not have held so much *laddu* in one go.

The sweet was warm and so sticky that it would be impracticable to save it up. We all ate it up, and it took some time to lick the stickiness off afterward. In fact, not until I washed my hands did they unstick. Sai Baba's hands seemed perfectly normal, however, when he signed photographs at the close of the interview. We heard the morning *bhajan* begin, a great wave of Oms swelling up around us from the thousands around the temple and compound. Baba reached for his "shopping basket" and gave each of us a large handful of small bags of *vibhuti*. I was also given *padnamaskar* again, this time the other foot. "I will see you tomorrow. Be ready!" Baba told me. Flustered, I could utter no more than "Yes. Swami," and not even so much as a thank you.

15

MARCHING HAPPY

Altogether, I'd been strangely unable to initiate any conversation with Sai Baba myself, so great an effect did his personality have on me. I know that this is the experience of many people, unless Baba decides that it should be otherwise.

Even those who have seen him daily for years, such as in connection with running his various educational institutions or the ashram, are silenced, simply by his wonderful presence. I heard a long description to this effect from the previous Vice Chancellor of the Sathya Sai Institute of Higher Learning, Professor Sampath, who has observed many leading figures in the presence of the Chancellor, Sathya Sai. Baba's well-known reputation for omniscience, being able at any time he chooses immediately to know what is on one's mind, can only add to the marveling awe he inspires in those around him. They are aware how all else but waiting upon the wisdom of his word would simply be a waste of very precious time.

Reidun and I had been unable to ask the shortlisted questions we had prepared in case we had a chance. Afterward this all looked quite unimportant, for the deeper self-confidence Baba had bestowed on us seemed sufficient.

The size of the ring on my finger made every movement of my hand feel ostentatious. After any interview there are people who want to see what Sai Baba has made, to admire and to touch it. After a while I thought that it might be best to take it off and avoid further notice for a while. I tried to slip it off but the same problem arose as when I had tried to put on the first ring Baba made, only in reverse. My knucklebone was too large to get the ring over. Naturally I wondered much about this. I felt it would be wrong to go and get soap and struggle to get it off. I could turn it around so the stone was inside my hand, but that proved highly impracticable whenever I used my hand, such as to grip a railing, etc. I later thought that such a ring is probably not supposed to be concealed. I have always tended to more "hide my light under a bushel" than move upstage, and when my awkwardness about wearing Baba's ring wore off, it certainly gave me more spiritual confidence.

It seemed most unlikely that Sai Baba would actually call us to a third interview the next day, and indeed, it turned out that he would quite simply see me, no more. One thing I wanted to know was whether or not I should try to take the ring off, for though it was not too tight, it would be hard to get it over my large knuckle. When Baba had put it on, moreover, he seemed very quickly somehow to have "rubbed it smaller" with a peculiar twist of his fingers.

During darshan the next day, at which most of the Danish group again drew row number 1, Sai Baba came up to me and greeted me. I was able to touch both his feet this time. In a second or less, Sai Baba glanced at my ring and said with a smile and an intense glance, "I know, I know!" I knew to what he referred—that the ring was on for good! Besides, I'm quite a muddlehead at times and have often nearly lost my wedding ring (not to mention my wife!).

As with other such rings, silhouettes of Sai Baba can be seen in it, sometimes with great clarity, his attitude varying much and very subtly with the lighting conditions. Shading it with a hand even often gives the appearance of the orange robe below the black hair, all set in a translucent green light! At times various types of crosses appear in it and also lotuses and Shivalingams. It is obviously a constant memento of Sai Baba, himself, and of what he stands for, and will lead us all to eventually: the jewel in the lotus (*Om mani padme hum*).

After Baba had put the ring on my finger, I actually managed to feel disappointment that it was not my favorite color, blue! Later I came to realize a number of things about the importance of the green color. One fairly mundane point alone is the difficulty that people—including customs officers, thieves, and muggers—would surely have in realizing that the stone is an extremely rare diamond of the highest degree of clarity, just short of perfection. Despite its size and brilliance, few persons apart from Sai followers have asked me about it during the past seven years. When persons knowing nothing of Sai Baba have asked what it is or where I got it, however, there has almost always been some remarkable circumstance involved. It has not always been easy to know at once what to answer in such situations!

Some people have called these stones emeralds, but emeralds are in fact never so translucently clear and bright, I have discovered. It may be of interest to know what others to whom Baba has given the same kind of bright emerald-green stone, and who have investigated the matter quite thoroughly, have thought about this stone. Through the years in the Sai movement I have seen perhaps twenty people with green diamonds given by Baba. Some have shown them to jewelers, but I have not heard that the jewelers have been able to say what the stone is. The stones are all of a similar shade of green, with a brilliance unknown in green gemstones anywhere in the world of commerce. One resident at Prashanthi Nilayam, who has a ring with a very similar stone of a slightly different green hue, was told by one of India's most well-known chemical industrial figures that it can only be a diamond, and I have established that its hue is very close to that of the Dresden Green diamond. These green stones that Baba makes are also held to be diamonds by an Australian who is recognized as a major world expert on opals. The stone is about 5 carats or approximately 1 cm by 1.2 cms and would be of huge value on the market, if anyone were willing to sell one or even risk trying!

No one knows the exact reason why Sai Baba gives any particular ring, for the most varied consequences have arisen for different people with what seem to be the same sort of ring. Some people think that this green color is connected with healing, or with the heart chakra, but the evidence both for and against this idea seems about equal, considering my case and others who have received green diamonds.

Since I began to wear the ring, several incidents involving it in dreams of Sai Baba have at any rate convinced me beyond any doubt that it is at times used by him as a medium to ensure that I make a right decision. He has said: "They are like my visiting cards and send me instant flashes when the person is in danger or in need of my help. Sometimes these gifts are made for special reasons: for the sake of devotees' health or I may give someone a gemstone so that the rays from it may constantly influence him or her to follow the right path. I want to tell you whatever Swami does has a purpose. He never does anything without reason."[1] Many accounts among the extensive Baba literature put the truth of this beyond any genuinely reasonable doubt.

Though I had long believed in Baba's many miraculous manifestations, I had now physically witnessed quite a few. Because some people are incurable skeptics who yet zealously believe that they know in advance what is and is not possible, even the old adage, "Seeing is believing" does not always hold true. Yet there *is* a difference between believing and seeing at first hand. I now therefore had the personal experience for confirming to others that these physical phenomena are empirical fact, not just something I believed in, at second hand, from the testimony of others.

The next occasion that Baba spoke to me was a full two weeks after the interviews, when over half of our group were leaving to return to Scandinavia. Again we drew the number for the front row, and Baba made *vibhuti* and distributed it to our group. I was last on that line. He gave me no *vibhuti* but asked me, "What is your program?" I had no idea what he meant. "Sorry, Swami?" He looked at me neutrally and said, "No program!" before walking on. That set me pondering, I can tell you.

It gradually became evident that it must mean that I was not following any strict daily spiritual routine there at Prashanthi. Therefore I decided to follow the full daily program of the ashram more strictly, from early *Omkara* in the temple until evening *bhajans*. I felt also I must add on at least one daily meditation under the bodhi tree on the hill above the temple. I "presented" my plan for approval one day during *bhajans* in the temple by asking Sai Baba to give a sign if he approved and give it the moment I mentally asked for the answer. Indeed, he looked my way *immediately*, looking at me where I sat many rows back amid a hundred people and giving some satisfied nods. Much later on again, I understood another and different meaning of "no program," which obviously referred directly to a private conversation in the interview room. This showed me again how Baba packs into a short phrase instructions for both the present and for future reference, too.

During the last few days of our friend Diney's stay, she decided after all that she wanted an interview so much that, since individu-

---

[1] Shakantala Balu, *Living Divinity* (London: Sawbridge, 1981), p. 296.

als were not usually called, she would if necessary return to England and join a group so as to return as soon as possible.

"I need an interview! I must have one!" she said so intensely and loudly that I suggested in fun that Baba must be able to hear her physically, even though we were inside a building and far beyond earshot. Just then it was time to go to darshan, so our conversation ended.

Since she got into a good position, Diney asked Baba, "Interview, Swami?" He asked her his usual question: "Where do you come from?" Next he asked: "How many?" She could only answer, "One, Swami." He said: "Go!" (for an interview).

From the 2nd to the 4th of January, 1987, Prashanthi Nilayam was visited by many hundreds of wandering *sadhus*—monks and renunciants—some of whom wander the highways and byways of the land. These were Telugu-speaking renunciants who had come from Andhra Pradesh State, having received Sai Baba's invitation to this unprecedented gathering, through their organization.

The atmosphere of their presence brought to life scenes from the ancient Indian scriptures. From the discourses that the most venerable of them delivered in Sai Baba's presence, it seemed from their eulogies that they held him in great respect and regarded him as a divine and spiritual leader. He also gave discourses for them, praising their sacrifices for the sake of fellowmen who have no other source of spiritual guidance. But Baba also firmly corrected various misunderstandings about the true qualifications and correct role of a *sadhu*, admonishing those who had taken to begging rather than serving their fellowmen (a few did try to beg in the ashram, but this practice—which is forbidden there—soon came to an end).

Sathya Sai made it clear that a true *sadhu* is not simply someone who gives up properties and renounces worldly ties, usually wandering about in an orange robe.[2] On the contrary, it requires an exemplary life and sincere, selfless service, which practice is superior even

---

[2] There is no one place to readily find more information. Readers may want to see Sanathana Sarathi, Feb. 1988, Discourse July 1, 1988, p. 32, where Baba spoke of sadhus as anyone whose deeds and thoughts are pure and are one, not merely those who don oche robes, carry the Gita, or merely mouth mantras. He has also said that, of the 500,000 sadhus, few are fit as gurus (see *Sathya Sai Speaks*, vol. 4, p. 411; or vol. 5, chapter 31, p. 172 in the revised edition).

to seeking one's own liberation. The *sadhus* each received a new set of saffron robes, a bag, and an umbrella—handed to each of them personally by Baba, to the delight of tens of thousands of devotees in the vast Poornachandra hall.

Some Westerners spoke with awe of the coming of these holy people, saying that we might, if fortunate, have a chance to serve them by working in the canteen where they were to eat. This opportunity did not arise, but we saw the *sadhus* daily, though we could not communicate with them much.

It seemed to me that the *sadhus'* visit had been a huge success, but I, too, had been seeing it through rose-colored glasses, for I later learned from a most reliable source at the ashram that it had been rather over-romanticized by those who did not understand Telugu. The leader of the Andhra Pradesh Math or society of *sanyasins* had accepted an invitation from Sai Baba to hold their normal yearly meeting at Prashanti Nilayam. Their concourse was cut short by some days, many *sadhus* evidently not taking too kindly to the strong advice of Sathya Sai to practice complete self-reliance and not be a parasitic burden on the common people and even the poor.

What remained of the Scandinavian group, fifteen people, continued to meet for mutual support and inspiration. During afternoon darshan on the 14th of January, I saw, to my surprise, my wife and the ladies of our group walking across the sand to the temple veranda. Another interview!

When Sai Baba came to the temple porch from his darshan walk he asked me, "Where are you from?" I answered, "Norway, Swami." But as I am British still and we were uncertain about whether we should move to England after all, I added, "I live in Norway." He was moving away from me when he commented "Norway!" in a slightly credulous but emphatic voice. He strolled around a moment then came back to me saying, "When are you leaving, sir?" "In March, Swami," I said. "Oh!," he exclaimed gleefully. "Plenty of time!"

Much later on I learned from a young Danish friend that, like many visitors to the ashram, he had also been asked, "Where are you from?" repeatedly by Swami. He had thought much about this and the next time he was asked, he answered, "From God, Swami." Sai Baba had smiled and said, "That happens to be the correct answer!" Still, one of the greatest and most energy-consuming dilemmas in my life had been, and still was, how I could—and whether I should—leave Norway and settle again in England, or perhaps elsewhere. My dissatisfaction with the situation had actually often caused me real suffering. Years later, I see that Baba was simply reflecting my feelings back at me, not giving any hints of advice. At the time of writing I am still in Norway, where I work in the Sathya Sai Organization group. The group still has only seven active members after ten years of existence, which fact itself in our experience certainly reflects something basic about attitudes in Norway to the kind of spirituality that above all requires selfless service without any form of remuneration or publicity.

Several people from Scandinavia, who would not accept the rules of the Sathya Sai Organization group, had come up to the *mandir* with us when we were called. When Baba had finished his darshan rounds, he came and picked them out, telling them to go back. One of them even tried to remonstrate, but Swami said gruffly, "Go away. Don't you think I know who is in the group?" (A week or so later, some of them were granted an interview together anyway.)

During this interview Swami conversed with a couple, asking about their relative Elsie Cowan, famous in Sai circles. One of them answered that she was 105 years old and very well. Sai Baba retorted, "She is not well at all. Hearing gone, bad sight, bad brain. All nearly useless and worn out," he smiled and swept his hand in an unceremonious way that made everyone laugh as if to say, "Well, the body has to go somehow, and what does it matter?"

Baba waved his hand, and out came a silver medallion with his head embossed on it. This time he cast it to an elderly Danish lady at the rear of the group. Another couple were then told to go into the private interview room and fight. "Sometimes he's crazy," Baba said, indicating the husband and screwing his index finger into his temple to illustrate the case. To the wife, he said, "Are you doing *japa?*" (i.e., repetition of a holy name). She did not understand this, but nevertheless Swami waved his hand and a large *japamala* (rosary) appeared, clattering through the air in wide circles. He told her that it was a special one of crystal with five-sided beads, showing her in detail and adding, "This is not an ordinary *japamala!*"

After that, we fifteen members of the Scandinavian group were all taken into the "private" room together, where Swami gave us about 20 minutes of teachings. He answered general questions, yet in such a way that his answers were evidently suited exactly to the understanding and special spiritual needs of the different questioners, so they were "private to the group."

This illustrated for me why Sai Baba's answers that we read in books sometimes appear to differ from one another fairly radically: they are evidently "tailor-made" for the people and each situation. So, when reading reports on interviews, one should allow for the particular circumstances, individual backgrounds, and problems of those to whom he addresses himself, for they differ very widely.

As an example, a question I asked was, "What is the way onto the Sai highway?" I had read about his having said that, once on the smoothly-paved Sai highway, there are no further problems or sufferings in life whatever. My question was designed to solve various considerations as to whether I ought to give precedence to social service activities or personal spiritual disciplines, and which ones. His answer proved to be perfect for me, reinforcing what I had always thought about this, before many new forms of *sadhana* came within my sphere. His immediate reply, given with the keenest of charming looks, was, "The *short*cut . . . is love, love, love." This truly confirmed and strengthened my own belief in what counts most in all forms of practice, social or personal. The remainder only depends upon circumstances, resources, and the like.

Baba then asked a youth if he knew what the cross he was wearing stood for, and explained, "It is the I, crossed out. Cut off the ego," and he cut sideways with a hand. Later, I asked him what exactly the ego is. "It is 'mine'—my this, my that," he said. "My thoughts, my feelings?" I asked. He answered, "Yes. My thoughts, my legs, my body, myself. When they are no longer 'mine,' then there is only love, everywhere love. What remains is the *Atman*."

Someone asked Baba what *he* wanted. He held out his hands and said, "I have everything here." He said he wanted nothing for himself, nothing but love. "I am nothing but light, love, peace, bliss," he told us sweetly. "All of us are nothing but that. Take away all the desires and what is left is love. Give love to everyone. God is wife, husband, mother, father, brother, relative, friend. Then all is peace. You are the embodiment of love, the embodiment of peace, and the embodiment of truth." The only question I can think of after that is, "What more can one say?"

Various people were corrected in their spiritual practice in a mild, loving way before we came out into the larger room again. As mentioned in an earlier connection, Phyllis Krystal gave Baba a copy of her newly published book, *Sai Baba: The Ultimate Experience*. He held it up for me to see, and holding it before his stomach, indicated clearly and yet without words to me that I would find it instructive, which took me both months and years to find out fully.

Once more we came out of the interview feeling as if we were walking on a cloud, nine feet above ground!

The question "When are you leaving?" is one of Baba's well-known favorites. He put it to me on four separate occasions during that stay alone. Each time it had an entirely different function or outcome. The second time I again replied, "In March," to which he responded smiling with, "Marching happy." This I took as a sign that perhaps my back problems due to walking would be solved, or at least that I would still be happy when I left.

Next, my wife was planning that we should leave India some week or so earlier than the end of the three months that I wanted to stay. She had indeed surprised me when almost begging Baba to let us stay three months at our second interview. But conditions had become very difficult for her, so I had agreed to change the ticket. But at darshan half an hour later, Baba came up to me and asked the famous, "When are you leaving?" The only date that would come to mind was that of the present tickets, the day exactly three months after we'd arrived. "Good!" said Sai with a big grin. That, of course, put an end to the plan for an earlier departure!

On later visits, Baba has asked me exactly the same question on at least four more occasions. In each case it has proven to have a special effect. It settled our departure date a second time, also just when we'd been planning to advance it. Sai Baba asked it with a hugely knowing smile, and slapping me on a shoulder, said a very emphatic "Good!" to the only date I could remember. During our next visit, when we were planning to delay our planned departure, he again sprang the question on me, effectively clinching the date originally planned. This was a bit disappointing, but months later we understood that we had fortunately been spared certain inconveniences that would undoubtedly have fallen to our lot if we had stayed on.

I managed to keep up the particular *sadhana* or "program" to which I had committed for some weeks, with my occasional bouts of back and neck trouble, until Sai Baba went to Brindavan near Bangalore. I must admit that what single-mindedness I had summoned began to wear down somewhat as time went by and alternative activities beckoned. It was particularly hard to maintain when Baba was there no longer. After a week we packed our bags and went to Brindavan too, able to hold out no longer. Some devotees arriving at Prashanthi Nilayam from abroad, however, propounded knowingly to us that it makes no difference, for "Sai Baba is always everywhere." I could not help asking myself sardonically what purpose could have brought them all the way to Prashanthi Nilayam! But I suppose they were trying to surmount or hide their own disappointment.

16

THE GOLD WATCH
AND THE HEART

I concur with all those who say that Sathya Sai Baba can influence one's deepest emotions, beliefs, and mental processes through the most subtle means, to bring emotional release, deeper understanding, and intensified awareness or joy. The span in time and content of one's internal or "subjective" experience that Baba may influence can be appreciated from the following nexus of events, which I shall cover as objectively as I can.

Inner reality is hardly at all accessible to any traditional scientific methods of study, because of unique personal combinations of events over time, whether in the waking or dream world. Sai *leelas*, which always bear some unmistakable hallmark, are likewise often of such an unexpected and fleeting nature that they cannot be studied scientifically. Investigation must instead depend upon a combination of attentive perception, notes, memory, and deep thought over long periods of time, along with careful interpretation informed by appropriate study and research. I therefore trust that readers will accept that what I write is not due to an overheated imagination or enthusiastic fantasy-fulfillment.

During my first visit to see Sai Baba I had a dream that came just after a turning point of that stay, which I think marked the clearing of one hindrance to improved self-realization. The dream related to my boyhood, the worst time of my childhood, when I was sent to boarding school in West Sussex. My parents were separating unbeknown to me, and my father was leaving Britain. One day, when I was 11 years old and had been boarding for two years, the

almost unbelievable and joyous news came that my father had come
to visit me. I could leave the class and go out of the school grounds
with him, something that almost never happened in the experience
of us boys.

He and I set off down the road, and I began to sense something
wrong. When he broke the news I was incredulous, then devastat-
ed. He was leaving to go to work in South Africa. I was to remain
where I was, and my mother would stay in England, too. My heart
was unprepared and defenseless. I cried long and most bitterly,
pleading with him to stay or to take me with him. Lovingly and
surely as gently as he could, he had to make it quite clear that there
was no chance of it, no money for it, and so on. I never dreamed
that this was also a permanent separation between him and my
mother. I somehow felt some of his own agony, too, for I never
thought of blaming him for anything. The fact was, he had lost his
position and had been ostracized because he would not agree to lie
on behalf of extremely influential and rich upper-class people in
England who tried to force him to help them cover up their involvement in a massive tax fraud. This I could not have understood then,
of course. At length I extorted from him, poor man, the half-prom-
ise of sending for me if things should improve, which became an illusion I lived on, and which softened the pain of the shock. Within
an hour I was back in class, trying to put on a cheerful face to foil
my keen questioners. I never did go to South Africa, but I did see
my father again very briefly during two short visits he paid to England before his death when I was 16.

Since those early days, I had forgotten an incident about a gold
watch. My father had promised, as some sort of consolation I suppose, that he would send me a gold watch from South Africa, wrist-
watches being the latest craze and mark of status at school at that
time. I suppose that this also gradually became a symbol of my
hopes and my dearest waking dream—that he would also send for
me later.

Though I wrote and reminded him, there was no sign of a gold
watch for weeks on end. One of my school friends doubted me one
day, saying that if I was to get a gold watch, where was it? I secret-
ly began to waver in my faith. Many weeks later, a package of mag-
azines came for me, postmarked South Africa. Sure enough, taped
inside one of them was a gold watch! But it had come too late, my
heart was already wounded. Besides, it had only a tiny second hand

of the sort we despised, but worse than that, the watch was not the small type I had fancied and asked for (in my innocence I didn't even know that small watches were only for ladies). At least I had some sort of face-saving proof to show, even though some boys teased me that it was not gold but "only gold-plated."

The following dream occurred at the ashram:

> There was a baby boy, perhaps about 2 years old, in critical need of a heart operation, his heart ticking irregularly, like an imperfect clock or watch. Sai Baba was present in his orange robe, asking what the matter was. Some surgeons were advising an immediate heart operation. Yet a 13 year-old boy was protesting against it, saying "No, no!"

The main significance of this dream was evident to me. There were still wounds in my heart from my childhood that needed healing. The 13 year-old boy's protest against the operation doubtless refers to the way in which, in some respects, I emotionally closed my heart for protection against the wound of realization that my father was not going to—indeed for genuine reasons could not—take me to South Africa, or perhaps would not even be able to be with me in the future at all. The overall symbolism seems clear, though: what had interfered with the ticking in my heart—the hurt represented by the gold watch—was now in the process of being removed. Indeed, the "heart operation" was already underway, in that I was regaining some lost faith in myself and in much else besides, the partial loss of which must have begun with that shock in boyhood.

Some nights after the heart dream, I also had a very happy dream indeed, set back at my old boarding school, the scene of so many boyhood trials. I met the headmaster again, as well as some boys whose charming friendship I had quite forgotten.

Much earlier in life some deeply cathartic experiences and emotional releases had enabled me to overcome the effect of various deprivations of fatherly love and support. This helped me benefit from the plus side of having had to define and realize my own manhood and to master various challenges. But the hurt had shaken my trust—not so much trust in my father as in the world that I held responsible for his fate. My feelings had then been gradually transferred more or less "irrationally" elsewhere, coming out in various ways, from bouts of despondency to an occasional irrational dislike of authority and a persistently bitter flavor in my emotional judgments toward many of the works for which the men of power are responsible.

I feel I can say that Baba's spiritual "open-heart surgery" lifted many a subtle and heavy shadow from my feelings, and he has helped me to act and react much more on the heart-to-heart level, trusting more to intuition and less to "the head," or the mere mind.

As to the gold watch, while at Brindavan, on February 2, 1987, I had a long dream in which, among other things, the following took place:

> Baba held me around my back with his left arm, and pressing his side to mine, lifted his brown and slim right hand, saying, "I will make you something. Yes, I'll make you a watch, hot from the hand." He was almost eager to make it, but I said, almost imploring him, "Oh! *please* don't make one, Swami." He then told me, while hugging me, "You are very close to the sea of peace, sweetness, and love!" He seemed to be standing in front of the gate of his residence Trayee Brindavan, and behind him I could view the beginnings of heaven reaching away into the distance, very wonderful looking.

When I awoke—naturally with a sense of great pleasure—I thought that a gold watch was something I certainly no longer required, so I inwardly said to Baba that he should give it to someone else who really needed it.

One morning, about a year later, on February 3, 1988 to be exact, I awoke from the following dream:

> I was sitting in lines of people on the ground. Baba came along from my left in front of our line, between us and the line directly in front of us. He materialized some object for the person on my left (I forgot what exactly). After this he asked me if I would like to see him do something else. I knew it would be for the person on my right. I said I'd love that. There sat a boy I once knew at boarding school, M., who had always been extremely sad, almost incapable of communication, and had frequently cried. Baba took from him his wristwatch, which was of steel, and rubbed it and its strap a few times. It became a smaller lady's watch, but now it was of gold. M. looked at it carefully in a characteristic neutral way, but now seeming a bit more lively and pleased than he used to be.

The atmosphere and degree of awareness felt in this dream simply told me that Baba was, as usual, giving a watch to someone who needed one. That it was a lady's watch indicated that it was in answer to my request. In fact he has materialized watches, both steel and gold, for many people, mostly young people and often his students. One must realize that in India a wristwatch is still often a highly-desired object for many people who otherwise would have no opportunity to possess one.

In 1988, I sat in the interview room next to a student from one of the Sathya Sai colleges. This young man was close to Swami's chair and received repeated and intense attention of the most delightfully conspiring and inspiring sort from Baba. During a pause, while Baba was giving someone else a private interview, I exchanged some words with that young man. A bracelet he wore caused me to ask if Baba had given it to him. He also showed me a very fine gold watch that he told me Swami had previously materialized for him. Somehow I immediately wondered if this was not a watch that I knew about, or that was related to my dream. I was convinced that, once again, Swami had somehow arranged that I sit next to a specific person for a definite reason. I feel this youth's presence simply made another opportunity for Baba to show me the operation of his omniscience and his loving care. Because of such incidents, I have faith that nothing Sathya Sai does, as he has affirmed himself, is without meaning. The limits of our understanding of his instrumentality in the organization of every detail surrounding him are drawn, I believe, only by our more or less wayward minds.

As Sai Baba often asserts, he is both our Father and Mother. Modern psychologists, who unfortunately still seldom understand anything much about spirituality, tend to "psychologize" the sublime guru-devotee relationship in such terms as "emotional dependency on a substitute father-figure." This is usually meant strongly to imply that there is something neurotic about it. I have been in various ways involved in psychology both in therapeutic practice and in broad studies of various forms of psychology as a science. What then of the so-called "father-figure" idea in respect to my own experiences?

My life situation necessitated a basic psychic and social self-reliance in me, which virtually immunized my mind against anything like accepting the authority of any spiritual teacher or guru, quite apart from the idea of actually putting into practice anyone else's teachings. In short, I had all the makings of a modern skeptic, with a strong interest in scientific thinking, despite (or even precisely because of) experiences I had had that were quite "beyond" the world of sensory objects.

My first approach to a guru had not been the result of any unconscious need for a father *substitute*. With my conscious and "critical" philosophical outlook, I had many reasons for avoiding any such figure. It was with difficulty that I overcame this bias when I was eventually driven, almost against better judgment, to seek *someone who really knew*, instead of scientific and philosophical know-it-alls who didn't even believe in transcendental awareness and knowledge of Truth, such as I knew existed beyond all possible doubt. When I first acted on the basis of budding spiritual faith, it led me to the swami as a temporary teacher and link to Sai Baba. I was eventually brought into the presence of the Universal Father, the truest progenitor of everyone.

Sai Baba has explained the complex and multiple etymology of the deeper meanings of his name with reference to several languages. A chief interpretation among the many associations is that *Sai* is itself compounded *(Sa-ayi)* of *Sa* from *Sarveswara* meaning "Sovereign" or "Divine," and *Ayi* meaning "mother." *Sai* also can mean Lord. *Baba* means "father" in a number of languages. Hence Sai Baba is the Divine or Sovereign Mother and Father. There are many other deeper interpretations of the significance of this, including his identity as the manifestation of *Shiva-Shakti* in the bodily incarnation, the unique unification of both the masculine and feminine energies at their fullest potency.

One morning at Prashanthi Nilayam, Baba was passing the chair where I sat. Suddenly he turned his head and gave me a brilliant shifting smile that warmed my heart, as if by direct energy, and also made me feel very familiar. As he went on by, I treasured it and only after some moments realized what the familiarity was. It had been the personalities of my departed mother and father, first the (visually-perceived) characteristic loving smile of the one and then of the other. It was a "two-phase" smile, which convinced me that each of them was somehow there "in" him. Yet the smile was also *his*, as "Sai Baba." It was a delightful gratuitous experience of great benevolence, in which I could simply bask with peace of mind and confidence in all things. It was also deeply mysterious, and wonderfully so.

The *actual* Universal Father-Mother Creator Principle is no "substitute figure" for a missing parent, for it is no less than the

Parent of all parents! Sathya Sai Baba teaches that the true Father of all being and beings is the *Purusha* or Spiritual Creative Urge, the true Mother is its counterpart, *Prakriti*, or nature upon which all life is founded at the various levels from the inorganic up to the most subtle matter or mind-stuff (*akasha*). The modern idea that acceptance of a Divine Teacher is necessarily some form of neurotic "father-fixation" is ignorant and foreshortened pseudo-psychology. Neither does adoption of Sai as Universal Mother imply any "mother-fixation." The 19th-century saint Ramakrishna Paramahamsa reportedly went to amazing lengths of self-denial and intensity of yearning in his worship of Kali as the Universal Mother. After years he was at last granted the supreme vision. Again and again thereafter he was able to achieve the superconscious bliss of genuine *samadhi*, completely lost to this world and transported to the ecstasies of who knows where at the mention of her name or at seeing her form in an idol. Even Ramakrishna could not stay in *samadhi* all the time, however.

Only a very few people are known to have achieved similar experiences through the direct grace of Sathya Sai Baba. One chief reason for this is doubtless that Baba holds true *samadhi* (*Sama* = same, *dhi* = thinking) not to be attainable in any such kind of temporary transport, for it is really total equanimity in complete awareness, maintained whatever the conditions and throughout all possible states of the soul.

17

A GLIMPSE OF SUPREME
SELFLESS DETACHMENT

The third time we visited India, we traveled with eight people from Norway and Sweden. We arrived at Prashanthi Nilayam on August 30, 1988 only to hear that Baba had not been giving darshan since the 19th, when he had fallen in his bathroom and sustained a hip fracture and head injury. However, he had appeared on the balcony of the temple once on Onam day (August 26) and then in a wheelchair at the Poornachandra auditorium, where he had actually pulled himself onto his feet and held over an hour's discourse standing at the microphone.[1]

Sai Baba has sometimes exhibited the symptoms of illnesses of many kinds, symtoms that have been witnessed by doctors. Once this even took place amid a conference of no less than twenty-five doctors called by the Governor of Goa to consult over Baba when he had a burst appendix and, hours afterwards, refused to have an operation. He was declared about to die by the doctor who was then India's leading medical authority. As is well-documented in various books, Baba nevertheless grew well again within hours and held a lecture at 4:00 P.M. the same afternoon.

While not commenting on the cause at the time of such illnesses, Baba has later let it be known in various ways or to different questioners that he has directly taken over the sufferings of great devotees who otherwise would have died, being unable to stand it. On a few occasions he has also named the beneficiary. For reports

---

[1] Account published in the monthly journal *Sanathana Sarathi*, Sept. 1988, p. 225f.

on some of the most dramatic illnesses that Sai Baba has reported-ly taken on, see the official biography *Sathyam, Sivam, Sundaram*, by Professor N. Kasturi.

The previous year (July 1987) Baba had sustained a severe heart attack and had been mostly in seclusion for some weeks. He even-tually informed some people close to him that he had taken on this attack for some unnamed lady in Uttar Pradesh, who he said was a great devotee and who had five daughters dependent on her. After his hip fracture, his attendants asked whose illness he was taking on. To their surprise, Baba said that this was not anyone else's illness and that his hip fracture was the natural consequence of his falling, being an accident of the sort that can occur to anyone who has a body. No one, whether emperor or poor man, can avoid hitting the ground when they slip on a banana skin, he had said with a smile.

We attended a lecture by Sri Narasimhan, one-time Editor-in-Chief of the largest English-language newspaper group in India, who has since taken over Professor Kasturi's function as editor of *Sanathana Sarathi*. A Telugu-speaker, and also a very widely-read person and a competent scholar of Sanskrit, he has often been with Baba as his translator at interviews. Sri Narasimhan told about Swa-mi's fall. He told us that Baba had said that he could cure himself straight away but had added, "If I rid myself of any ailment instan-taneously, people may comment, 'What sort of a selfish person is Sai Baba? He cures his illness immediately. But he does not remove the pain of others.'" There are thousands, he had said, who suffer even for months from such a fracture, so in solidarity with them he would go the whole course.

He had denied any treatment or medicines for himself, letting the body heal itself in the natural way. He was only taking care not to put undue pressure on the hip (except during the Onam discourse), sitting 24 hours a day on a sofa while reading a mountain of mail from devotees. He had explained how he could ignore his body and thus not feel its pain, by being totally absorbed in others, their joy and also their pain. Thus his self was totally ignored in all respects. Complete equanimity was the key. Likewise, he had insisted that we should not worry about him or his condition. "Nothing can do me any harm. . . . If you realize the true nature of Divinity, you will not feel that Swami is experiencing great pain and that he should take some medicine." During his Onam Discourse, held within days of the fracture, he made what will surely come to count as a historic pronouncement: "This body is not mine. It is yours. Hence I am unaffected by what happens to the body. Your bodies are in me and when you experience pain or pleasure, I share that experience.[2]

Sri Narasimhan answered a question about Swami's omniscience concerning why Swami had not known in advance that the piece of soap that he slipped on was there and that stepping on it would cause him to fall, saying that there is much misunderstanding about Swami's omniscience. Baba is not conscious of all things equally at all times. Narasimhan's experience was that Swami can at any moment be fully aware of any event, time, or place he chooses, as soon as he wills it. But this does not mean he is always aware of everything. (This also illustrates why it is important to direct one's prayers to him in a distinct manner, preferably in definite words.)

Another question put to Sri Narasimhan was whether Swami's accident could be regarded as the workings of *karma*. From his reply I understood him to mean that, by definition, a sheer accident has no cause other than chance; it is a here-and-now event that is caused according to the natural laws of physics. Though the avatar is free of previous *karma*, his having taken on a body in a physical environment subjects it to instant *karma*. Presumably, instant *karma* affects the body but not the self-illumined Atma that Baba himself always fully is. Sai Baba mentioned instant *karma* in a discourse in Secunderabad in August, 1992, as follows:

> Taking food is Karma, relieving of hunger is the fruit of the action. But between the action and the fruit, a number of events take place. These events may be immediate or spread over many years, or lifetimes.[3]

On Saturday, September 3, Krishna's birthday was celebrated. Swami gave darshan from the *mandir* balcony, where he was greeted by the richly-caparisoned elephant Sai Gita with a loud trumpet of welcome in his direction, as soon as she saw him on the terrace above her. Students and others led a dozen or more cows into the compound, and a troupe of gifted musicians with shenai, trumpet, and drums played very lively music on the temple porch.

---

[2] *Sanathana Sarathi*, Sept. 1988, p. 288; p. 225.
[3] Published in *Sanathana Sarathi*, Sept. 1992, p. 200.

In the afternoon our group was among those foreigners who were given special access to Swami's discourse in the *mandir*, which was otherwise packed with students, staff, and residents. When he came in, Baba surprised some of us by waving in welcome directly to us. After a speech by Narasimhan, Swami told about his accident again, laying emphasis both on the laws and the mysteries of nature. The latter are very difficult for humans to understand, he said, but this is why humans take birth. Unfortunately, people forget the purpose for which they are born. Among his memorable statements were also the following: "All things are equal to God. One cannot distinguish between Nature and God," "Everything in Nature has a message to man," and "It is Nature which is the primary preceptor of man." This attitude that nature is divine is enshrined in all Indian religion and culture, he explained, and spoke of the "foolish who think Indians foolish" for their worship of God in every animal, from the ant to the elephant—and even in the form of stones. This is a precious gem of ancient Indian culture.

He pointed out that "God's actions depend on the devotee's understanding," and said, "You should be full of the feeling of divinity at all times and places, whatever you do," and "Whatever happens is bound to happen. Treat it as a gift from God." One should forget the past, for it is no more, and one should ignore the future. The future of others should be our concern. The unity of the present is his concern—the past and future are only "omnipresent."

On September 7, Reidun and I were called via the office to an interview with Sathya Sai (just as I had dreamed on June 6, 1986). It took place very early in the usual room, together with thirty people from various places (Italy, Germany, Greenland, Denmark, U.S., Dubai, Calcutta, Bangalore, Kerala, etc.). It was the first interview given since Swami's injuries. He was still not appearing for darshan or bhajan. He called to us eagerly from inside the room, "Come on. Very happy!" and we soon saw his beaming smile where he stood to welcome us. He was walking most slowly and with a slight limp. It was certainly remarkable that, without medical aid of any sort, the healing process had progressed so well that Baba was walking with his fractured hip like this, only 19 days after the accident! The explanation of such rapid healing, he has told people, lies in a life of complete purity and of entirely selfless thought and action.

While we were finding places to sit, one young boy who had stepped forward to a place close to Baba's chair was sent by him straight to the back of the interview room with a strict reprimand: "Naughty boy!" On the other hand, one of his teenage students was given the most wonderful welcome and a continuous series of smiles, rapid-fire comments aside in Telugu, and loving and playful looks throughout the entire interview.

He made *vibhuti* for the ladies nearest him, and one got a lot to take to the others further back, as he was not walking about unduly. He was truly full of charm and gave most of his teachings in Telugu, which Sri Narasimhan translated. Swami corrected him now and again, giving him occasional mock blows for getting it a bit wrong.

Two boys at the primary school had written to him, Baba told us, asking if they might be allowed to clean his bathroom for him daily. But, he said (in English), "I clean my bathroom floor myself, and it is just as clean as a mirror!" So it was that, when he stepped on a piece of soap, his legs parted; he showed with first and second finger how he had, so to say, "done the splits," and his hip was fractured (that was on August 19 at 4:00 A.M.).

All of the following he told us himself, bubbling with pleasure as he illustrated his words (in Telugu—translated by Sri Narasimhan) by the most expressive gestures: There was about twenty feet to cover to his outer door, which he bolts every night after his staff leave him. He pulled himself to the door and opened the lower bolt. But the higher bolt could only be opened if he stood full height. As he forced his legs to raise him to open the bolt, he felt a shock wave of pain through the body, which he ignored, saying, "I am not this body" (he did not once mention the head injury which Sri Narasimhan had told us was serious and had caused tufts of hair to fall out due to damage to the roots).

His attendants saw that something was wrong and were very worried, he told us. They called the doctors, who came in and shed tears at his plight. They wanted him to go to the Prashanthi hospital, but he told us that he had said "no" to that. Then they insisted on an X ray and called in a mobile unit from Bangalore. He agreed to be X-rayed, and this took place at 10:00 A.M., the result showing a so-called hairline fracture of the hip.

He said "no" to urgings to go to Bangalore or to accept any medical treatment, due to the arrival of thousands of very devoted people from Kerala to celebrate the Onam festival. He told us that he had ignored the agony when he had pulled himself to his feet to hold his Onam discourse, which he did because of the intensity of the devotion of the thousands of Keralan pilgrims there, whom he was simply unable to disappoint.

He told us how the spiral staircase from his room has such narrow steps that he had to sit on them and lever himself down, step by step. He was able to ignore his bodily pain each time a shock wave hit it, because he is totally concentrated on the pain of others, never his own. "This is possible for the divine to do, but not for you," he told us all.

An American asked how Swami's "legs" were now. "Perfect. See!" said Swami, wriggling himself in lively demonstration of this. He was beaming all the time he spoke and was more full of energy than I had seen him before, even at interviews. "I'm not worried about myself. It's all you that *I'm* worried about." That got a good laugh.

The first time he turned to me during the interview, he asked, "Where is your son?" I said, "Norway, Swami." He tossed his head a bit and said, "Norway" in a somewhat gruff tone. (I had asked Kai two weeks before we left what I should say if Swami asked, "Where is Kai?" Kai had said that we could count on Swami not asking anything like that! It would be "the last thing he'd say!") He asked the elderly Dane beside me where his sons were, too. They were in Denmark. He asked an Indian gentleman where *his* son was, and the man named one of India's three major cities. "No!" Sai told him. "He is in Srinagar." The man almost jumped with surprise. Baba went on to tell him that his son was associating with bad "friends" and gave a masterly imitation of the friendliest of charming smiles. "False friends who only like him because he has money."

An Italian lady was questioned by Swami about her brother, who was in the Middle East. Baba gave her a small brown *lingam* for him, which he produced in the "normal" hand-waving fashion. He gave the usual instruction about leaving it overnight in water and taking a tablespoonful daily. Baba also manifested a silver medallion embossed with his head, complete with chain, which he gave to a lady from Calcutta.

One teaching he gave was very graphic, with beautiful illustrative hand movements and expressions, in which Swami first said one word in English, then illustrated while he talked Telugu. It went: "Bee," and he told and showed how it sought nectar until it found a flower. Then "rain," and how it fell onto a hill and ran down in every direction until it found the stream. Then "creeper," which

twisted and turned as it strove upward toward the light and the su..,
followed by "stream," which wound here and there, growing as it
went, until it found the river and the ocean. This illustrates how all
things seek God, as does mankind too, because "Nature is the very
best teacher."

Baba talked about how we are all actors on the stage of the
world and that we must play our parts well. He gave many very
blissful looks at the middle-aged lady who had received the *vibhuti*
for distribution and talked to her a good deal now and again. He
turned to me and said, "This lady is a very great devotee and has
been for twenty years. She is a great actress, too, and has also donated a trust fund for the college at Brindavan." Shortly afterward
he announced, "I do not need any gifts from you. Everything is
here!"—he held his right hand up high for all to see. Some moments later, as if to demonstrate this, he turned and waved his hand,
making a diamond ring in a golden lotus setting for the Danish gentleman beside me, amusingly saying that it was "1.1-carat diamond,
48-carat gold!" Though the gold standard Baba was using was fig-
urative, of course, the literal value of such an item is naturally felt by
the recipient to exceed any known worldly measure.

Baba was gruff and strict-sounding later, when he told one
young Western man that he was often depressed and had a bad
mind, not just a monkey mind, but a mad monkey mind. Afterward
he said, "Psychiatrists are tricksters," and explained that, for example, when a married couple who have been having trouble together
come to a psychiatrist, what he does is to get them to bring out all
the negative things, all their worst thoughts and actions, and lay
them open before him and each other. In this way they lose their
self-esteem. "Self-esteem is very important," he concluded. "Are
there any psychiatrists here?" he then asked playfully. No one replied! He talked about the personality being like a house, where the
foundation is self-confidence, the walls are self-satisfaction, and the
roof is self-sacrifice. He also said that we need first, self-confidence,
then self-satisfaction, then self-analysis, leading to self-realization,
and ending in self-punishment. (I take the last to mean *tapas* or self-
denial, which can include such "self-punishment" as voluntarily
compelling oneself to put up when necessary with other peoples'
unpleasant or offensive behavior.) He concluded, "The Selfless Self
is the True Self."

Swami brought a young, newly-married couple to the front,
where they sat at his feet; he asked them where their wedding rings

were. They had left them in the room, the young man said. "What!" said Swami, wagging his finger at them in a sportive warning. Then he created a gold ring for the man's ring finger. Later, in between some discussion, he suddenly circled his right hand again and made another gold wedding ring for the lady, which was put on her first finger.

Swami asked the question, "What is the way to God?" No one answered. Mentally, I sent an answer to him, whereupon he turned round to me immediately and asked it again. I said, "Through *sadhana.*" "What?" he queried, leaning closer as if unable to hear. I had to repeat it and Sri Narasimhan did so too. "Yes," and he went on: "What is *sadhana?*" I said, "Love, Swami." He quickly pursued it further: *"How* does one love?" I said, "By seeing God in everyone." In a flash he asked,*"How* do you see God in everyone?" I said, "You try your best to see. . ." "No!" he cut in with a big smile, "you *must* see God in everyone! You must! Hear no evil, see no evil, speak no evil."

Since our previous visit, the only thing I had thought I would ask of Swami in an interview, if I got the opportunity, was to sing the *bhajan* "Love Is My Form" for us. I had seen the Italian film *Love Is My Form*, in which he sang it in the interview room in a sweet and soft voice that had appealed particularly to me. As if in answer to this six-month-old unexpressed thought, Swami suddenly began singing it . . . but in even softer and sweeter tones than in the film—like a small innocent boy!

A more humorous teaching was about non-attachment, as follows: At first you are a man and you are free. You have only two legs. You get married. Four legs—an *an*imal! Husband and wife, an animal. You get a son. That's six legs—a scorpion! Next comes a daughter, eight legs—a cockroach! He explained how (worldly) life is like a series of compartments, one connected to the other. Once you get inside the first box, you are led on to the next one and you lose your freedom.

He asked someone if he felt well now. "Yes" was the answer. "That is due to divine vibration," he said, indicating by his hand that we were within its sphere. He looked at a tray on a side table and amusingly complained, "No peppermints?" So he took a single clove from a small dish there and popped it into his mouth. Since Baba says he never says or does anything without meaning, I thought someone present might have wanted him to materialize peppermint sweets, as he has often done. On the tray was a yellow rose, which he picked up. He told us that it is not correct to say that God is within us, because then we imply that we are bigger than God, as the hand is bigger than the rose it encloses. "No. We are also in God, like the rose (inside his hand), not only the reverse. Everything is God," he said.

He urged us to experience supreme love, transcendental love, super love, love for its own sake. It is not intellect, not *buddhi*, but love. Without love it is living death. In the *mandir* talk four days previously he had said some striking things about love: "Love is its own reward," "Love is a witness of love," "Love is full in itself," "Love lives for itself," and "There is no selfishness in love." He talked about doctors and knowledge, science, and intellect, and explained that thinking, knowledge, the power of discrimination, and all of that is not the highest. It can give wisdom, but out of wisdom, love comes. He looked benignly at me and said, "You have become *jnani*; then you become *bhakti*." (Baba once said in a discourse that there are not really any *jnanis* today, but it is said as a courtesy term.)[4]

Again I noticed how being in the presence of Sathya Sai was like having an anaesthetized ego, a release of my true self. The mind was simply stopped, and I gazed and listened in wonder and thoughtless happiness. When he talked to me, I could only react without forethought or afterthought, yet my answers later seemed

[4] A *jnani* traditionally meant one who masters spiritual knowledge or *jnana*. *Jnana* means the "universal wisdom" of the discriminative faculty of understanding—the highest, living, self-revealing truth. "There is no full jnana in the world! He is in no need of the world itself; then, why does he need all this? . . . Jnani is a term applied by courtesy; a full jnani does not exist in the world" (*Sandeha Nirvarini* by Sathya Sai Baba, New Delhi: 6th edition 1975, chapter X, p. 73). On the same subject, Baba has said: "This is the crucial test. It is not enough that the intellect nods approval and is able to prove that Godhead is all. The belief must penetrate and prompt every moment of living and every act of the believer. Jnana should not be merely a bundle of thoughts or a packet of neatly-constructed principles. The faith must enliven and enthuse every thought, word, and deed. The self must be soaked in the nectar of Jnana." (*Sathya Sai Vahini,* Prashanthi Nilayam: Sri Sathya Sai Books & Publications Trust, n.d., p. 69).

to have come as if formed by some foresight and reflection, being exactly what I would have wanted to say in any case.

He gave many of those present private interviews of varying length. He called in those from "Denmark." This meant a couple from Greenland who were celebrating their 25th wedding anniversary that day—with their teenage son—as well as Reidun and I. (We five were those present who belonged to the Scandinavian Organization then centered in Denmark.)

In the private interview room, when Baba shook hands with me and was so friendly and natural saying, "Very, very happy," it was hard to realize the tremendous extent of his greatness in the way I have often done when I was far away. Many times I had felt intense joy when reflecting on the wonderful events of his childhood and youth, with their self-fulfilling clarity and the depth of loving bliss his every boyhood word and act expressed. Though he also became awe-inspiringly distant for some moments when he sat before us, and though I later bowed before him to touch my forehead to his feet, the sense of sheer ultimacy of this super-divine Being would not sink in emotionally, as it were.

I had not wanted to ask Baba to be cured of my illness if it were a *karma* that I should nevertheless have to fulfill at some later date or in another life. I had figured that, if it were possible for me to be better able to serve, then Baba would also see to it that my state of health would be sufficiently good actually to do so. I had therefore already pruned and boiled down my list of priority questions to one key request—to ask for an opportunity to do better service.

He then asked, "How are you?" I said, "Very happy, Swami." He clearly knew how I had decided not to ask for health for—after speaking to me some more—he turned next to Reidun and asked, "How is your husband?" She said, "He is not very well; his health is not good!" He replied, "Don't worry about his health. I will look after it." He turned to me and said, "I give you a very long life. Happy life, healthy life!" He later promised the same to Reidun and to our Danish companions.

Baba now asked me the famous question again: "What do you want?" Though unexpected, this time around I was not lost for an answer and I put my key question to this great giver of all possible boons. "I want to serve better, Swami," I said. He looked very pleased and said, "Good. That is the way to God. I will be with you in everything you do!" After paying me a personal compliment, Baba added, "But sometimes he thinks, thinks, thinks, thinks,

thinks." He smiled at me and said, "Don't think." (I'm still thinking how best to achieve this!)

Swami had said he was giving the Danish couple a present in celebration of their anniversary. They came out puzzled, for they did not receive one. But someone else had gotten a large picture of Swami signed by him as a present to them. When they opened it to look, after the interview, *vibhuti* was issuing from it around his hair.

After the private sessions were over he signed pictures, including one for us that he had promised to sign "next time," after the previous interview about 18 months earlier. He blessed some things offered to him, including a computer diskette I remembered at the last moment to offer him. It contained about three hundred pages of writings, including the larger part of the present book. He gave it just one quick look with an almost puzzled expression as if to say, "How do you think I can know what this contains?" Then, with a big amusing smile, he swung his arm rather like a bowler at cricket and slapped his hand firmly down on the diskette, much as he sometimes slaps people on the back. (Later, I could not help wondering whether he might by this even have erased some (or all) of the data. But when I tested it again on returning home, all the contents were intact.) The entire interview had lasted about two hours, ending shortly after morning bhajan singing was heard to begin, a great wave of Oms swelling up from outside the interview room.

Before he had fully recovered from his hip fracture, Sathya Sai went to Brindavan, where he started giving darshan again, though his hip fracture was still not completely healed. He was nonetheless as natural as the day, as unaffected as if he were with an informal group of old friends, rather than in front of a continuous and changing mass of people of almost every description from the four corners of the earth. Everyone waited for him as long as need be, sometimes singing his name for hours under the great Chinese banyan tree. His every movement is naturally followed by everyone until he withdraws from view, for one may witness wonderful happenings at any unexpected moment.

In fact, during the darshans here, he smiled more sweetly, wore more mysteriously blissful expressions, and was less often remote than we had often experienced at Puttaparthi before. Some long-term devotees say that he is outwardly often more joyous and playfully Krishna-like at Brindavan and other places he visits, while at Prashanthi Nilayam he is outwardly more the teacher of selfless renunciation and appears more in the Shiva-like role of a "destroyer" of illusion and ego. This certainly concurs very largely with our experiences.

Throughout this visit there were many other coincidental details and smooth-running events that seem to happen very often to those who visit Baba. The return journey also brought a number of lesser *leelas*. There was the propitious "empty seat" beside us on the flight to Bombay. Next, I went to try to book one of the very scarce resting rooms at Bombay's domestic airport and, due to my condition, asked for Sai Baba's help in this. While speaking to the airport manager, a boy was sitting beside us, and I noticed that he was wearing a large silver ring with the head of Shirdi Baba on it! This sort of "coincidence" made me feel Swami was looking after us. We got the last vacant room, though the manager said we were very lucky indeed that it was vacant just then.

That evening, the flight was postponed until the following morning, so we were housed at the Centaur Hotel in a luxury suite and given meal tickets. This was the occasion of another of those subtle *leelas* that cannot be proven, but nonetheless cannot be forgotten. It turned out that the dinner ticket allowed us to use up to 80 rupees each, while the breakfast ticket was worth 28 rupees each. That adds up to 108 rupees each. Baba has often explained how the number 108 signifies the Divine, the sum of the digits being nine, which is the numerical symbol of Divinity. As the food was so good and the cash so liberal, I'm afraid I gorged myself on panir curry, exotic ice-creams, and so on, causing indigestion on the rest of the journey.

18

ENIGMAS OF SUFFERING
AND HEALING

In the months after I learned of Sai Baba's miraculous appearance
to my mother, I became more and more convinced that he is a divine incarnation of the very highest order. I read again the literature
I had, and I also obtained much more. What had been fascinating
but somewhat incredible previously, began to appear in a quite different light to me. I was sometimes transported with wonder as the
significances of this astonishing saga and the teachings of this sage
of sages began to "sink in." Extremes of joyous feelings were awakened in me by hearing the details of Baba's selfless care for others
and his greatness, goodness and wisdom from his earliest years onward.

I soon came to have full faith that his *vibhuti* could be the vehicle of many a cure of normally incurable conditions, if only he
chose to effect one. This was put beyond doubt for me later, in that
I met so many persons who could attest to this fact, sometimes to
cures so dramatic and clear as to be quite indisputable. Of course,
there was the removal of my own symptoms directly after eating
materialized *vibhuti* during our first visit. Though mine was not a
full or permanent cure—lasting only for the better part of three
months—I already thought it likely that *vibhuti* was not itself necessarily a physical medicine but rather an outward sign that Sai Baba
could be effecting a cure, whether full or partial, permanent or temporary, by some means beyond our powers of direct perception.

From what some Sai Baba followers say, they seem to think that
anyone who is still ill after some visits to Baba must lack sufficient
belief in the *vibhuti* and in Baba's divinity, for it cures *all* illnesses.

However, it is not recorded in any reliable book or authentic source that Sai Baba has ever uttered that sweeping generalization. One can safely say that this is an ill-informed exaggeration that can itself cause unnecessary and unhelpful confusion and guilt in those who receive no cure.[1]

To call *vibhuti* a universal medical panacea is to mislead and even cause unnecessary disappointment and doubts to those who really do believe in this, but are still not cured by it. Many have complete faith in the curative potential of what Baba produces, without presuming to know whether they will be cured. It may be a necessary condition for some persons also to have total confidence in God and that they *will* be healed, whether or not they regard themselves as being fully worthy of this. None can be sure what is sufficient to remove the particular *karma*. While Baba has insisted that increasing faith and confidence in God gives the possibility of increasing energy and health, he has also made clear that he often "only" mitigates the effect of an illness by reducing the suffering it causes. Baba has also compared his grace to a drug that removes the pain, but not the illness (i.e., the *karma*, which must run its course).

It can be a spiritual solace to suffering persons, despite all, to make it known that even persons physically very close to Baba through decades have sometimes suffered very considerably. To mention just two examples, such was the case with Mr. Kutumba Rao, who was head of Baba's ashram for over twenty years and suffered in pain from spreading cancer in the years before his death in a Madras hospital in 1988. Even one of the nearest and dearest, Prof. N. Kasturi, had weeks of intense physical suffering before he died. Devotees with chronic and other serious illnesses mostly report, however, that Baba has given them the strength in one way or another to withstand their ailments, such as by having found lasting peace of mind, as in my own case.

---

[1] Incidentally, *vibhuti* which manifested on a photo of Sathya Sai Baba at a temple in Srirangapatnam, was taken by a German TV team (who made the film *Der Mysterium der Shiva?*) to a scientist, Dr. Jurgen Evers of the University of Munich, in 1987. He carried out an advanced form of atomic analysis on it. The complex graph it produced on a spectrometer screen was seen to be exactly the same as that of a sample of pure quartz crystal powder. The doctor stated that such crystal is found in the human body only in the most minute quantities.

Sathya Sai has made it clear on many occasions that some serious illnesses have to be suffered. It is attested by many, including many leading Indian and other specialists, that he has cured almost every type of illness, whether through his holy *vibhuti*, his nectarine *amrit*, or through a number of other apparent medicines, amulets, or *lingams* he produces. His cures have not always depended at all upon the faith of the individual, either, for he is known to have effected quite a number of cures on "non-believers," such as on my mother. The evidence also shows without reasonable room for doubt that cures of the same sort of illnesses have frequently been effected by Sai Baba's will without the aid of *vibhuti* or any other known physical medium. His comments about his healings tend to support the view that it is above all a matter of divine will *(sankalpa)*, whatever the "outward means" by which he demonstrates this will for the particular individual.

This can be due to *karma*, which Baba has said that he deems best usually *not* to remove. All scriptures hold that the means of assessing the status of a person's "karmic account" or what is in a person's heart is not known to anyone but God. To remove an illness today can mean that its equivalent must be suffered later sometime, even in a later lifetime; I am reliably told that Baba indicated this in an interview, to someone to whom he even gave that very choice. Not to remove illness can be best, because it is itself actually an aid to that person's spiritual development, a blessing in disguise! For example, some devotees say they would probably never have actually visited Baba had they not needed his help in bearing an illness. Further, if one fully believes that Baba is all he has said he is, it can take some courage to travel there to meet him face to face, not least because it faces us without ourselves to an uncommon degree! Illness may help some take the leap. Through increasing richness of the inner life, we can also learn better to disregard the inevitable ills of the body.

> You might say that the karma of previous births has to be consumed in this life, and that no amount of Grace can save you from that. Evidently, someone has taught you to believe so. But I assure you, you need not suffer from karma like that. When a severe pain torments you, the doctor gives you a morphine injection, and you do not feel the pain, though it is there in the body. Grace is like the morphine; the pain is not felt though you

go through it. Or the Lord can save a man completely from consequences, as was done by me for the bhakta whose paralytic
stroke and heart attacks I took over in that Guru Purnima week.[2]

According to Phyllis Krystal's understanding of his role in dealing
with her own sufferings, Baba perhaps even accelerates an illness, so
that sufferings that are supposedly unavoidable sooner or later are
made shorter. If this is the case, one can see how much better it
would be to undergo whatever is necessary, while having the aid of
freedom from anxiety and the confidence to withstand pain that he
can confer.

My long-term illness began in 1981 and can serve to illustrate
some of the questions about suffering and healing in relation to
Sathya Sai. Compared to some illnesses, mine is not so serious as to
cause very great suffering. Yet it incapacitated me for a normal
working life at the so-called height of life and is often painful
enough.

During these years of physical ailments I have gone through a
number of positive mental, social, and spiritual changes. Suffering
has made me more acutely aware of all the blessings of life, which,
even if I did not take them for granted before, I nevertheless tended to forget. Chronic illness necessitated alterations in my lifestyle,
which was always moderate but became less hurried and much more
peaceful. I examined more intently to what extent I really was practicing the true values in life and getting the greater benefits they
bring. Some words of Baba illumine this:

> Agony is more potent than awe in leading you Godwards. Grieve
> for lost chances, lost time; move on, every day, forward to the
> goal.[3]

---

[2] Sathya Sai Baba. For an account of the stroke and heart attack incident,
see N. Kasturi, *Sathyam, Sivam, Sundaram: The Life of Sathya Sai Baba*,
Vol. II (Prashanthi Nilayam: Sri Sathya Sai Books & Publications Trust,
1973), chapter 5.

[3] Sathya Sai Baba, Discourse Prashanthi Nilayam, Feb. 3, 1963, *Sathya
Sai Speaks*, vol. IV (Prashanthi Nilayam: Sri Sathya Sai Books & Publications Trust, n.d.), p. 14. New Indian edition ISBN 81-7208-151-0: vol.
3, p. 15.

What illness has taught me about others is also important, in that I now have a more open-minded and sympathetic understanding of what other chronic sufferers, whose lives are changed by debility, must undergo both socially and inwardly. Such experience gives a good personal basis for consoling other sufferers on their own terms. Being ill also brings out different qualities in friends and acquaintances.

For the record, I add that I have been taking a pinch of Sai Baba's holy ash almost daily for years and have occasionally taken the water in which Baba's materialized *lingams* have been immersed. Whatever effect these may have had has not been possible to judge with any accuracy, partly because my condition has varied a good deal both in the short and long term. Baba has given various grounds to believe that *vibhuti* sometimes acts as a protection against illness, too, which fact cannot be investigated by any normal observations, unless one knows which illnesses one otherwise would have suffered from.

Sai Baba was quoted by Dr. S. Sandweiss in *The Holy Man and the Psychiatrist* as follows:

> Do you think I would confront you with pain were there not a reason for it? Open your heart to pain as you do now for pleasure, for it is my will, wrought by me for your good. Welcome it as a challenge. Do not turn away from it; turn within and derive the strength to bear it and benefit by it. It is all my plan— to drive you by the pangs of unfulfilled need, to listen to my voice, which when heard, dissolves the ego . . . and the mind with it.[4]

As Baba teaches, illness can be necessary for personal development. While cutting off some possibilities, debility may instead actualize other and positive alternatives that would not otherwise have been tried. For example, I would most likely not have fulfilled certain lifelong desires for artistic discovery and self-expression without becoming ill. The sense of duty to stay at work, combined with my need to keep on making a living in the industrious and restless society of Norway while still healthy, had kept me teaching at the university. Obligations incurred in life had always, until my illness, held me back from indulging fully in personal creativity. Yet the chronic

---

[4] Dr. S. Sandweiss, Sai Baba: *The Holy Man . . . and the Psychiatrist* (San Diego: Birth Day Publishing, 1975), p. 202.

condition that confined me day in and day out to our bungalow, also gave me an opportunity to pursue my interest in writing and recording music at home, to the extent that my condition allowed. The fact was that there was little else with which I could occupy myself. Sai Baba later gave his blessings to the results of both these home pursuits. My musical activity I have since directed more toward devotional songs and *bhajans* (viz. from *"Bom! Bom! Bom!"* over to *"Om, Om, Om"*).

The actual occasion of making the journey to Sai Baba was my worsening spinal problems, which were like "the straw that broke the camel's back," so to speak. My untreatable and undiagnosable illness had caused natural anxieties, which were removed through the advent of Sai Baba in my life. Instead of the prospects and plans that my debility closed off for me, came a greater boon even than my previous excellent physical health!

Later Baba conveyed a whole range of various ideas, hints, balms, reassurances, convictions, and suggestions to me by means of *leelas* and in dreams, as follows:

Early on I had a most special dream in which Sai Baba somehow "redrew" the shape of my spine in light, using a finger of his right hand, which he did in all twenty-one times. In another he took my head and neck on his lap, where I rested it fully as he stroked away the pressures. Later on in another dream, he laid his hands on a crucial point in the middle of my spine. Such dreams often gave brief improvements, but always a lasting sense of joy.

> *Dream of August 18, 1985*: I was in our living room with Reidun and my son Kai. Baba came in and spoke to them, whereupon they withdrew into another room. He came over, bent forward to where I sat, and put his mouth to mine. He breathed into my lungs long, slowly and very deeply, then drew the breath out of me again. I was able to perceive a sort of brownish, gaseous fluid being drawn up from the very root of the spine (the *muladhara chakra*). This poisonous substance was fully drained off, and Sai Baba looked at me as he swallowed it, appearing momentarily just like the imposing Shiva with a blue throat and the characteristic pile of hair.

Comment: I awoke, immediately, very early in the morning. The experience in the dream left a very strong impression on me. The meaning of the "kiss of life" in life-saving is symbolic, so the dream suggests that my life was saved. In the Bible, God gives actual life by breathing into the body fashioned of clay, and the origin of the Vedas, the first holy teachings, was the breath of Brahma. The Vedas call the individual life-principle Atma, which is divine consciousness. Some philologists relate this to words in the Indo-European language group relating to breath, as in the German *Atem* for air or damp air, the Greek *Atmos,* and the English derivative, *atmosphere.*

What ailment it was that this "dream operation" can have cured me of is uncertain, but I had been awakening at night in a feverish sweat and a truly awful sensation that some sort of poison was gradually rising up my spine. It was so real to me, even though the sensation went away when I awoke, that I felt that it could even mean death if it rose much further up the spinal column. The last time it occurred, just days before the dream, I had called out for help from Sai Baba and had also taken several spoons full of *amrit* (which we had saved from my visit to the temple where it issued from a locket).

Though I have no further evidence that this was a real life-saving operation, I am much inclined to think it was. On the other hand, it did not then result in any appreciable improvement in my back and neck problems. Yet I have not experienced the feverish and painful awakening from "rising poison" again.

A lady who was staying with some mutual friends happened "coincidentally" to tell Reidun of a dream in which Sai Baba also drew the breath out of her with his mouth. She was surprised at herself and said she wondered what had prompted her to tell her dream, for it was so private, and none but her husband knew of it! Of course, we then exchanged our accounts. She claimed that it had almost cured her of long-standing vertebral problems incurred from her early years when she had crashed step-by-step down a flight of stairs on her spine.

Directly after my crisis in August, Reidun dreamed that she was at a *bhajan* where Baba gave her darshan and she asked him to cure me. He agreed and sent off a disc (of the sort Vishnu rotates on a finger, called a *chakra*)[5] toward me, where I was on the men's side

---

[5] Vishnu's *chakra,* known as Sudarsana, was supposedly itself endowed with the character of Vishnu. It was connected with life and death, usually being used as a weapon, as related in the *Srimad Bhagavatam.* On the other hand, devotees at Prashanthi Nilayam have at least once seen a chakra-like shape moving toward Sai Baba, which he has explained as being "the soul" of a devotee.

of the compound. Reidun asked if I would know what it was. Sai
Baba said that yes, I would know, definitely.

> *Dream of June 11, 1986*: In a shady room somewhere, Sai Baba
> appeared quickly, and touching my forehead at the "third eye,"
> he immediately set about "operating" on my neck with his bare
> hands. He plunged them in at the throat and removed some-
> thing. Turning me over, he did some similar thing on the back
> of my neck. It was all over in about 10 seconds. I "saw" it as if
> from outside myself, and I felt no pain. He went off to wash his
> hands in a small washroom like the one in our home, but the
> shelves were full of medicaments. I followed, standing at the
> door while he washed his hands like a doctor does. Holding my
> hands in the *namaskar* greeting, I asked, "Did it have anything
> to do with my lungs, Swami?" He shook his head without turn-
> ing. "It was something the body (or the blood) could not rid
> itself of," he said. He added that I could be "quite ill for a cou-
> ple of days."

Comment: The previous evening I had prayed to Baba for some
healing because the pain and physical tensions had become so intense.

Also, I should add here that through the years I have been both
to "normal" doctors and specialists and to a wide range of therapies
and treatments including six chiropractors, three acupuncturists,
two homeopaths, three naturopath/osteopaths, and a number of
"healers" of various persuasions. Nothing succeeded in improving
my chief condition more than very temporarily, and I thereby discovered much about serious deficiencies in the medical profession
and health system. The same went for all the other treatments, too,
which were all disappointing in terms of actual results. The only
help I could rely on to ease a crisis was, and still is, the deep-mus-
cle massages of the back and neck that my wife is able to do.

Due to the biases of modern medicine it is very difficult for
people with certain spinal-structural ailments to be accepted as genuine sufferers. In my case, I know that it is a peculiar combination
of several long-standing spinal prolapses and subsequent displace-
ments caused by a number of falls, compounded by a slight short-
ness of one leg, a problem in the bone structure in one foot, and not
least, a type of "spinal bifida" deformation. The condition worsens

whenever I walk any distance or stand for long. This ailment tenses and inflames muscles and sinews, which try to compensate for the unevenness. These symptoms are very like those of fibrositis.

I was subjected to professional mistrust and sent to a neurologist who, when I got there, proved also to be a psychiatrist! This was months after Baba warned us all at an interview that "psychiatrists are tricksters," which had confirmed my own previous ideas about the pseudoscience and strengthened my resolve in dealing with it. I was sent from pillar to post and back again before my application for disability benefits was finally granted after five years of uncertainty. The mainly-mechanical explanation seems to be thought an impossibility by most doctors, who all had surprisingly few and narrow ideas about spinal-skeletal-muscular conditions. Doctors nowadays tend to write off most of what they cannot diagnose easily or treat with drugs, and turn amateur psychologist instead, putting all they do not understand down to "some psychological origin."[6] Eventually my own diagnosis was supported by Baba.

This support came mainly in connection with our third interview with Baba and the book *Sai Baba: The Ultimate Experience*, by Phyllis Krystal. I found there the direct answers to several questions I had written down prior to that interview, but that I had not had the opportunity to ask. One of these was: "Is there any remaining psychic element in the cause of my illness?" Phyllis Krystal writes:

---

[6] This sorry state of affairs has to do with the deepest assumptions upon which modern Western psychology and psychiatry are based and with some unfortunate social functions they frequently fulfill as a consequence. Neither psychiatry nor psychology fulfill the conditions of strict scientific knowledge, and the nature of the case is such that they will never meaningfully do so, however much those who represent them lay claim to their being reliable sciences. Compared to the practical-theoretical understanding of human reality, society, and health at all levels of the soul provided in Vedanta, as Sai Baba also teaches so strikingly, Western theories must still unfortunately be classified as relatively "amateur psychology." Those who are interested in these questions are referred to my forthcoming book, *The Human Whole: An Outline of the Higher Personal Psychology*, a study of the psyche and its transformation that attempts to bridge scientific theory, psycho-therapeutics, and the philosophical psychology of Vedantic thought.

> Towards the end of the following morning we were called in to
> an interview. We again discussed my continuing ill-health. He
> assured me that the headaches were not the result of anything I
> was thinking or doing wrong, but were due to a weakness. He
> further stated that they were mechanical-physical and not psy-
> chological. This assurance was a great relief to me. As if reading
> my thoughts he added, "Don't let anyone tell you that."[7]

My brand new copy of the book actually fell open at that page from
the start, so the above passage was the first one I read. In brief, I at
once "knew" inwardly that the answer was also for me: my condition was not psychically caused, and I must on no account let anyone convince me otherwise. The reference to headaches, which I
had begun to have increasingly at that time, and the use of the
words "mechanical-physical," which I have often used to try to explain my condition to specialists, removed any possible doubt that
Sai Baba wanted me to perceive this as his answer to my question.
That the text I found was the answer and not merely my imagination is beyond doubt for me, because of the detail and precision of
the parts of the text that apply.

Thus, Sai Baba communicates with exactitude, precision and
timing across time, proving how he knew the idiosyncracies of my
mind. Every gesture, every word he addresses to anyone, it seems,
has a meaning that will be clear sooner or later, even a meaning
within the meaning. This helps one penetrate matters, both through
deep self-analysis and contemplation of relevant facts.

> *Dream, November 1986*: I walked along beside Baba, him clad in
> orange, across a thinly-grassed, sandy open space. He led me to
> some sort of table where I lay down. He touched my forehead
> on the third eye. The next I knew was that he had operated on
> me somehow while I was "unconscious" of it. He put some sort
> of plaster/gauze around each of my thighs and around my waist.

Comment: This dream was perplexing, and I began even to doubt
whether it had any real meaning. Not until the following June,
months after our three-month visit to Prashanthi Nilayam and Brin-

---

[7] Phyllis Krystal, *Sai Baba: The Ultimate Experience* (York Beach, ME:
Samuel Weiser, 1994), p. 134.

davan, did I fathom its meaning. It proves to me that while I was in Norway, Sathya Sai somehow actually carried out an operation on my lower spine, which had quite tangible results. The facts are as follows:

While visiting England in June, I went for investigation to the College of Naturopathy in London to one of its founding teachers, Mr. Kylie, who is an osteopath and master of various other disciplines. He impressed me as a true expert, because during his examination of me, he diagnosed my condition more fully than anyone else, and this took him not more than ten minutes in all.

Almost at once he claimed that neither of the two sets of my X rays from different years were mine, because in them the lower spine was in a much more serious condition than I proved to have when he examined it physically. It showed an excessive curvature and a lower vertebra that was badly and permanently displaced. He was even surprised that I was able to walk about with it! Without any comment whatsoever from me he remarked, "I would have staked my professional reputation that these X rays are not yours!" However, my name was photographed into each one. He asked what on earth I had been doing—how the great improvement in my spine had been achieved. I told him I had hardly been able to walk much of the time, let alone exercise. He shook his head and said, most perplexed, that anyway there was simply no method or exercises he knew whereby I could have made the condition so much better. He made a thorough examination of my spine and hip, including a great deal of expert manipulation of the joints and long perusal of the X rays. He seemed quite confused about it for a while, but then he passed on to other questions and made no further comment on the inexplicable.

It was not until afterward that I remembered the dream of the operation "under anesthesia" and the bandages on thighs and midriff on either side of the crisis point in my lower spine! Before the "rat in the drum" episode I had even been unable to walk about the house for long without having to lie down. Yet within the month I had gone to India, sitting in airplanes and walking for hours in a day without more than a few tensions! Though I had felt sure that Baba was helping me, I had not realized how radical a change this had required to my anatomy!

Baba's statements: "This body is yours, not mine," and, "When your body suffers, I feel it," are mysterious, not least because he has said many times—and most convincingly demonstrated—that he is *also* beyond all suffering and is permanently established in eternal bliss. However, I have had several proofs from Baba that he can somehow "feel" my pains wherever I may be. Summarily, these were as follows:

On an occasion in the Prashanthi temple, sitting cross-legged amid a large crowd during *bhajans* and feeling severe shoulder and neck problems, I sent a mental prayer to Baba, who was seated about twenty yards off before me. Directly his eyes looked straight toward me and he put his hand on his own shoulder, exactly where my aches were worst. I felt no improvement but knew that Baba felt it, and this helped me to persevere.

By 1987 I experienced another degree of worsening of neck tensions that had moved to the left side, where the muscles and ligaments had become as hard as iron in a straight line from behind my ear down to my left shoulder. I had sent in a short article to the editor of *Sanathana Sarathi* (titled "Science and Spirituality"). This appeared in the March 1987 edition. To my amazement and "by chance," I noticed that my name was printed on the inside cover so that, when closed, it fell against the photograph of Sai Baba's head on the opposite page, to cover *exactly* the same line along which the new tension was most painful! (This fact can be checked by examining the issue in question.) The caption of the picture was, "Why fear when I am here"! The same phenomenon has occurred with two other of my contributions since then, indicating to me Swami's awareness of the shifting pains in my head and neck. It is always very reassuring, as if he is saying, "I know. It's all going according to plan."

In other incidents too many and subtle to recount here, both during darshan at his ashrams and in dreams and *leelas*, his presence has reassured me and sometimes has actually given me sudden physical relief when things were bad. The relief obtained has in fact often occurred in connection with Sai organization activities. Once, for example, I was returning by plane from a meeting of the European Sathya Sai Organizations in Ghent, Belgium (to which I had gone only because of a dramatic dream in which Baba very angrily made it clear that I must). The strain of all the activities and travel had stiffened virtually every neck muscle, so I was in considerable discomfort and pain. At one point our friend Bente, with whom I was traveling, began to feel such powerful heat in her hands that she confusedly and urgently asked permission to release it by touching my neck. The heat I felt was considerable too, and the cure was immediate, lasting long enough to enable me to reach home without assistance, whereupon the normal symptoms gradually returned.

That sort of healing has not happened before or since, either to her or to me, though various people have tried to help me in that way. For me, this incident supports the conviction that it is God who relieves and heals and who decides the due time, place, and circumstances, whether from within or without. My experience has shown me repeatedly that a person whom God may use as an instrument for a healing now and again, does not actually heal, and therefore cannot honestly lay claim to being a "healer," as it is becoming an ordinary custom for so many to call themselves these days. History shows that even fully-realized saints do not themselves lay claim to such abilities or titles.

During the private interview, when Baba promised Reidun to look after my health, he also tapped me on the head once while I was taking *padnamaskar*. A day later I was laid out with intense tensions and pains in the spine and head, plus a strong dose of "Delhi belly" for good measure. The spinal pains were worse than any before, and they laid me up for about a week.

I lay in the room we occupied at Prashanthi Nilayam, listening to the steady downpour of South India's heaviest monsoon in decades. One night I rolled back and forth in much pain, drowsing in and out of sleep. I became aware of Sai Baba's presence, in his orange robe, superimposed on my body and taking away the pain in my spine as I rolled to and fro. From then on I recovered from the worst of it. I also experienced a (for me) very strange emptiness of mind, in which there was absolutely nothing I wanted to think about or do. Every decision that faced me, however trivial, seemed irrelevant. There is no proof, of course, that either this condition or the period of increased illness were "caused" by the tap on the head, but it may have been. Perhaps Baba speeded my illness-*karma* for a while, as well as helped me in the dream to bear it physically. Without going into further details, I am of the opinion that through my illness I am working off *karma* from a previous lifetime. I am concerned that it should not be healed only temporarily (i.e., postponed) by whatever means, but that I should be able to suffer it through now, while I have the spiritual support of the living avatar himself.

At the time of writing this I can add that, as long as I keep within my tested physical limits, my condition seems to have stabilized, apart from fairly predictable ups and downs. I have no fears or worries to mention, for these left me virtually for good in 1986. The problems, as I explained it to a bewildered ex-colleague, are fortunately "only physical."

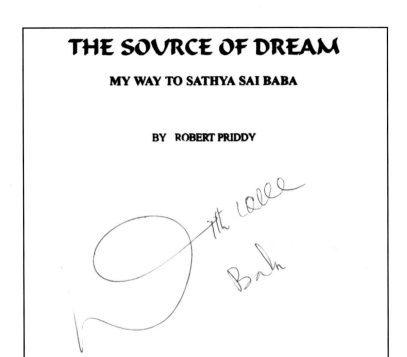

THE SOURCE OF DREAM

MY WAY TO SATHYA SAI BABA

BY ROBERT PRIDDY

Title page of the first edtion of this book, signed by Sai Baba.

An interview in Brindavan where Sai Baba signed books, including the first edition of the present one.

Two angles on the green diamond stone set in a gold lotus ring, showing different facets. Materialized by Sai Baba on December 23, 1986. See pages 130-133.

The form of Sathya Sai Baba, masked in, for aid in recognition.

The (unmasked) book cover, in which the above form is seen (see the description on page 212).

My finger pointing at the small green wax *lingam* that was formed on the candlestick's drip tray. Note the silhouette of Baba's head and shoulders in the ring's stone (hold the picture sideways).

19

LIVING AND LEARNING AT THE ASHRAM

Staying at Baba's ashrams is to live close to the great on-going event, being able to see and wonder at Baba, always graceful and unruffled by the thousands who daily watch him going tirelessly about his activities.

Of the many with whom I have become acquainted who have visited Prashanthi Nilayam more than once, practically all admit to considerable mental and emotional swings during their visits when "lessons" arise, usually at intervals, calling for self-assessment and change. Yet the hills and dales still seem markedly more negotiable than those of life at home under usual conditions, where the energy and inspiration is not so high. The shifting atmosphere and conditions in the ashrams are subtly conducive to exposing the rougher edges of the ego.

What Baba has called his "repair workshop" can seemingly involve almost any type of personalized physical, mental, or emotional overhaul. We have met at least a dozen people who have had accidents, bouts of sickness, and even serious illness during their visits to Puttaparthi, yet who have often claimed that they learned something invaluable by its occurring there that they would not have, otherwise. Baba often makes it clear in one of his many ways that the person's problem is known to him. This itself can give faith or self-confidence.

Baba behaves in such a way that I am not in the slightest doubt that he is aware of the process I'm in and is waiting for me to go through with it! At the other end of the tunnel, so to say, he will notice me and maybe smile lovingly to me again. The trials of ashram life, one realizes eventually, are challenges holding personal, tailor-made opportunities for improvement and stabilization of one's emotional and mental condition. The perfect tailor cuts his cloth very finely, too. I do not think he ever takes a wrong measurement, nor ever fails to provide the fitting garment for the right occasion. But the cutting can be painful and can go on for some time until realization dawns. How it is possible I do not know, but many can confirm that if one refuses to learn while at the ashram, the pressure simply grows.

Whatever "gets to me" about other people will eventually be provocated forth by situations at the ashram and not leave me alone until, somehow or other, I face and resolve it—or at least have a fair try at it. Under the guiding presence of Baba, however, I have also found that what comes up in me is part of an intensified cleansing process that eventually brings some benefit, such as more equal-mindedness. In discovering my own quirks, failings, and egoistic insensitivities, it becomes easier to be detached from the seesaw of an undisciplined mind, as Baba teaches we must do in our own and everyone's best interests.

Considering how most people at Baba's ashrams regard him, it is no wonder that there are very strong desires and motives for wishing to see him, to get as close as possible, and to have his attention. Not surprising either is the wish to feel that Baba shows his grace to oneself personally. To be seen as someone whom Baba (at least apparently) ignores is itself a test. Similarly, hearing all about the grace that someone else has received can be an inspiration to others, but it can also awaken feelings of self-pity and jealousy. These are also tests to grow on. Those who have some inner experience of Baba will know, however, that public signs of Baba's attention are not all, and that often "appearances are deceptive." The number of interviews a person receives may be a reward for goodness or may also be an indicator of how dire a person's need is, or even of the amount of loving inspiration required by those who can only accept correction from him in person. Baba has occasionally said that good *karma* from past lives, unbeknown to us, is what brings us to him and is why he helps us to improve or remove the remaining bad *karma* that we are here to work off this time.

Also, what is seen and heard to go on around Baba is not easily understood. Just when I think perhaps that I have figured out an event or someone's behavior, there will be a surprise and a turn-around, which will show me how incorrect or incomplete my under-standing was.

Others' behavior in Baba's vicinity can pose riddles and rouse both strong positive and negative feelings. For example, one may see that undisciplined, selfishly pushy, and talkative persons some-times receive Baba's repeated blessings during darshan or are called to interviews. This can be hard indeed to understand or accept emo-tionally, especially when one has been visiting and hoping for an interview oneself, perhaps after years of waiting. However, we do not know the depth of a person's need or possible suffering, nor do we realize what Baba's purposes are. He is here to teach, inspire, and transform both the good person and the not-so-good, even the evil-minded. I have also observed the same persons whose bad be-havior Baba has overlooked—or even seemed to reward—trying for his attention again for weeks on end without any success whatever. I have also sometimes seen the same persons back again years later, behaving in a civilized and disciplined way!

Some think that it is completely wrong to notice any failings at all in others, because one of Baba's most oft-repeated and categor-ical teachings is to see, hear, and think only good of others. I often found this hard to interpret in daily life, for it seemed to imply be-ing naively ignorant of most of what goes on around us in the world. Could it mean, say, that one must accept a theft as not be-ing a theft but something else, something good? Furthermore, if I see only good, how then can I avoid bad company, for I first must have seen the badness of it. I have learned something about solving this dilemma, I feel, from staying at Prashanthi Nilayam.

It seems to me that I may always observe and judge for myself the words and actions of others, and that this should not actually be to judge others *as people*, but only their behavior. We notice the lie or the theft, but do not see the person as "a liar" or "a thief," with-out recognizing that this is also a person who has the potential for the transformation that is always in each of us. If someone lies or steals, it is of course still often one's common-sense duty to give warning or take other precautions. The same is even more obvious where major crimes like rape and murder are concerned. Yet even then, we must still see God in every human being.

To be honest, we cannot actually avoid using our own judg-ments of others' behavior in life and acting accordingly too. Yet I must always look beyond temporary acts and facts into a wider perspective to try to discern or imagine what positive purpose or cause could be involved, despite appearances. I also find that, simply by watching others, I can, upon inner reflection, avoid certain mistakes myself and also discover mistakes in myself. Nor does this preclude me from learning about positive qualities that I lack or from learning new ways of behaving from my evaluations of others' behavior.

When some rush to get anywhere near Baba in the hope of a word, a blessing, or to touch his feet, whether or not he grants them permission, I must then nonetheless exercise patience and have sympathy with these poor misguided fellows of mine. When taking up positions for the daily darshans, one can occasionally see even elderly gentlemen rushing uncontrollably to bag a front place. This is an extraordinary sight, which can be either aggravating or moving, depending on my mood (and sometimes perhaps on where I am in the line!). It makes me think of Baba once having said, "Swarm like bees but don't leap about like frogs!" What can make them so keen? It's clear that they are certain it is the *real* honey that can be had from this flower of perfection. Once I saw Baba walking along a row of devoted and intensely eager Indian gentlemen. Waving an arm to include them, he announced (in Telugu), "They're all mad!" They all laughed together.

Personal experience leaves no doubt that many of those one meets at the ashrams or who work there in one or another way are true followers of the teachings of the avatar. The norm practiced is that of civility, helpfulness, and care. People seem more peaceful and happy in an unobtrusive way than at any other place I know where many people congregate.

Nevertheless, one of the most common tests visitors have to undergo is the indiscipline of other persons. While ten thousand individuals remain silent and comport themselves with dignity and consideration, there will usually be a few who do not. It is quite hard to concentrate only on the goodness of the ten thousand when someone who chatters, pushes, or elbows you constantly is sitting right next to you!

While at the ashram, tests of self-control in how to ignore the bad (i.e., "to see and hear no evil") and thus overlook others' failings, often fell to my lot. During one visit, I kept finding myself sitting behind a person who insisted on standing up in front of me just as Sai Baba was approaching, despite repeated instructions from the staff to remain seated. He would force his way forward, treading on

people and acting so selfishly that I wondered how such a p
ever came to be at Prashanthi Nilayam at all. Baba ignored this person and eventually glared at him outright. I'm afraid I also added
my own look of disdain afterward. An hour later, however, Baba
gave him the most loving smile, spoke to him, signed his picture for
him, and let him touch the lotus feet. Years later I happened to see
him again, this time sitting in line in a very orderly fashion with a
group that was later called in to an interview.

Again, at *bhajans* I would find myself beside someone who be-
haved as if he were Caruso and who bawls out with a foghorn voice
not quite in tune, or someone who claps with ear-splitting intensity—usually almost anywhere but on the beat, ruining it for everyone. Once, when both these phenomena occurred beside me and
went on ceaselessly, evidently disturbing practically everyone within earshot, I at length felt it a sort of civic duty to request the person concerned, not unkindly, to sing and clap less loudly. He
reproved me straight away with, "Swami says always speak sweetly
and softly!" A public-spirited little demon in me was quick to make
me reply, "Sing sweetly and softly, too!" That only cramped his
clapping style for a short while, though.

One way Sathya Sai lets us know that we must correct our behavior is simply by ignoring us day after day. I know from experience that he sometimes does this very pointedly, standing right in
front of a person and looking at others all around for up to half-a-
minute, yet without his eyes ever alighting upon that person even
for a second. On other occasions, one only has to think: "Can't you
just give me one look, Swami," and his eyes may flash toward one
without a split-second of delay.

The lesson can, however, be enjoyable and laughable, too. One
day, while a large group of overseas devotees was cleaning out the
long-unused foreigners' canteen building at Prashanthi Nilayam, I
became involved in a ridiculous charade of petty attachment. I was
detailed to scrub and wash some food counters, and the organizer
went to provide me with a plastic bucket, a cloth, and soap for the
purpose. Therefore I assumed there was an ashram store of buckets
and so forth provided to all the helpers.

Washing with one bucket only was most ineffective: I needed
one for soapy water and one for rinsing. At last I saw another bucket
that was not in use, so my work began to speed up beautifully. An
Italian devotee, however, came and insisted the bucket was his, so

he took it back—only to leave it standing unused some way off again. I took it back again, and shortly he reappeared and insisted on having it again. I searched about and found several buckets not in use, so I requisitioned another one. Much the same happened, a different Italian appeared and said it was his bucket. I protested that I had found it, and it was required for my task. He insisted on having it. Never thinking that it was not a communal bucket, I simply refused to give it up—my work was slowing and it was all most irritating. By then the man was almost begging for his bucket in sonorous tones and with much Italian waving of arms. It was a mystery to me. And when I turned my back again, I found the bucket had gone! I kept my eye on another one that I saw was not being used and eventually procured that. In a few minutes that one was simply taken from me by yet another gentleman!

Eventually I had to finish the job with the one bucket, which I left vacant when I went out. Outside I heard my wife saying we had lost "our bucket"! "Do you mean to say that you brought *our* bucket when there are so many here already?" I asked her. I soon learned that everyone had brought their "private" buckets; there were no public ones! That explained people's desperation! I had to laugh. Then it dawned on me that *our* bucket was in there somewhere, and we might lose it and have to buy a new one. My whole attitude altered, and I searched around everywhere until I discovered what I was almost sure was our bucket, standing forlornly, full of water. I grabbed it and left. No sooner was I outside than an Italian lady came rushing after me—it was *her* bucket, not ours! It was, too. I had made an unfortunate mistake in my zeal to recover *our* bucket—my wife had found ours already and was standing with it waiting for me!

All this brought home to me how extraordinarily attached we can become, even to a plastic bucket that we have bought very cheaply for only temporary use on our visit. "Me" and "mine" are indeed very powerful identifications. I felt a peculiar conviction that this little comic bucket ballet had been especially choreographed by an unseen hand.

Another incident shows Baba's omniscience at work in instruction for transformation. I would point out here that I go to Prashanthi not least in the hope of receiving such lessons whenever necessary, for I have firm faith that the benefits therefrom are much more than can ordinarily ensue.

My son Kai was on his first visit to Prashanthi and was waiting to hear when a return booking was available. We came to learn of it only hours before he would have to take the taxi to Bangalore, some 140 miles away, to catch the plane. Reidun decided to stay so there would be no problem about leaving the room unattended.

However, at the last minute she decided to accompany us both. I was relieved, as my health was poor and the marathon taxi journey would make me really need a neck massage. We locked the room we had been so fortunate as to be able to occupy over the whole Christmas period and, seeing we had no time to vacate the room—which the accommodation office might well have required of us—we decided just to inform our neighbor that we'd be back by the following afternoon, in the unlikely event of the owners arriving at this stage to claim it.

Having seen Kai safely off, we arrived back the next day just after noon. The neighbor told us that friends of the owners *had* arrived and we were to vacate the room, but that they had not told anyone that we had been away since the previous afternoon. Straight away we felt there was more to this than chance. We went to the accommodation office and were met by one of the staff who had in fact greeted us when we were leaving the previous afternoon. I forgot this, and instead of apologizing and explaining our motive, I tried to cover up our overnight absence. Embarrassingly, I eventually had to admit that we had left almost certain that we would stay away until the next day.

At the next darshan, Baba gave me a very quick and definitely serious look of displeasure. It was some days before I was in his good books again enough for him to smile my way, which he did the very same moment I mentally apologized and thanked him for the lesson when he was passing me at darshan. As everyone close to him says, he is a stickler for truth in all things, and down to the very last detail. This rubbed in the medicine I needed and made me even more determined to try never to diverge one iota from the truth!

It may be an emotional pain that gets dissolved in the "workshop" or again it may be that one has to be made really to see oneself from the perspective of someone else. The problem could be a so-called "external irritation," such as some door-banging, night-chattering neighbor. If one puts up with it and mentally asks Baba what to do, the chances are that the next minute you'll get to know something that will explain to you a reason for it of which you had never even thought. Or it could instead turn out that your beloved neighbor suddenly has to leave because the permanent occupier of the room has returned and you are left in peace at last. If you get angry instead, it may very well turn out that you have to leave your room for the same reason. The chances are, when your desperation peaks and you just give up the ego struggle, another room will fall vacant soon that is preferable to the first one. Such turnabouts as this occur at all levels frequently to practically everyone I know who has stayed there long enough to give it a try.

I have also often found that the externals of a problem situation remain the same after its solution; it is just that they appear differently because some mental blockage is removed in myself—for example, that I have managed at last to give up mustering whatever stubbornness I could. Part of this process is due to the adjustments and changes necessitated by the proving ground that the ashrams provide.

What matter if dogs fight over the refuse bins to destroy the night silence, if blaring music or angry speakers from distorting loudspeakers from the adjacent village shatter one's meditations, if 5,000 vociferous crows argue it out outside your shutters before dawn? During darshan the opposite extreme can be experienced: ten thousand people sit, often in perfect unbroken silence for an hour, awaiting their Lord. Sometimes, however, such as on festival days, the extra large crowd, swelled with villagers from many miles around, will be buzzing in a lively mood. Baba will approach and—making some of his characteristic movements, like weighing the air with one or both hands—he seems to refine and raise the atmosphere. All will be stilled within seconds while a peacefulness seldom, if ever, met elsewhere arises. Above all, Prashanthi Nilayam is a world spiritual center, a city of light, the true "Jerusalem"—at least it is when Baba is in residence.

Selfless service is given for the benefit of visitors by the ashram staff, who work ceaselessly and almost always show great tolerance and cheeriness, even when faced with the stresses and strains that dealing with thousands daily can involve. This also goes for the members of the Sathya Sai Seva Organization at Prashanti Nilayam, which is impressive.

For example, each fortnight a different Indian State was, in 1992, sending 1,000 Seva Dal members to guard and help at the ashram—500 men, and 500 women. They paid their own journey and expenses, and many of them spent their holidays from work for the visit and lived cramped together in halls. Many of these volunteers were civil servants and professionals; others were ordinary workmen, and some were casteless. They worked sixteen hours on and eight off—often standing at the same spot or doing the same task—guarding the halls, apartment blocks, gates, and like tasks for a week or more at a time. Most of them did not even get to darshan or to see Baba until the last day, when they were relieved by the next batch of 1,000. Then they sat for hours in formation until Baba came out and, going through the lines close up to each of them, allowed touching of his feet (*padnamaskar*) and gave each one some packets of *vibhuti*, some sweet or fruit he has blessed (*prasad*). Sometimes the group would receive some useful article, such as a sari for each of the ladies.

At the special darshans for all such Seva Dal volunteer workers, Baba invariably looks at each of them, smiles, and he may say a word or two. At this, they all seem to be immensely grateful and happy, many shedding tears of joy. They work together tirelessly under the leadership of ashram staff, without any sitting at darshan waiting for interviews. The demands taken on by these voluntary service workers at Baba's ashrams are impressive indeed—what a brilliant example they set up for these selfish times! What a lesson in devotion and application for most of us over-pampered Westerners!

While some people are always near to Baba physically, it does not necessarily indicate prominence of spiritual status. There are, of course, many devoted and blessed residents in the ashram who have been with Sathya Sai for decades, even from his childhood, and who can regularly bask in his grace. Yet divinity itself evidently doesn't *just* "rub off" merely through being there or gaining regular physical proximity, because Baba has occasionally said that to have been a constant resident of his ashram for so-so many years is in itself no qualification for spiritual grace. He has also said that some live in his ashram while making no real effort to do his will—or even to do anything useful—and yet hope for progress toward divinity.

Baba has occasionally said that the good attracts both the good and the bad. Since the avatar has come to transform erring humanity, one cannot expect to find only good persons going to the ashram. Among the hundreds of thousands who visit, I know about criminals, thieves and even murderers, who are known to have visited Prashanthi Nilayam. Quite likely, some are moved to go there despite themselves and receive help that they may need most direly. This reminds of Jesus' allowing even great sinners to approach him and be changed.

Though all love to be near Swami, even his physical body is nonetheless ultimately only an appearance, because Baba is ever reminding us that, being Universal Spirit (*Paramatma*), the avatar is not really bound by any physical conditions whatever. Day and night he is contacting an inestimable number of people all around the world. Baba assures everyone that practice alone counts in getting and continuing to receive his grace, and that includes selflessly serving others, and non-attachment (or the curtailment of selfishness).

Sathya Sai speaks publicly with enthusiasm about many devoted people around the world who travel thousands of miles just for a sip of nectar. He has also said that they can be just as close, even without coming to see him in person. We all know, too, how sometimes "distance makes the heart grow fonder." Baba has also warned those who know of and accept him not to feel superior for the reason that we have come to learn about and gain the faith to accept the avataric advent, for there are many devout people who find their own ways to God, in whatever form they may conceive of him.

Amid the outpouring of his love, he also upbraided the vast gathering of somewhere over half-a-million people at his 60th birthday celebrations for thinking and speaking of themselves as the "Sai family," because it is a form of exclusivity. He has often told that he has come for the benefit of the whole world and everyone in it, and that God cannot be limited. So there is no "cornering of the market" on divinity. Others who worship and follow God in other forms or as the Formless, are equally liable to benefit directly from his grace, whether or not they can make any sense of avatarhood or accept that Sai Baba is himself the fullest possible incarnation of the Godhead.

There are still at least hundreds of people alive who in the past half-century have had the privilege of being able to live in close proximity to Sai Baba, as was possible during the earlier years. I met a gentleman who had been living at Prashanthi Nilayam who once used to have three-hour interviews like family gatherings with Baba. He told me that those days are past for him, as they are for many who knew Baba in his younger days, though this gentleman still sees Swami daily in the mandir. Nor can anyone come and go in anything like the old informal way, though I don't think anyone was ever really "informal" in any off-handed sense with Baba. His presence is simply so exceptional that even the closest servitor stands awaiting his will, quite simply in loving awe of his personality. Though he has reportedly always had this air about him that inspires respect and reverence, there were times when his days were less full of duties and he appeared to have time to spare for all manner of informalities. Yet even now, he never gives the slightest feeling of being in haste; he appears to have "all the time in the world."

People who have lived at the ashram for a decade and sometimes much longer can hardly get more than a brief exchange with Baba every few months. Meanwhile, more and yet more groups of foreigners arrive to whom Baba gives much of the time he daily sets aside for interviews. Of the thousands of his students, hundreds are also always present at darshan, waiting for the opportunity of personal attention, which Baba daily showers if not always on all, then on some of them at least. He has said that he divides his time respectively 3 to 1 between his students and all other followers.

If I have made ashram life seem somewhat less than always idyllic here, let me reaffirm the nature of the overall experience: within the ashram there is an inner sense of being removed from all the unrest, strife, and problems of the world at large. There is a great sense of spiritual security at being within the charmed circle at the unruffled "eye of the storm" that rages in many ways elsewhere across the world. This remains so, even though mundane security precautions have been introduced after a serious gang attack at Prashanti Nilayam in 1993 and due to the widespread terrorism that has been troubling India.

At Prashanti Nilayam, one's thoughts are insulated from the concerns of the news or all those items of which I heard Prof. Kasturi once say were "the sweepings of the world pushed through one's letter box every morning" (and he added with a smile: "over which I throw myself avidly"). Days at the ashram remind me of accounts of soldiers during World War I who would suddenly be posted away from the daily terror and despair of the trenches, to which they had become so dully accustomed. Not thirty miles behind the lines, the peace of pristine nature ruled, and there life again invigorated the spirit with peace and a great confidence of hope, which one had long since put aside. Similarly, one's awareness can alter when one enters the domain of Prashanthi Nilayam which means literally, "The Abode of Supreme Peace."

The place name has led many newcomers to imagine mistakenly that nothing that happens there is, or can be, otherwise than good. Yet it seems clear enough that the Supreme Peace to which the name refers is none other than the being of Sathya Sai Baba, his own very reality and essence . . . and not the physical or social institute of the ashram itself. Nevertheless, there amid the good company of Baba's devotees, where many seekers of truth try to learn and to practice the essential values in every action, there is a great difference from the demands, attractions, and useless diversions that meet us in the modern world as soon as we have to leave again to face them and carry on with our allotted duties, until such time as we shall one day finish the game.

SAI "PREMA" IS SUPREME

Sathya Sai is himself the center of the great event. From all corners of the earth, people travel to its center—which is geographically not so odd a statement as at first it might seem. Situated almost centrally in India's triangular southern Deccan plateau, the region in which Puttaparthi lies has virtually always been near the center of the earth's land masses, according to the geological theory of continental drift from the earliest single landmass of Pangea, the Deccan plateau having apparently not moved far from its original location at the center of Pangea, while all the other continents have spread out from it.

Like a central magnet, Sathya Sai exerts the supreme attraction of Universal Love (*Prema*). The name "Krishna" comes from the Sanskrit root "to attract," and in this, Baba certainly lives up to his forerunner, of whose life he can tell and explain every detail to a level that confounds even Indian savants. People from outside India who have been drawn to him must already number somewhere in the tens of thousands, while Indians who have visited him number in the millions. Baba's unlimited variety of "divine sport" are also an expression of his love and a bait to attract. His paranormal influences have evidently resolved the doubts of thousands. They inspire people to actions guided by the confidence that arises from faith and can also pose mind-breaking enigmas to keep the persons concerned "spiritually on their toes."

Those from abroad who are fortunate enough to have been drawn into Sai Baba's sphere in one way or another, and to observe sufficient of him and his works for some length of time, will know

*Prema = Universal Love

how amazingly varied and widespread the evidence in support of his omniscience is. Every visit to the ashrams brings one into contact with people who most convincingly tell what otherwise would be incredible legends or myths. Even a visit to practically any Sai center or group around the world produces the same results—namely, more and more testimony of events involving Sai Baba, of a nature and on a scale that simply surpasses the scope of any feasible plan of systematic observation, checking, and collection.

As there can hardly be such a thing as a "Spiritual Who's Who," only at best a spiritual "Who am I?," one cannot rank or meaningfully list the qualifications of all those who have witnessed and accepted the great miracle that Sai Baba himself is. The list of famous visitors covers all fields of endeavor, though the great majority are "ordinary" people who also have come, seen, and "been conquered." This shows how Baba is an authentic and unparalleled master, operating on and behind the scenes of the contemporary world, and that he does indeed bring with him everything that he has announced he does.

Sathya Sai has made it clear long since that worldwide TV coverage of his work would not change hearts, which is the only level from which real, lasting improvements can arise. Media sensations come and go, seldom leaving any motivating impression. In the light of this we can understand something of why Sai Baba never seeks publicity and rather shuns it and delimits it by the subtlest of methods, which I have now and again seen or heard of. Had the amazing ways of this avatar become "common knowledge" to watchers of TV and readers of the papers from the start, the laws of supply and demand might have made access to him in general far easier for the economically and politically privileged and most difficult for the needy and the devoted. In fact, Baba appears somehow to be able to control his own public image in ways that are quite remarkable.

For example, I must admit that the appearance of Sai Baba in printed pictures and photographs did not originally attract me at all. On the contrary, they tended if anything to make me both skeptical and perhaps even somewhat fearful of this figure. They were still somehow memorable. Some even report feeling repelled by photographs of Sai Baba, including people who are attracted in other ways. However, actually seeing him is something *entirely* different. By comparison one would have to say he must be unphotogenic—except for the equally inexplicable fact that hundreds of photos of him are available that are exquisite!

For some unknown reason, these lovely photos, which sometimes *nearly* do his physical appearance justice, have not, in my experience, previously achieved as wide a circulation as others that are neutral or even make him look powerfully unapproachable and almost scowling. One sees beautiful pictures on the shrines of devotees and in people's private albums. What the camera cannot capture is what I can only call personality, the emanation of caring love that envelops those around him.

In his presence my mind is stilled as I absorb the moments in peace and clarity of consciousness. The fascinating effect of his personality, so natural even during his "supernatural" miracles, makes one become somehow more open and integrated while in his vicinity; self-assertive ideas disappear or appear for just what they are.

All admit that no one can exert pressure on him in terms of whom he will see, what he will do, or when he will do it. He has often said that only he knows the time and place at which each of us can obtain the greatest benefit from knowledge of him and eventual arrival in his presence. He is ever surprising all who are around him in many ways, not least those on whom he bestows gifts and attention.

According to what he has said, any difficulties in contacting him are entirely due to shortcomings in the seeker, and yet he has given the guarantee of his attention in one or another form to anyone who makes the genuine effort to follow some of his precepts and approaches him with a pure heart, whatever other failings one may have. We cannot know with any certainty who has and has not attained to real "spiritual seniority" in his eyes. However, it is surely unlikely that he would have accorded special privileges and showered his grace in public on certain people, as he has done, without their having the requisite spiritual qualifications at some point in their lives (either this and/or previous lives). Certainly, no one close to him claims to have a superior right to Sai Baba's attention or to the inner boons he can bestow.

However, anyone who wishes seriously to follow up whatever clues Sathya Sai Baba has given, by way of letting his presence be known to them, will eventually and surely be able to confirm that we are dealing here with an entirely unprecedented opportunity. And it is not too late to investigate, for Baba will still live among us in the present body until he is 95 years old. According to his own declaration of his "Task," which he first made over four decades ago to his elder brother in a famous letter that is still preserved, he assures that he will "never give up those who attach themselves to me." I refer the reader to other extensive literature for the documentation of these facts and accounts, and of so many other historically-unprecedented public miracles, that even a mere list of the best-testified of them would occupy several chapters![1]

As Sathya Sai's followers everywhere will comment, the most impressive aspect of his life work is really the spiritual revolution that is taking place as an inner transformation of millions. The activities of the hundreds of thousands of devotees in the various Sai Centers must constitute virtually the lowest profile mass movement operating globally. Baba insists that we should spread his message, first and foremost, by ourselves being examples of its fruitfulness, i.e., through practicing his teachings. Evangelizing of any sort on behalf of a new religion or Sai Baba sect has been strictly forbidden by him.

According to many accounts, some people have discovered him and become close "overnight" without any apparent mental effort or other specific preparation of which they can give any account. Others have been "fetched" by him more gradually. Yet few persons does one meet at his ashrams who have nothing unusual to relate concerning what brought them there. Many occurrences in the lives of seekers who arrive there are so uncommon that it is often a relief for them to be able to meet others who do not look on them oddly or show signs of skeptical disinterest when they talk of what is filling their hearts and minds.

It is a disappointment to some that Sathya Sai Baba does not demonstrate his powers for science "under laboratory conditions." Various scientists who have not even met him have criticized him for not submitting to laboratory investigation. Some want to test his powers, others ostensibly want to give humanity the benefits that could arise if science were to find out that—and just how—he materializes things.

Some have suggested that such powers as immediate healing of terminal illnesses and materialization of medicines, foodstuffs, and so forth could, if understood and employed by science, help eliminate most of the world's need and suffering. Experience, however,

---

[1] See N. Kasturi, *Sathyam, Sivam, Sundaram*, vols. 1–4 (Prashanthi Nilayam: Sri Sathya Sai Baba Books & Publications Trust, 1960–1980); S. Balu, *Living Divinity* (London: Sawbridge, 1981); E. Haraldsson, *Miracles are my Visiting Cards* (London: Century, 1986; Revised edition, New Delhi: Macmillan, 1996).

indicates that such knowledge would soon be monopolized by special interests and would probably end up only making the rich richer and the dispossessed poorer. History proves that scientific knowledge, alas, has *so far* never proven itself to hold any guarantees of just or even distribution of its fruits. Many scientific establishments and multinational conglomerates would doubtless like to possess the secrets of divine power (and, after all, who wouldn't?), and it is no exaggeration that they would not be above stealing God's very thunder if it could be done—and preferably without having to make any spiritual efforts at self-improvement.

In his posthumous works, Dr. Paul Brunton suggests that Sai Baba would do more good to bring humanity out of the danger of total war by demonstrating his healing miracles "under world inspection" than by preaching.[2] That opinion is clearly untenable. Not only has the danger of total war evidently passed since Brunton wrote down his doubts in his then-private notebook, but even though many prominent surgeons, doctors, and scientists already have testified in writing and on film to the indubitability of hundreds of Baba's miracle cures, the world has not really discovered much about this yet. If we suppose that Baba were to hold publically-advertised demonstrations of physical-healing miracles, allowing full documentation and press coverage under controlled laboratory conditions, and so forth, one can hardly imagine the community of Western medical authorities actually crediting this, when they are collectively so skeptical toward anything that challenges their supposed medical wisdom or professional interests. Yet were this nevertheless to come about, and were the media to present the facts with a high degree of objectivity (not so likely!), how would there then be any room left near him for spiritual seekers? Baba has given the guarantee that he will always be close to his persevering followers, and he can be seen to have kept this promise despite the steadily rising tide of new seekers coming to him.

Baba has explained in various discourses why he does not use his Divine Will on every occasion or, for that matter, cure all sufferers and remove all world problems overnight. If God were to do so, there would be no real personal growth or spiritual development, which can thrive mostly only where there are challenges. Removing all the symptoms of humankind's "illness" would be futile if the

---

[2] Paul Brunton, *The Notebooks of Paul Brunton*, vol. 7 (Burdette, NY: Larson, 1987), p. 42.

causes were not removed, and the causes are all human, he says, resulting according to the universal karmic law of action and inevitable reaction, whether from our actions in the present or previous lifetimes. Furthermore, Baba has said that the creator has to conform to the rules laid down by him for creation:

> In the great drama of cosmic life, the Cosmic Director, God, is also an actor. The Cosmic play is governed by certain rules and regulations. Because He is the Almighty, God cannot behave in an arbitrary manner. His actions have to be in accordance with His role in the cosmic play. There are certain rules as to how one should act according to the time, place and circumstances. He cannot behave according to His whims just because he is all-powerful.[3]

Is it not divinely ironic that divine power is a great "open secret" that is already at work in laboratories and everywhere else throughout creation too? How it is so widely thought to be "only natural" as a result of accidental causes is another great irony of the times.

Now that we can learn of and observe the avataric mission, it takes little further imagination to understand why Baba's acts of grace are necessarily largely so difficult to reconstrue or record exactly. Not only are the ways of God mysterious, but the real relationship of man to God always remains a heart-to-heart and intensely personal, "private" affair. If every act of his grace were made a public event (numerically impossible in any case on mere practical grounds), there would be no need for the purposeful educative struggle to develop faith by oneself. Baba is always insisting that we develop a minimum of faith in divinity, or at least an open mind and heart toward it, if we are to experience the boons this alone can confer.

Many people who have known me well for years and to whom I have therefore told some of my experiences with Baba, behave as if it were all a fairy tale. Rarely has doing so led to their wanting to investigate for themselves, let alone actually go to India, even years after I have first lent them a book or showed them a film. It is easy to understand how hard it is to credit all the facts that seem—and in one sense are—virtually "out of this world." Many followers of

---

[3] Sathya Sai Baba, Discourse Prashanthi Nilayam, July 21, 1993, in *Sanathana Sarathi* journal, Aug. 1993, p. 199.

Baba feel this frustration, at least until they learn that it is just not within our power to bring followers to the avatar.

Not so surprisingly, perhaps, Reidun and I have found that as we become more involved in trying to do Baba's will, and always giving priority to work in the Organization, various friends have drifted away and make no further contact. I admit, I could sometimes use more self-control in hiding the crazes of enthusiasm that his life, message, *leelas*, and grace often inspire in me. Our awkward position of trying to explain this inexplicable divine incarnation and the convoluted and incredible proofs of it that he often provides us with, is itself a divine comedy, a joke both at our expense and yet to our advantage. But I am genuinely sorry for those who cannot yet taste the honey of truly seeing, believing, and knowing!

A small story can illustrate: When Sai Baba was a youth and was many miles away from a certain lady devotee, he sent her a promised tiny photograph of himself attached to the legs of a bumble bee. Imagine the difficulty of the lady in explaining this event to others. Imagine, too, the quality and intensity of her joyous awe! Thus, I have to be judicious as to whom I talk to about the rat-in-the-drum *leela*, for example. Several people I know who have visited Sai Baba are even anxious about sharing anything at all when asked about their visit, so difficult is it for people in the West, particularly highly-educated or professional people, to credit even the simplest *leela*!

Some societies in northern Europe are now so fundamentally materialistic in thought and belief, so uninformed even about paranormal facts that have been well-known in other cultures and throughout history, that most of their members have been educated into cynicism and cultural bigotry. I leaned somewhat in that direction myself when I was a much younger and less experienced fool than I may appear to be now. While studying philosophy and science, my views tended at times toward the academic norm and the intellectual's peculiar brand of misplaced and commonplace common sense, which I now recognize as most unhealthy in the long run, because it conceals from oneself the very purpose of life, or even that there is one! On two occasions already related, when people who had been in India and experienced some of the wonders of Sai Baba came to tell me about it, my supposed breadth of scholarly achievement and comprehensive reading, etc. etc., kept me from following up on the matter. Now that I am at the other end of the stick, I can sympathize with those who continue for whatever reason to forego the opportunity and thus lose many precious years of access to the marvel and the love of Baba.

The scale of necessary mental adjustments to all the Sai Baba phenomena and to what his advent implies is evidently very considerable for many people. The more educated and scientifically-minded are at a special disadvantage in this case, as Baba himself has often said. In order to appreciate how difficult it can be for "intellectuals" to even approach, let alone embrace, the advent of the avatar, I have only to consider how many years it took me mentally and emotionally to acclimate myself sufficiently to the unusual culture of India where this is occurring. This whole idea of Divinity actually being incarnate today affects one's view of oneself, one's behavior, and the whole range of beliefs about the purpose and meaning of life and the cosmos altogether.

The effect that Sai Baba's unqualified and pure love has on the open-minded seeker is known best to themselves and to Baba. I can speak only for myself in confirming the miracle of personal transformation that Baba stimulates and supports in us. To that end, among the chief gains from Baba's advent in my life is genuine and lasting peace of mind, through being increasingly able to let go of many "things"—from futile thoughts and moods to fruitless wants and ambitions—and discovering a richness of life that would otherwise be clouded by the products of egoism. A subsequent benefit has been an inner strength, with which I can now more successfully ward off undue demands, from whatever quarter of existence they arise, and with which I can better disperse various problems that arise around me.

Baba has established in me what I feel to be an unshakeable faith in the omnipresence of the Divine, including its reflection in other people—and myself. Furthermore, a sense of security in the cosmos and confidence before the world and all its ills has increased, and indeed passed a threshold some years ago, so that I am now convinced that I will not lose it. And, not least, I have gained growing insight into the challenges presented by my altered physical and social circumstances, for the consequent redirection of my activities and mind have, in fact, much improved the quality of my life. In all, I now flow with life more easily, find pressures have relaxed from within, and have also been able to know the self-fulfillment of realizing certain of my dearest dreams. All this grace, through Baba's love, is beyond repayment, I feel, by any other form of thanks than following up his call as best I can.

THE UNIVERSAL WORLD TEACHER

For the first time in recorded world history, the entire globe has become virtually one intercommunicating and interacting unit. The crucial steps in this development were doubtless the globalization of world trade and its many consequences, culminating so far in an age of widespread mobility through public air travel, and of instant communications via space satellite. This material unification of world society, so to speak, forms a background for the appearance of a true *world* teaching, crossing all boundaries of culture and religion and becoming available to persons in every corner of the globe through various media. This must, indeed, be the "machine age" predicted in ancient times and recorded in the Bhagavata Purana and in other extremely old Indian texts, such as the age-old palm-leaf manuscripts (*naadi*) by Brighu, Kumar, and Shuka. The same texts predict in unmistakable detail the coming of Sathya Sai Baba as the avatar of God in this Age of Kali. That he is known to millions, says Baba, is unique for any avatar within his own lifetime.

The spiritual teaching required in this age of unparalleled splintering and pulverization of cultures, faiths, and beliefs must be one that unifies the essential truth and goodness found at the core of every religion. It must recognize and embrace the necessary fact of human and cultural variety, despite the divergences and conflicts that have arisen. Only such a teaching can be a truly universal world teaching that may heal the wounds of history.

The very highest requirements one can set for a teacher at this universal level are to be an impeccable example, to have unlimited knowledge of all cultures, and to demonstrate perfect, inclusive love of all beings. That the teacher always is himself observed to act in perfect accord with his teaching, that he can convincingly answer questions that arise in any area of human endeavor, and that he demonstrates unfailing insight into any problem, individual or collective—these are qualifications that ought to suffice for the title of "Universal World Teacher"!

Sathya Sai Baba's "students" include a great range of all ages who absorb his every word and who study and practice in their own countries. Many of the people I have met, who have come to Baba in their 40s or later, have been through wide-ranging searches for the highest truth and are convinced that they have at last found the ultimate person from whom to learn it. The sheer range of people and their backgrounds must surely make the gatherings, wherever Sai Baba goes, unique among world movements. There seems, at least at the outset, to be not one recognizable sociological or psychological factor common to Sai Baba followers. It may seem an indiscriminate collection of individuals to some, and indeed it is, in that in principle no color, class, creed, age group, or status is either discriminated against or privileged more than others.

To judge by the written and transcribed testimonies of an impressive range of firsthand observers, Sai Baba's call is heard by people from all walks of life, of every shade of wealth and poverty, and of any degree of learning. A catalogue of most respected leading figures in Indian life and government, science, and the arts, and many of the greatest spiritual leaders throughout India have met Sai Baba since he began his mission as a 14-year-old in 1940. All have testified to the literally overwhelming impression of his great personality, his remarkable powers, and his universal love.

Sathya Sai Baba's practical teachings inform us how to be, what values and goals to aim for, and how to achieve them, including what sort of situations and activities to avoid and how to relate to all types of problems and difficulties. All this he relates within a program of five "human values," which are the universal values that form the quintessence of the worldview that Baba holds forth. They are espoused as ideals in one form or another in every known human society, even though they may only be partially agreed upon or practiced only to a limited extent. These five—truth, right action, peace (of mind), active non-violence, and love—are so fundamental that they neither can be, nor need to be, justified by reference to any other values. All other values, whether moral standards or intellectual criteria, can be seen to be subvalues that derive their validity from these five basic human values. The five major values are unsurpassably universal because, taken together, they express and circumscribe the meaning of Goodness. The eternal idea of the Good cannot be explained without reference to the five values and subsequently to the host of subvalues that they embrace.

From his public discourses and talks to varying groups of people, it is always possible to discern Baba's central message to all, whatever their age, race, or religion. Yet each discourse is also designed for a specific public. The discourses recorded in the collected volumes of the *Sathya Sai Speaks* series and in *Sanathana Sarathi* have very largely been for Indian audiences, and as such they often exemplify themes and expound in terms well-known in the Indian culture. From this, and from the avatar's continued insistence on the primacy of the Vedas' message for civilization, one may regard him as a Hindu. This is a truth with modifications, for he teaches to an unsurpassed degree the unity of religions and insists on the inclusion of all that is good or laudable, true or beautiful in human life anywhere and everywhere. Essentially, Hinduism has always held and practiced just this universalism. Thus, Sai Baba makes the Vedic teaching clear and accessible as one of great pragmatic, social, and spiritual depth, having relevance to modern life everywhere.

The reasons for this concentration on reviving the best in ancient Indian culture and spirituality can be discerned by cross-referencing many of his comments over the years. Firstly, it is in India that Baba's mission started and it is there that he (at least, his physical body) has remained, except for one brief visit through East Africa to Uganda. He has asserted that the full avatars never incarnate anywhere but in India, for which he gives many reasons, explanations, and examples. Secondly, it is in India that morals must be regenerated first, to regain in practice the traditional universal spiritual values that were founded there as part of the earliest religion known to humankind. Only then will the mutually-skeptical sects of all religions and cultures again be able to find the truly non-exclusive approach.

It is easy to guess the reaction of some "fundamentalist" sects— or the fanatically self-righteous—to these facts and statements, which seem to put the Indian Vedantist religion above all others. However, Sathya Sai makes clear that the essence of truth and goodness is in every religion. The reason for the advent of the avatar is precisely that this truth has been clouded over everywhere and certainly in India, too, causing the huge global spiritual decline that has produced the unprecedented excesses, madnesses, and ills of the 20th century.

The overall aim of Baba's mission is the re-vitalization of humanity's understanding of the unchanging true nature and purpose of human life, and of existence altogether. These truths were first realized and propagated to humankind by *rishis*, a handful of unsurpassed sages who lived in the mists of time on the Indian continent. They discovered the ultimate truth through meditation and sacrifice, and they gave this divine knowledge the verbal formulation known as the Vedas.

According to the accolades of today's Vedic scholars and Brahmin pundits, Sathya Sai Baba's teachings are most pure and give the easiest access to those scriptures, which Baba often refers to and has done constantly since age 14.

This illustrates Baba's repeated assertion that his mission is above all a reinstatement of the *dharma* of the holy Vedas, which means all forms of right living and good action. This is a regeneration of ancient peaceful traditions, not only as the basis on which to raise India's present civilization to its very ancient great glories, but also through this to re-establish genuine religiosity throughout the world. These assertions and the actions with which Baba backs them accord with the original promise of God Vishnu to incarnate in a new form on earth "whenever evil threatens to vanquish good" and to "save *dharma* from decline."

Sathya Sai Baba has in recent years frequently confirmed that he is the avatar of this age, an embodiment of all of the forms of God "rolled into one," who has come according to his age-old declaration to turn around the world crisis and save humanity from self-destruction through the reinstitution of virtue *(dharma)*.

The regeneration of faith, hope, and charity is taking place on the backdrop of a whole era of history and at the very turning point of the ages, itself involving the three nearly consecutive Sai Baba incarnations that together will probably span around 250 years. There was an eight-year period between the passing over of Shirdi Sai Baba at the age of about 83 in 1918[1] and the 1926 birth of

---

[1] According to the reported discourse of Sathya Sai, given at Prashanthi Nilayam on Sept. 28, 1990, Shirdi Baba was born September 27, 1835. In a subsequent printed discourse, however, the date appeared as September 27, 1838.

Sathya Narayana Raju (later Sathya Sai Baba). Dozens of writers have reported that, after his passing on at age 95, Sathya Sai Baba has stated that he will return as Prema Sai Baba. Most of them assert or assume that there will be an eight-year period between the Sathya Sai and Prema Sai avatars. There is confusion about all these assertions. On various occasions Baba has allegedly said that his life would last 96 years. (Note that the way of reckoning or stating a person's age in India differs from the Western norm. In India a person who is 95, yet is in the 96th year, is said to be 96 years old.) In two early discourses in 1960 and 1961 respectively, however, he himself gave the length of his remaining life as 58 and 59 years. In both cases, this adds up to a life-span of only 93 years. Professor Kasturi announced in a lecture in January 1985 that Baba had recently pointed out Prema Sai's future birthplace as they passed by it in a car together. That was Chandrapatna in Karnataka State near Mysore. Further, some writers also assert that the future birthplace is called Gunapalli or Gunaparthy in the Mandya district of Karnataka, also near the town of Mysore on the banks of the Cauvery River.[2] Though Baba has told that Prema Sai will not be publicly known until his teens, despite his having given the time and place of the birth, many persons alive today will be able to witness the return of Sai Baba in the form of Prema Sai. Baba has already materialized several objects bearing images of a bearded Prema Sai Baba, most notably a ring with a gradually-changing image of Prema Sai for Dr. John Hislop of the U.S.A.

Some may ask what difference the presence (or "omnipresence") of Baba makes to the "man on the street"? Any answer must take into account that the advent of Sai Baba is not, according to himself, an event taking place only at the observable, worldly level. It is a process of assisting the change in heart of individual men and women who call on or need the help of Divinity itself. The spread from person to person of the immeasurable ideas and transformative impulses originating in the love and light of the Sathya Sai Baba avatar cannot therefore systematically be traced or measured by anyone. Neither empirical observation nor penetrative reason will be able to provide incontrovertible proofs about the extent and nature of the avatar's task and actual achievements. Yet, to the "trained observer"

---

[2] Baba's words are quoted in S. Balu, *Living Divinity* (London: Sawbridge, 1981), p. 29. The original source is not stated.

who specializes in the subject or practice that Baba playfully dubs "Saience," unmistakable influences can already and increasingly be observed across the globe. Not least, it is seen in the faith of at least tens of millions that Sathya Sai Baba will become recognized as a figure of unsurpassed stature in world spiritual history. The process initiated and watched over by the avatar, we are told, is turning the world's people gradually back toward God. So the "man on the street" may therefore eventually be brought off the streets and into the temple; if not an actual one, an inner spiritual one.

Others ask why we cannot yet clearly observe the beneficial influence of the avatar on the corrupt world of India's public life. When questioned whether a new age of peace and love is really possible, considering the huge problems current in India and also in most other countries of the world, Baba told the elderly editor, Sri V. K. Narasimhan, that his work proceeds slowly because it has to lay a sound foundation for centuries ahead. That foundation is his thousands of students whose high spiritual ideals and public achievements are beginning to make them the natural and much-sought-after educators and leaders of their country.

At the time of writing there are *relatively* few people who have been in the physical presence of Sathya Sai Baba. I say this because an estimated ten million individuals or so who have had the opportunity to visit one of his ashrams or be present at a discourse and darshan still represents only about one-fifth of one percent of the earth's population (officially estimated as having surpassed 5,500 million as of 1994). It seems most likely that the number of fortunates will increase considerably before A.D. 2020.

Baba has asserted that without his will, no one can come to him, while no one knows how the flow of visitors is regulated. He told Dr. Hislop that the Indian authorities were aware of him and his miracles, and that they were playing it down in the interests of avoiding an avalanche of visitors. With Baba's famous visitors of recent years, such as a half-dozen heads of State, however, it seems more and more likely that such an avalanche will occur. The construction in 1990 of an airport capable of landing jumbo jets just four kilometers from Puttaparti, and the opening beside it in 1992 of the world's most advanced Super-Speciality Hospital, presumably herald a much greater influx yet to come.

The prediction Baba made in his youth to a few hundred followers (who could not credit it at all then) was that the crowds seeking him would be so vast that he would one day be but a speck of orange in the distance to them. The celebration of his 60th birthday at Prashanthi Nilayam saw crowds of several hundreds of thousands while equally huge crowds attended both the 65th and the 70th birthdays. Back in November 1970 Baba said:

> I have been declaring for six or seven years that the day when millions will gather to benefit from the Avatar is fast coming; I am advising you to garner and treasure all the Grace and all the Bliss you can, while you may . . .[3]

A great deal has already been said and written about why God takes on human form and the value derived from being in the physical presence of the avatar. In the case of visiting Baba, a "charging of one's spiritual batteries" definitely occurs, as he also asserts, in that one's inspiration and confidence in the value of spiritual living and activity is always renewed.

The many features and details of this universal teacher and Divine Being's life and work, with his Biblical "sword of truth" and his "blood-red robe," concur with the avatar predicted in several ancient Indian texts, such as the *Mahabharata*, in which the Lord prophesies that he will be born into a family in South India in the age of Kali to inaugurate a new era of truth (*Sathya*), and the *Vishnu Purana*, which predicts the Vishnu will incarnate and reside in a village worshipping the cowherd form of Krishna. Various other sources can be interpreted as referring to Sai Baba's advent, among the most impressive being that recorded as Mohammed's discourses in a work titled *The Ocean of Light* where, in volume 13, a long list of unmistakable characteristics of Sai Baba are found as prophesied by Mohammed to distinguish the coming Great Teacher.

Unlike gurus who often tell disciples what to do or not do in a traditional way, Baba teaches and tests individuals by more subtle and indirect means. The ways he plays with us in what he sometimes refers to as "the game of life," shows that he can call our bluff at any moment and raise the stakes so that staying in the game demands improved equanimity. This sort of interaction can happen wherev-

---

[3] Sathya Sai Baba, Discourse Prashanthi Nilayam, April 18, 1972, *Sathya Sai Speaks*, vol. VIII (Prashanthi Nilayam: Sri Sathya Sai Books & Publications Trust, n.d.), chapter 18, p. 114. New Indian edition ISBN 81-7208-159-6: vol. 11, p. 27.

er we are in the world and over any period of time. After a lesson, he gracefully allows dedicated players to win some of the "jackpot" of bliss. This is surely also why his followers hang on every word they can hear him utter. But even . . .

> A glance from the corner of the eye is enough to get things go-
> ing towards a successful conclusion.[4]

Baba does indeed give glances from the corner of his eye, sometimes so memorable and full of unspoken meaning that they keep coming to mind ever afterward. Hard though it is to understand, one look from the avatar can have a deeper and more lasting effect on one's life than can a whole two-hour interview. It all depends, of course, on the particular look! Others have agreed with this, but how it is possible no one can quite explain. This applies both to his "corrective" looks and—even more so—his exceedingly blissful and divine glance.

The look in his eyes can be lambent and suffused with understanding. At darshan on two successive days he looked at me from close by, somehow fluttering his eyelids in the most charming and beautiful of expressions. I have never seen him do this before or since, nor have I seen anyone else express anything like it. I feel that these glimpses of intense sweetness and love surely have the same attraction that the poets have tried to convey about the Krishna avatar.

> Every gesture, word and activity of mine, however casual it may
> appear, is motivated to move you towards the fulfillment of your
> lives, and endow you with the Ananda (Joy) that your Atman
> (Spirit) is.[5]

This has been exemplified for me time and again on anything up to fifty occasions when I saw Baba "writing in the air," as he is accustomed to doing. However, they kept occurring, in many peculiar

---

[4] Sathya Sai Baba, Discourse Prashanthi Nilayam, Oct. 11, 1970, *Sathya Sai Speaks*, vol. VIIB, (n.d.), p. 71. New Indian edition ISBN 81-7208-158-8: vol. 10, p. 186.

[5] Discourse Prashanthi Nilayam, Feb. 22, 1971, *Sathya Sai Speaks*, vol. VIIB (n.d.), p. 213. New Indian edition ISBN 81-7208-159-6: vol. 11, p. 70.

ways, just after I happened to think about whether he wanted me to write this book. Sometimes he would make the writing motion when just in front of me, or when I glimpsed him passing between two pillars or the like. Before I left in 1989, I was getting frustrated at not being certain that these signs really applied to me. At last he "answered" my question by once more writing in the air when about thirty yards off, immediately thereafter turning and giving me a quaint smile, definitely directed straight at me. This was also a comment on how I should rely more on my intuition and on these tremendously economical ways of communicating with me. He developed this further during our next visit, when he repeatedly wrote in air when approaching me, or just before and just after looking into my eyes. Before I traveled to publish this book, Baba appeared in a dream and did the same. Again, as I was doing the final polishing of the manuscript, I often saw his right-hand index finger busily writing when I glanced at a picture I have up beside my computer. Yet in the picture his hand is actually forming a *mudra* with the palm upward. All this exemplifies well how he urges and inspires and helps one make up one's own mind and develop confidence until it is almost "a foregone conclusion."

It is not therefore absurd to conclude, as many have done before me, that Baba himself subtly presides over and aids in the very production of literature which, though doubtless never perfect, is at least not incompatible with his mission.

While compiling an extensive index of Baba's words, Reidun and I were reading the texts and making notes daily. One evening, tired after a strenuous day, we felt like dropping it, but recalling Baba's call to duty and self-discipline, we carried on with the work. The candle on our shrine must have burnt so low that we overlooked it when we retired for the night. The next morning, to our great perplexity, we saw that a small, green, and perfectly-formed Shiva *lingam*, about one-and-a-half centimeters in height, had formed from the candlewax. It must have dripped from the candle as the flame gradually sank and gutted out. The *lingam* was of tapering shape and even had ring-like markings, as seen in some Shiva temples. This was evidently a leela, because wax never ordinarily drips in that way. (See color plates.)

My son Kai was intrigued and tried to work out the physics of it, coming up with the explanation that it could have formed by gradually smaller drips as the flame sank. Two weeks later a candle in his own flat also produced a *lingam* of the same size and color.

However, the wax would have had to drip four times the distance in that case, which makes the physics of it incomprehensible. Perhaps the *lingams* were not formed by the drips at all? How the two *lingams* were of the same shade of green is also inexplicable. Incidentally, Kai had previously worked tirelessly on preparing a data program for making the index.

A second *leela*, which we felt was a form of recognition by Baba for our carrying out regular study of his teachings, occurred similarly one evening when we plodded on with our reading, even though we were very tired. My eye was suddenly drawn to the form of Sathya Sai in the clouds of an evening sky on the front cover of a book that I had recently read. The book is a deeply spiritual account of life and death in a Japanese prisoner-of-war camp by Laurens van der Post, titled *Night of the New Moon*. It is curious, too, that the night of the new moon is known in India as the night of Shiva. The figure of Sai, leaning forward as if to dispense vibhuti, can be figured out from the background. (See color plates.) When I returned attention to my place in the text, it read:

> Each person has a different conception of God and of Goodness, according to his upbringing and the state of purification of his impulses. All such conceptions are valid; when water is let into the fields, you will find sheets of different shapes—circular, rectangular, oval, square, according to the shape of the fields.[6]

[6] Sathya Sai Baba, Discourse Prashanthi Nilayam, Aug. 2, 1963, *Sathya Sai Speaks*, vol. III (Prashanthi Nilayam: Sri Sathya Sai Books & Publications Trust, n.d.), p. 33. New Indian edition ISBN 81-7208-151-0: vol. 3, p. 100ff.

UNDERSTANDING BABA'S TEACHINGS

It is not my purpose to attempt a presentation of Baba's actual teachings here. The subject is altogether too broad, and there already exists an adequate literature, both by Sathya Sai himself (translated from Telugu to English) and by various editors and commentators. It is rather the teachings' general nature and questions on interpreting them as a whole that I will discuss here.

It is truly impressive how, wherever Sathya Sai Baba has spoken and whatever his audience, his vision has always had a one-pointed focus. At that focus is our relationship to God, the purpose of life, and the means of fulfilling it. It is exemplified in sublime sayings like, "Love is Divinity," "God is present in everyone as a seed," and "Everything is the substance of God." Therefore, to realize all this and thereby realize oneself, one should always "Be good, see good and do good." This leads to reunification with the Godhead, which is the ultimate Liberation.

Baba has varied his approach and his examples, yet has held to that overall message, unvarying for over thirty years! I base this on my studies of all available materials to date. Having once spent six years to get a Masters' degree in philosophy, I decided in 1987 that Baba's teachings were worth at least as much study. I have since spent many years at this "higher self-education," and in the process also made a detailed index of Baba's own words from all his extant writings, discourses, and other authorized sources. The index, with the title "Back to the Source," contains over 18,000 separately-detailed entries.

Unlike other major educators or spiritual masters whose lives are known from youth, Sai Baba has never had to modify any tenets of his public teachings or to develop them through time. Such confident consistency is truly striking.

Rationalistic critics have discounted Baba because his teachings are not original or novel. They are not "original" in the sense of being previously unheard of, but are so in a deeper sense of being authentic and expressing Vedic truth that is coeval with human religion itself. He claims only to be renewing the age-old Vedic *Sanathana Dharma*, which means the "eternal religion," the combined form and essence of all virtuous living.

A clear majority of Baba's stories and illustrations are freely recycled from well-known scriptures or from great Vedic and Brahmanic spiritual forerunners like Ramakrishna, Ramanuja, Adi Shankara and others. This does not detract from their truth or force—in fact, the reverse is true, because Baba's daily life exemplifies for us and clarifies the values they taught. Various biographies of Baba provide abundant examples of how his avataric activities often illumine the meaning of doctrines in a new and more vital way than commentators have previously been able fully to grasp. At the same time, he continuously uses the most inventive and striking new examples of his teachings from almost anything that is close at hand or from aspects of ordinary situations that are well-known, but were previously unappreciated.

Because audiences have so far mostly been composed of Indians, many of the examples and explanatory references are based on their unique and deeply religious social and cultural history, so unlike the West's. Baba draws upon all the great richness of the Indian treasury of folk tales and the *Puranas*, including classics such as the *Ramayana*, the *Mahabharata*, and the *Srimad Bhagavatham*. These latter receive the most attention and explanation from Baba, who is ever showing how well he knows more than everything that is otherwise known about their authors, and not least about their heroes! He uses these materials with telling surgical accuracy, often adding surprising twists and turns to correct mistaken traditional associations or solve contentious enigmas.

Baba's own writings, at first penned on the spot when Professor Kasturi asked for material to put in the journal of which he was the editor, are more general in style. These works help to enrich the spiritual culture of the West by introducing the deepest insights of Vedanta in ways that show how very rich and multiform that culture is by comparison.

Comparing the thousands of discourses, one sees how Baba has repeated the same explanations, admonitions, and stories, time and again. Critics of this constant hammering in of the same basic lessons may reflect that this is probably because the audiences have not really been listening in the correct way. Baba always insists on his followers not merely listening, which is a futile exercise, but also putting his guidance into practice. Repetition is also required while there is a constant stream of newcomers who have not previously heard or read Baba's words.

Though all the same themes have thus always been present in Baba's message, some have been given increasing emphasis and development. In recent years he has put much weight on the need for self-inquiry and self-control—limiting one's desires through self-examination and eliminating egoism through doing voluntary, selfless service to those who are really in need. Other forms of religious discipline that Sai Baba recognizes, such as devotional singing, repetition of divine names, worship of divine forms, and prayer were originally much more to the fore. That they once seemed to play the major role in Baba's mission is perhaps due to the fact that the great majority of his devotees in the first decades were mostly local people who were accustomed to various traditional forms of worship, such as decking out idols or pictures with flowers and fruit (*puja*) and devotional singing (*bhajan*), from which they more easily derived spiritual inspiration. These practices are nowadays recommended less frequently by Baba. Though he has said that *puja* and *bhajans* are at the spiritual kindergarten level, he still encourages all to partake in singing of *bhajans* at the twice-daily half-hour sessions at Prashanthi Nilayam and as a frequent and regular activity in the Sathya Sai Organization worldwide.

The theme of expansion of the heart to include all creation as being the primary means to realization of self and the blissful vision of omnipresent divinity, has increasingly been developed in Baba's discourses. Since his 60th birthday, Baba has said that the criterion which will separate "the grain from the chaff" among his followers is to be whether one's actions are dedicated genuinely in outgoing selfless service. Nevertheless, the various phases of Baba's message overlap, and they represent a shift of accent, without his thereby rejecting practices of which he made much more of a point in earlier days.

The spiritual scope of Sathya Sai's explicit and recorded teachings is immense. In his public discourses, he seldom goes into much scientific or esoteric detail, choosing rather to stay at the essential, universal level. Reports from some of the many thousands of interviews he has given and from other talks, of a more or less private nature, make it clear that he at times will convey entirely specific and detailed knowledge, apparently on any subject he chooses, demonstrating mastery of any aspect of the world's scriptures, literature, languages, and sciences to those who are so fortunate as to be allowed to question him in depth. Students and teachers of the Sathya Sai Institute of Higher Learning are among the relatively few who get such opportunities nowadays, while in days gone by when the crowds were small, even some very skeptical visitors had such access.

Only since Baba was 30 years of age, when he first devoted himself explicitly to giving public discourses, have texts become available. That phase in his life, as he explains and had predicted earlier, always occurs after childhood and youth in the life of an avatar.

Baba's way of teaching is unique and uncommonly attractive, in its dealings with everything from everyday problems to the deeply mysterious, from the most serious questions of life to the humorous. No one to my knowledge gives such directly simple, yet deceptively deep and subtle, answers to the most enigmatic of questions, nor does so in more straightforward and powerfully-convincing ways than does Baba. Through the years he has discussed every vital aspect of education, science, knowledge, wisdom, spirituality, and many unusual and esoteric subjects, too, always angling them toward the same vital overall perspective, wherein the priorities of human values and self-realization in practice are clearly brought out.

He speaks primarily in what he calls the "language of the heart," not the dry and precise words of the intellectual. This language communicates by virtue of spiritual qualities such as friendliness, sympathy, understanding of others, good humor, chivalry, emotional honesty, supportive vision, and constructive wit—in short, the eloquence of the love of all. No spiritually-interested person who reads Sai discourses or writings can fail to be impressed by the clarity and simplicity of these teachings, which bear comparison with any known higher spiritual teaching. In a talk to devotees before Baba in 1991 at Kodaikanal, one of his students referred to the uniqueness of the teachings, in that they are delivered with the impact of a master, so that they strike deep within one's heart. It is the nature of Baba's personality that packs the power behind the teaching.

Many of the discourses deal directly with (and solve!) the key issues of what would otherwise be the most abstruse philosophy, yet they are always understandable, even though the perspectives they open are sometimes so deep as to be unfathomable.

The highly-specialized intellectual or the scholarly academic who expects to find high-flown and sophisticated conceptualism in his writings is likely to feel frustrated by the way in which his message always transcends any artificial limits set by concepts or logic. The multiplicity of his reason soon leaves the over-analytic thinker behind, by showing the boundaries of what man can know and where the always-impenetrable mystery begins. Nonetheless, the great questions of life and death, of creation, history, and mankind, and above all of mankind's relation to God, are all answered in the most striking and ultimate sense. Some insights surpass those to be found in any scripture or comparable work known, at least, to the present writer.

On the whole, the main thrust of the discourses is toward the practice of living virtuously, thus applying to all of humanity. When we consider that the teachings of a major avatar are said always to last through entire ages, as for example have those of Rama and Krishna, we see how pointless it would be for Baba to go into all manner of detail publicly about matters that have only fairly temporary relevance. Culture and society, the viewpoints of science, and human standards all change radically over quite brief spans of time. Therefore, what Baba could well say that is relevant to the world of today may only be confusing and seem very outdated to future generations. This would explain why all of the Sathya Sai Baba writings and the major part of his public talks repeatedly dwell on universal concerns, timeless questions, and eternal teachings. Baba points out how to select from his fund of advice:

> Every one of you is a pilgrim on that road, proceeding at your own pace, according to your qualification and the stage reached by its means. The advice that appeals to one of you or applies to one of you might not be appropriate to another, who has traveled less distance or reached a more advanced state. When I tell one person to follow one line of Sadhana (i.e., spiritual practice), it is specifically for his benefit; do not take it as prescription for your own benefit also, saying, 'Swami told him thus; let me also

adopt it.' Each has a different make-up, mental, physical, and spiritual.[1]

We can only imagine how helpful such advice would have been, and what horrors and absurdities might have been averted, had it been included by the authors of what became the various major religious scriptures of world religions!

It is natural, when trying to follow spiritual teachings, to apply generalities to individuals. This is very difficult to do in an impeccable manner, because such application depends on deep understanding, which arises only from long-term trial and error in practicing them.

It is also easy to misinterpret the *exact* intention of each of the many generalities that can enter into even one spiritual discourse. One should preferably master the language, know well all the common sources of error that can arise in any form of verbal communication, and also have broad knowledge together with a keen intuition. Therefore one can surely assert that spiritual teachings require very regular study, continual practice, and genuine self-examination—then ever more continuous repetition of this process, whatever one's age or status!

Though Baba always insists that the truth is eternal and changeless, he also naturally makes allowance for differing interpretations of the truth, as embodied in the great scriptures of world religions. We can distinguish two main sets of issues on which correct interpretation of his teachings depends:

1) The accuracy with which these teachings have been recorded and whether they have been handed down correctly in the authentic form or have been subject to mistranslation, errors of copying, censorship, selectivity, and so on.
2) The degree of relevance of religious observances or rules of law laid down in the situation of origin, when later applied to altered and changing societies, cultures, and individuals.

In discussing the social codes and individual guidelines laid down by those sacred Indian scriptures, the *Smrithis,* Baba wrote in *Paramartha Vahini:*

---

[1] Sathya Sai Baba, Discourse Bombay, March 3, 1974, *Sathya Sai Speaks,* vol. IX (Prashanthi Nilayam: Sri Sathya Sai Books & Publications Trust, n.d.), p. 58. New Indian edition ISBN 81-7208-160-X: vol. 12, p. 179.

But, in the process of time, the Smrithis suffered change, by omissions and additions and by differences in emphasis. The sages allotted for each era (Yuga) a particular Smrithi as authoritative, for, too many Smrithis with divergent counsel caused confusion and doubt. . . . When centuries roll over the land one after another, new problems arise, new situations and predicaments confront man and so, the laws and limits of the past have to be altered here and there. Indeed, such adjustments are part of the Design. The people have to be shown the path to spiritual progress under the altered circumstances, and so, the Smrithi that suits the new era is declared as binding.

Nevertheless this has to be borne in mind and carefully noted in memory by the readers: The Atma Dharma enunciated in the Vedanta is eternal, unchangeable. . . .

The moral codes and ideals of good conduct, the practices (Sadhanas) that man can adopt to control his mind and senses and purify his intelligence have, however, to suit the conditions of the people, the bonds they cultivate among themselves and other groups. With the changing face of social conditions, they too have to undergo adjustments and modifications.[2]

Sai Baba has seldom given talks in English, except in interviews, which makes exact and sound interpretation difficult for those of us who do not master Telugu or other languages such as Malayalam, Tamil, Kannada, or Hindi, in which Baba has once in a while given discourses. Baba reportedly spoke in Swahili when his interpreter was lost in a crowd during the visit to East Africa. (Incidentally, in 1992, Reidun was one day sitting in the darshan lines in front of some Japanese ladies who had recently been at an interview, when they mentioned that Baba had spoken Japanese. Reidun asked the lady if she had heard her correctly. The lady affirmed this, telling that Baba had used an interpreter, whom he had interrupted when his words were mistranslated, himself giving the correct Japanese phrase. He had also said a few sentences in Japanese.)

After questions of language and transmission come the usual difficulties of interpreting teachings of such generality and universality. These are the timeless quintessence of the "truth contents" of all the great and age-old scriptures of the world. Yet what is most special about them is how they are the truthful reflection of Sathya

---

[2] Sathya Sai Baba, *Sathya Sai Vahini* (Prashanthi Nilayam: Sri Sathya Sai Books & Publications Trust, n.d.), p. 80ff.

Sai's own perfect loving example and impeccable conduct. Also, his words—written or spoken—bear the force of conviction of certain knowledge, of *totally* self-confident omniscience, which can be observed in many different ways. Some of his declarations are entirely unprecedented in human history and are of such surpassing authority that they could surely not have been made by any ordinary human with such impunity.

The same truth, says Sai Baba, lies at the very root of every religion of the world. The source materials of a religion may sometimes have been tampered with, severely misinterpreted and mistranslated, or obscured by historical aberrations in theory and practice from the original pure intentions. On Christmas Eve in 1972, for example, Sathya Sai Baba spoke publicly about the origin of Christ's supposed announcement that he would come again, as follows:

> There is one point that I cannot but bring to your special notice today. At the moment when Jesus was emerging in the Supreme Principle of Divinity, He communicated some news to his followers, which has been interpreted in a variety of ways by commentators and those who relish the piling of writings on writings and meanings upon meanings, until it all swells up into a huge mess.
>
> The statement itself has been manipulated and tangled into a conundrum. The statement of Christ is simple. "He who sent me among you will come again!" and he pointed to a Lamb. The Lamb is merely a symbol, a sign. It stands for the Voice—Ba-Ba; the announcement was the Advent of Baba. "His name will be Truth," Christ declared. Sathya means Truth. "He will wear a robe of red, a blood-red robe." (Here Baba pointed to the Robe he was wearing!) He will be short, with a crown (of hair). The Lamb is the sign and symbol of Love. Christ did not declare that he will come again, he said, "He who made me will come again." That Baba is this Baba, and Sai, the short, curly-hair-crowned red-robed Baba, is come. He is not only this Form, but, he is every one of you, as the Dweller in the Heart.[3]

[3] Sathya Sai Baba, Discourse Prashanthi Nilayam, Dec. 24, 1972, *Sathya Sai Speaks*, vol. VIII (Prashanthi Nilayam: Sri Sathya Sai Books & Publications Trust, rev. ed. 1982), p. 172. New Indian edition ISBN 81-7208-159-6: vol. 11, p. 346.

Avoiding sophisticated scholarly terms and references, Baba brings a fog-piercing clarity that dispels many a modern religious dogma and confusion. His writings impress by their startling directness and uncompromising truthfulness. Their simplicity is often deceptive and can make one feel superior in understanding, until perhaps he touches one's very sore points, hitting home at our human failings. The will to accept such home truths and honestly apply them to oneself, is surely the biggest hurdle in progressing toward inner vision and confident strength, which the knowledge he conveys can build in the aspiring learner.

Since Sathya Sai Baba mostly teaches from the basis of non-dual philosophy (*Advaita*), special problems of interpretation arise for anyone trained in strictly systematic thinking or logic.

All the major traditions of European thought lack the conceptual flexibility for grasping the highest non-dualistic philosophies, and therefore one easily finds any such different ideas and their modes of expression to be "contradictory"—from which it is natural for rationalists to conclude that one or another of the assertions must be false. However, this is not necessarily the case.

Western education relies upon reason, which is based entirely on the principle of "either/or, but not both." For example, if matter is said to be real, by this eliminative principle, then non-matter (i.e., spirit) cannot be so. However, both spirit and matter are real, yet are so in ways incompatible within the limitations of normal conceptual reasoning. Sai Baba explains both that the world in which we must live out our lives is real, not an illusion, and yet *also* is illusion, due to its impermanence, which veils the unchanging eternal that underlies it. Mere logic cannot allow that both assertions can be true. In fact, however, both are meaningful and valid within each of their quite different frames of reference or "paradigms."

Baba makes clear that no system of thought can ever grasp or contain the whole truth about God or existence. Presumably this is why he does not preach any single system or doctrine, preferring to encompass all faiths and valid philosophies, restating their essentials or universal truths in his discourses. In philosophy, many examples crop up of how reason itself causes apparent contradictions, especially when applied to first and last things, which ultimately teaches only that there are many different possible approaches. Baba is ever approaching the same questions from various avenues and providing apparently new and surprising answers.

The only sort of understanding that can harmonize the outward contradictions due to the inherent limitations and ambiguities of the written word, or due to differing systems of thought and religion, is one that leads to practical solutions and to what people can and should do.

In January 1987, Professor Kasturi answered at length a long list of questions, which, in the interest of future students of the works of Sathya Sai Baba, I had formulated and delivered to him previously concerning the many publications in which he was involved, either as transcriber, translator, or editor.

Some of the questions concerned the source materials and the degree of their authentication and accuracy. As to the former, when my wife and I visited him, Sri Kasturi told us that Sathya Sai Baba had himself, almost invariably in Kasturi's presence, personally read and authenticated every one of his discourses published in the monthly journal *Sanathana Sarathi* since its inauguration by Sai Baba on Shivaratri Day in 1968 (which that year fell on February 16). If Baba was dissatisfied with any result of Kasturi's editing (or in later years, Sri Narasimhan's), he would indicate corrections and alterations.

Though *Sanathana Sarathi* appeared from the start in English, Baba's discourses in it were translated from the Telugu. Only later were sound recordings made of the discourses, with all transcripts and translations being based on these. Until about the mid-1970s, Professor Kasturi's own notes, taken on the dais while simultaneously translating Baba's words during public discourses, were the only source from which he had to work in preparing the English versions for printed publication. Now, anyone who has been present during a Baba discourse and heard the amazing speed and fluency with which the interpreters must work—their sentences often cut short by the flow of Sai Baba's next sentence—will realize the nature of the feat Sri Kasturi performed during the decades when he was most often the interpreter.

Naturally, a question was included about the accuracy of results from such a rapid process for, as Kasturi pointed out, he never had time to transcribe more than a note or reminder while these two-hour marathon discourses were under way. I did not ask whether his notes were mainly in Telugu or English (or in Malayalam, Tamil, or Kannada, which Kasturi also spoke and translated from on occasion). In any case, Kasturi said that Sai Baba not only often corrected his translators on the dais, but also sometimes altered the original itself for the purpose of publication, and that Sai Baba had even altered *verbatim* transcripts of his song-poems as recorded on tape, saying that his meaning had not been properly conveyed.

For the record, I would report that in 1987 Kasturi told me that Baba once asserted that the recorder had *misrecorded* what he had actually said! I am aware that accepting this may seem to be credulity to some. Yet those who have experienced instances during interviews or darshan where different persons have actually *heard* quite different sets of words from a single one of Sai Baba's utterances will find it less difficult to accept. At one interview, as mentioned earlier, a phrase Baba said to me sounded like two quite different sets of words to me and yet two more different phrases to the gentleman beside me, so that I could not be sure which of the meanings was intended. In fact each of the four sentences proved to have significant meaning! (See chapter 12, "The Inner Sanctum").

According to Kasturi, the reasons for such alterations varied. Sometimes it would be to protect those who had come under Baba's criticism in public, during the spoken discourse, from unnecessary further publicity. More often it would be to avoid undue repetition when several very similar discourses had, on his directions, been compounded and compressed. Kasturi remarked that Baba's discourses tended to go in cycles; they might often concentrate on the same selected themes for a week or a month, yet with altered presentation and examples according to different types of audience—whether lawyers, teachers, farmers, students, foreign devotees, etc.—all to suit their various levels of language, experience, or understanding. The same points would be made in a variety of ways, sometimes differing only slightly, sometimes considerably.

Though given full editorial freedom and responsibility regarding all other contributions to *Sanathana Sarathi*, Kasturi told us that Baba always demanded the very highest standards of editorial integrity and exercised strict control if any incorrect material were passed for publication.

The available translations of the works of Sathya Sai Baba, printed in various editions and occasionally translated by others than Professor Kasturi or V. K. Narasimhan, may sometimes lack stringency, which can be seen from occasional vagaries of expression and from some incorrect English grammar and terminology that has now and again found its way into these publications. Printers' errors also occur, especially in some Indian editions. Such errors can pose a severe test of faith for some people. For example, on several occasions Baba has said that in the past 5,000 years there have been 15,000 wars—itself surely quite an eye-opener for many historians! Yet in one instance the printed version diverges from the others in making the number 15,000 wars in 5,500 years. Yet this is the sort of point a critic may jump at as a "proof" that Baba is inconsistent.

The proof of accuracy of texts for future definitive editions of the avatar's words may lie partly in tape recordings. The earliest tape recordings of Baba's discourses—in Telugu, with on-the-spot interpretation by Kasturi and recorded directly by him—were donated by Kasturi to the Sathya Sai Institute of Higher Learning for research purposes, in all between fifty and sixty tapes. Since then a tape library has apparently begun to be collected.

Professor Kasturi also recounted for us a number of personal experiences concerning how Baba had made him the official biographer. He had been told of his future role fully twelve years before Baba eventually asked him to produce the material for publication. Baba had arranged for him to get to know a wide variety of devotees from the earliest years, including Baba's parents, brothers, sisters, and other kin. Meanwhile Kasturi witnessed many marvelous and joyous events in the presence of the avatar that only gradually opened his eyes to the magnitude of this incarnation. Baba only revealed his "identity" step by step, thus unfolding deeper and deeper aspects of his being, of which we can read in the literature, particularly in the four volumes of biography, *Sathyam, Sivam, Sundaram,* which Kasturi, the long-serving professor of history, was thus "re-educated" to write, and also in his own subsequent remarkable autobiography, *Loving God.*

Eagerly awaiting the signal to begin writing the biography, for years Sri Kasturi was teased and tantalized by Baba about his future authorship while also being given to know that the time was not ripe. Kasturi told me how Baba had told him that people would think the history was all some sort of "Arabian Nights Entertainment," some imaginative fairy tale concocted between himself and Kasturi! Baba added that they should let the message spread by word of mouth awhile yet. In good time there would be enough hunger for the meal; then Kasturi would be called on to serve it.

Not until twelve years after the first mention of the matter did Baba one day call Kasturi to say that some devotees had just been praying and "pestering" him to allow some literature on Swami's life to be put out for devotees everywhere—so what had Kasturi been doing all this time? Hadn't he produced any material yet? With great joy Kasturi understood at once that this was the signal for preparing the first volume for the public.

Professor Kasturi's biography is a highly-reliable sourcebook for the major events in Baba's life through about 1980. Kasturi had retired from his chair of history at age 50 in 1947 and came then to live close to Baba. As Kasturi wrote in the preface concerning the time lapse between his retirement, and his beginning on the collection of materials and publications some years later, "Baba always speaks of personal experience, not books, as the best way of knowing Him, and this has been, in the main, responsible for the delay."[4] Kasturi was thereby also in a position to hear first-hand accounts from literally thousands of witnesses of Sai Baba's life, including many from the earliest years.

---

[4] N. Kasturi, *Sathyam, Sivam, Sundaram* (Prashanthi Nilayam: Sri Sathya Sai Books & Publications Trust, 1961), Foreword.

SCIENCE AND SPIRITUAL KNOWLEDGE

When I studied Sathya Sai Baba's views on science and spirituality, it was a relief to find that they confirmed those that I had arrived at myself through many years of researching and contemplating these matters. But Baba also redefined the relationship of science and spirituality through deep new insights, all stated very pithily to boot. My interest here is to show further how Baba's critique of science highlights some of the shadows science casts and the limitations from which it suffers. We are all left too much "in the dark" about these aspects by the protagonists and believers in science who seem to rule the intellectual roost these days. However, realizing these shortcomings is an unavoidable preliminary to understanding the role science must play in future and what part spirituality will have in its development.

> Many describe science today as a powerful acquisition, but, science holds before man a great opportunity, that is all. It cannot be as great a power as it is imagined to be. If it is devoid of character it brings disaster.[1]

It is held that "truth" is the sole aim of science, along with an insistence on neutrality toward all other values. But is not truth with-

---

[1] Sathya Sai Baba, Discourse Prashanthi Nilayam, Aug. 29, 1981, *Sathya Sai Speaks*, vol. XI (Prashanthi Nilayam: Sri Sathya Sai Books & Publications Trust, n.d.), p. 132. New Indian edition ISBN 81-7208-163-4: vol. 15, p. 97.

out goodness a sort of contradiction? This may not be logically contradictory, but it represents a clash between two values. Science is
held to direct itself toward the common good. Yet it often contra-
dicts this by excluding from its assumptions and practical goals all
other positive and universally-known human values, such as non-violence, love of humanity, peace of mind, and rightness of action.
Scientific neutrality toward values is maintained as its policy, supposedly in the name of "objectivity." In fact, the pragmatic justification
underlying natural scientific research has rather been technological
invention, which itself has definitely been used for ill as well as for
good.

Sai Baba points out that, though science is sacred and gives
great opportunities, it is also a danger and is being used for harm-
ful ends. Science has contributed many goods to the world—many
material goods, much know-how, and also a few less tangible good
qualities. However, more than enough has been written to boost
one-sidedly the positive image of science today. Wherever the Western lifestyle is an ideal, science has assumed the role of a sacred cow,
a sacrosanct provider that exists only for the material good of the
world. But anyone can see that science has also had many unfore-
seen consequences, often very dangerous and socially-destabilizing
ones, and also that scientists have released many ills upon the world,
too, even if often unwittingly. Baba has often remarked of science
that it ridicules a science of spirit and fails to seek the creative reality behind the appearances of the physical universe, while having itself catered to selfish desires and having failed to remove ignorance
and conflicts throughout the world.

I have long held that the sciences today rely on an underlying
philosophy that is far too narrow and incomplete. For example, the
industrial and technological marvels that publicize the natural sciences and build the public image of science are not matched by any
comparable achievements in the humanities or "social sciences,"
particularly not in terms of effective, proven, and beneficial applica-
tions for society. Even psychology has shown itself remarkably weak
in understanding how to assess and improve lasting mental health or
quality of life, while sociological researchers can hardly do more
than observe the degeneration of values and the madness of excesses of every kind the world over, often without even deploring it.
Also, inadequacies of the social-scientific theories of Marx and En-
gels have caused much suffering and have historically also lent

themselves to misuse on a worldwide scale, with results in terms of suffering comparable to those due to nuclear and other ghastly weaponry developed by the aid of physical scientists.

Sathya Sai Baba has mentioned science's claim only to describe very precisely *how* things happen, while rejecting any questions of *why*, i.e., the reasons and purposes inherent in or "behind" what scientist's study. Because of the (unproven) materialistic assumption that is built into the theory and method of "science," the urge to know is limited to externals and the cosmos is regarded only as the physically-observable universe. This is seen, most definitely in the excessive public promotion of physics, astronomy, and molecular biology, with billions of dollars for vast cyclotrons, space telescopes, etc., all supposedly to answer the riddle of the origin of the universe and life, but most absurdly presumptuous of all, to claim thereby to know the very mind of God. Somehow one had hoped for something more!

"What *is* the cosmos and *why*? Can I know what or who I really am and for what purpose I am here?" Something much more than the mere theoretical riddles of black holes and the Big Bang is certainly provided by Sathya Sai Baba, something more near, dear, and real than that! His universal vision is backed up by sublime knowledge of the deepest of mysteries, including the creation of matter and of human souls. In December 1973, for example, he said during a discourse:

> The energy with which the most elementary and subtle particles are bound with each other is Divine. The individual separation of these individual particles is absolutely precise and cannot be altered by anyone. Any separation or merger would mean nonexistence of Creation. This Divine Energy is God.[2]

Perhaps yet more vital is the question, "How can I know what is right and wrong?" Partly out of the uncertainty caused by supposing mistakenly that the theories of the various sciences are neutral with respect to all values, (i.e., "value-neutralism"), academic institutions will not willingly touch on vital questions of moral values except, at best, out of sheer historical interest. But science itself supports, implicitly at least, certain types of idea systems against others

[2] E. Fanibunda, *Vision of the Divine* (Bombay: n. p., 1976), pp. 99ff.

and is certainly not free from intellectual and cultural fashion. So science is necessarily involved in values, despite its own underlying "neutral" ideology.

It is obviously true that no one can absorb every theory and subtheory, or know the vast host of empirical details of science. It is further widely held that science is so vast that no one can have a complete overview of its scope. This latter, however, is a mere myth of scientism, a self-defensive argument to fend off criticism that strikes at some of the basic assumptions of the sciences. I studied for many years before I found to my own satisfaction that no theories in any science, however sophisticated and apparently flawless at first inspection, were capable of defining more than what amounts to mere cross-sections of the fullness of reality, and even that amounting to mostly only temporary validity and, more important, disregarding entirely the richness of the mental and inner quality of human life, particularly as it is when perceived from heightened states of consciousness.

The paradigms and parameters in each of the special sciences also tend to delimit what one may and may never know by their aid. The very vastness and subtle intricacy of the full design of creation is either left unapproached or is denied a place in "science" because it is beyond reach of the physical senses and the analytic mind.

> Faced with a universe which is fundamentally mysterious, which
> he feels must be endless and beginningless, which he feels must
> be infinite, the scientist has to accept it, though he cannot form
> a real picture of that kind of universe.[3]

It has been my experience that the more one seriously inquires into a science, the more questionable many of its theoretical and practical claims are found to be. Even the clear-headed "layman" often plainly sees the shortcomings in the achievements and claims of professional scientists and is sometimes better placed to notice the failures of scientific experts to understand or solve the great majority of our human problems. Science's piecemeal "analytic" approach

---

[3] Sathya Sai Baba, Discourse Prashanthi Nilayam, Sept. 30, 1960, *Sathya Sai Speaks*, vol. I (Prashanthi Nilayam: Sri Sathya Sai Books & Publications Trust, n.d.), p. 190.

and its specialization has the disadvantage of often serving to keep it from addressing or understanding the real causes of the greatest problems, such as ecological imbalance and pollutions, the ill consequences of much industry and technology, many physical and mental illnesses, social disruption, economic crises and much more besides.

However, the true origin of these problems lies in the minds and hearts of each of us. The cause of all this and its continuation is not to be found independently of the thoughts and desires of the individual persons who make up society!

By way of another example, though clinical medicine has advanced in many respects, through specialization it has also lost sight of very basic health needs and simple but effective forms of treatment. Baba points out that personal care, love, and respect are the essential elements in all genuine forms of "health care" and his hospitals provide care on those bases. Modern medicine tends strongly to depersonalize people through its specialized bureaucracy and estranges itself from them, making many previously unheard-of blunders as a result. Through highly doubtful priorities that award the most scientific prestige and money to profitable hyper-technological developments, such as genetically-designed drugs and super-high-tech machinery, it all too often neglects the majority interest and care of the needy of the world.

There does exist research that aspires to noble results in practical improvements of the world, which does good. There is also that which desires knowledge through uninvolved, "disinterested" observation, which probably does neither good nor ill as such. Yet the much-vaunted "freedom of science" can be—and unquestionably still is being—very widely abused. This occurs, for example, in the ungodly desecration of life in experiments on animals, for which—if really necessary—human beings could volunteer instead.

Scientists should also recognize the meaning of the fact that we all have to die of something anyhow! Our desires must have limits, and the extent of our human rights cannot be unlimited, for we also have duties towards God's creation. Then there is the scandal of patenting creatures and plants as if they were human inventions, so the rich can have economic control over them. The freedom of science has not least of all allowed the aberrations of almost every area of the physical and biological sciences into all forms of warfare. However, is high time that such freedom be redirected dutifully instead. Our duty cannot be other than towards the essential core of high moral principles, including awe and respect for the Creator's will, as expressed in all the world's major religions.

All in all, from the higher of philosophical viewpoints, the theoretical "holes" and blind spots that remain throughout the entire body of science look, if anything, larger and blacker year by year.

> "Science is highly fragmentary, and its approach to reality is through Maya,[4] and this is a highly dangerous procedure. Science does not even know the truth of chemistry and physics. Each ten years or so, the old truths are discarded or modified because of research results. So, when a man tries to compare science and the spiritual world, he is comparing a science whose finality is not known, with spiritual truth of which he is also ignorant. . . .[5]
>
> . . . Religion begins where science ends. In science, when one door is opened and a passage is revealed, ten doors are discovered in that very passage, and each one of them has to be opened in turn. Science transforms things, rearranges them, studies their composition, regroups their parts and releases the energy that lies latent in them. But I create the things themselves! And they are as lasting as any that are found in nature! That is this, but this is not that. Nature is Brahmam, mistaken to be nature. . . .[6]

Even today, scientists without the metaphysical bent who are skeptical of anything as yet unperceived, that is, of a purely spiritual nature, fail to see how their own initial assumptions (about scientific

---

[4] *Maya* may perhaps be defined as the subtle interplay of the mind's natural "mental projection" and the "objective illusion" of the natural world, which appears as given to observation, in cooperation with the mind. *Maya* is thus easily identified with nature itself, the ever-changing play of events that the mind—when not strictly controlled by sense disciplines and higher intelligence—seeks to diversify, embroider, and "objectify" as the only reality.

[5] Sathya Sai Baba, quoted in J. S. Hislop, *Conversations with Bhagavan Sri Sathya Sai Baba* (San Diego: Birth Day, 1978), p. 43.

[6] Sathya Sai Baba, Discourse Prashanthi Nilayam, Oct. 17, 1961, *Sathya Sai Speaks*, vol. II (Prashanthi Nilayam: Sri Sathya Sai Books & Publications Trust, n.d.), p. 82. New Indian edition ISBN 81-7208-150-2: vol. 2, p. 73.

method or the nature of reality and knowledge) affect their scope, robbing them of any genuinely holistic understanding of phenomena, and eclipsing the place or relations of said phenomena within progressively wider scopes, up to and eventually including the overall purpose of life in divinized nature. This shortcoming in vision and sublimity is what also accounts for most questionable experiments with both plant, animal, and human nature, from the horrific to the immoral and even obscene, carried out with the barest minimum of self-knowledge and wholly lacking in spiritual insight.

New discoveries are always showing how wrong the experts were about what is and is not possible, even in subjects that have long been supposed to demonstrate a great degree of precision and predictability. Take, for example, all the expert assurances about the impossibility of accidents in modern nuclear technology before the Three Mile Island and Chernobyl disasters took place. Only a handful of the more intelligent physicists warned against such a likelihood—and were treated by the established scientific community as outsiders.

Meanwhile, supposedly established theories in what are thought to be sound subjects, such as Earth's geological evolution, archeology, paleontology, biological evolution, medicine, physics, and the astronomical sciences, are full of very doubt-inducing gaps that tend more to widen than to close, while the reappraisal of one dogma after another is frequently forced upon the established scientific punditry by circumstance or chance discovery.[7] In addition comes the pressures on the scientific community seeking work and prestige from the many vested or state interests and research-financing bodies, affecting the overall directions of science toward economic productivity and financial profit (sometimes even causing the "cooking of results"). In all this, science easily becomes less than a servant of truth and all the more unconcerned about responsibility toward the greater good.

Social prestige is obviously one of the worldly aims of many scientists and anything that tends to challenge the authority of their

---

[7] See, for example, the increasingly-popular work *The Structure of Scientific Revolutions* by Thomas Kuhn (Chicago: Chicago University Press, 1962), in which it is held that the paradigms by which science at any given time organizes its descriptions or explanations of phenomena are always subject to modification and even very radical "revolutionary" changes. These views are almost mere truisms today.

supposedly superior knowledge of what is possible or not, is usually either ignored or pooh-poohed. It is hardly surprising that some
people who call themselves "scientists" have stated that it is impossible for anyone to materialize objects and have argued that such
events must be sleight of hand, deception, and even "mass hypnosis"—the latter being a favorite argument of psychologists, who
seldom have much actual knowledge of hypnosis of any kind. This
vague idea—never experimentally demonstrated or explained in any
convincing manner—is often used to write off and defend the mind
against anything that surpasses everyday experience.

However, while Sai Baba has been challenged by scientists to
demonstrate his powers, he has stated that he never simply demonstrates them and that they are always only an expression of his love
and care for the person who benefits from them. That Baba never
challenges anyone is obviously because he has no need to do so
whatever. He does not submit to experiments, obviously because he
has no interest in "proving" himself. Besides, why should he waste
his time, so precious to devotees, on people who try to approach
him in an imperious, challenging, or otherwise offensive manner? It
would fulfill no genuine need, as the critic with preconceived beliefs
is not motivated by fruitful aims but by mere self-justification. Thus,
challenges only rebound on the challenger.

Nonetheless, there is not a single scientist in the world today
who has been able authoritatively to disprove Baba's supernormal
acts. Those scientists who are known to have visited and made firsthand observations, have become convinced of the genuineness of
the materializations, at least, and there are many such who testify
formally to this. The others, who lack the firsthand experience, are
unable even to give an informed opinion, because science must always crucially depend, in the first and last instance, on the proof of
observation. Yet the causes of such phenomena, Baba has repeatedly
explained, cannot be known by the human mind; such realities can
only be apprehended at all through intense spiritual practice and in
a supramental state of extremely blissful realization, which is entirely
beyond the pale of outward-directed scientific investigations.

Sai Baba has pointed out that science is itself caught in a changing process and operating within narrow limits, which means not
least that it cannot grasp the universe, for as it advances, the mystery deepens. Modern philosophy of science has recognized that scientific knowledge is conditional, never absolute. No knowledge
about the supposedly "objective" world of physical nature exists

that is not itself "subjectively-organized" by the human mind in the context of some era of time and society. Nonetheless, science expresses certain values in its involvement with society, and scientists are forever airing publicly and via the media their "evaluations" of what may or may not happen or be achieved, which is more often than not itself a highly unscientific sort of guessing game. When these, as so often, are divorced from spiritual insight, they become a force that can be as dangerous as it is blind.

Through research work in the sociology of knowledge, I found that a large proportion of psychological and social researches were often futile for most intents and purposes. There is an over-reliance on what appear to be objective methods (quantitative statistical analysis). However, when the object of study is itself the conscious human subject—or many persons in the form of a society—it is qualities and values in life that matter and are unavoidable in any sensible judgments. Social "scientists," always hoping for the status of "objective" scientist and hence for social authority and influence, are loath to recognize this fact and to draw the right conclusions. Yet their assumptions are *always* formed at basic levels by the values of the particular society and beliefs wherein they grew up or that they have assimilated and adopted. Consequently, the only solution to the dilemma between "fact" and "value" is to research both facts and values, and then, to do so *only* on the basis of good and clearly-enunciated positive values. Otherwise, the divorce of theory and practice and of confusing conflicts can only continue, because observers who are merely trying always to be neutral, can at best only describe things fairly neutrally—yet they themselves do not recognize this fully, and so they fail to either assert the good or refute the anti-values.

Ultimately, through the systematic study and well-organized practice of positive values, a new type of experience must be gained that goes well beyond the assumptions of "physicalistic" natural scientism, without thereby becoming a moralistic free-for-all of dilettante theories without relevant scientific controls. The future of academic-scientific culture, if it is to be fruitful, must lie with the re-introduction of the basic and universal values of love, non-violence, peace of mind, and virtuous action for the common welfare, starting at the basic level of education and research. No less than a newly-spiritualized orientation toward the human being and nature is urgently required.

Science owes its success and credibility largely to its accurate observation and measurement of physical nature. Only in fairly recent times have these methods been applied widely to the study of human society. Instead of ever describing and measuring past and present tendencies, we now require imaginative hypotheses and forward-looking approaches for truly valuable change in the human or social sciences—with active participation not just to understand but also to positively influence events through the scientist's own actions and example. Just, think, if only half as much time, effort, and money as has been poured into specialist fields like microphysics or organic biology, were to be invested in cultural bridge-building and active peace research, such as the systematic testing of lasting forms of friendship and fruitful cooperation between people who are separated, estranged, ideologically-opposed, or in other types of conflicts, the world would probably be vastly different and much better altogether today.

Human nature combines the outer and the inner, body and soul, matter and mind through action and interaction. Culture, or communication between human beings and groups within an interactive environment, ultimately springs from and relates to the inner world of the spirit and therefore cannot be studied intelligently or fully merely on the basis of natural scientific assumptions.

Any researcher has only to refer to almost any one of Sathya Sai Baba's discourses from 1955 to the present day to find convincing examples of potential improvements in human life and society that cover a vast range of ideas, any one of which may form the starting point for fruitful action-research hypotheses in the sciences. The systematic study of what improves the *quality* of life is an essential task, particularly where material prosperity is no longer the dominant problem. In this sense, "quality" can really only be assessed (not accurately "measured" as if it were a quantity) in terms of people's evaluations, such as what attitudes and behavior promote tolerance, respect, chivalry, and so on, in relations between persons of different backgrounds, classes, and ages, and between the individual and public servant, patient and doctor, and so on, through all the variations of human association.

Because science even programatically eschews its only proper partner, which is spirituality, in practice, it has become like a half-blind leviathan stalking on the road of worldly ambitions and preying on anything in its path—be it human or beast, plant or mineral—that it can turn to material advancement and profit. This mostly hastens the exhaustion of resources and extinction of species by those who stand to gain financially.

> Science without discrimination and a society without morality and integrity cannot bring about prosperity. Therefore you should have discrimination along with science. Along with discrimination there should be humility.[8]

The vital question that must be answered in every area is: "How can the aims of education and scientific research be channeled toward the realization of human values?" At the most general level, Sai Baba answers that the transformation of every heart and mind through awareness of the divine cause, nature, and purpose of all entities *alone* can bring peace and happiness to the world. This guiding law must be applied throughout the spectrum of human research and learning—and only when science enters such a symbiosis with practical spirituality can we look forward to a safe and secure global community.

---

[8] Sathya Sai Baba, Discourse, "Education and *Seva*," Nov. 22, 1987. This is a pamphlet published by Sri Sathya Sai Books & Publications Trust, reproduced in part in *Sanathana Sarathi*, Dec. 1997, pp. 325ff.

EDUCATION AND
TRANSFORMATION

As a dissatisfied educator at university, Sathya Sai Baba's philosophy of education came to me in my late 40s, as both a support in my disillusionment with much in the present system of higher education and as a strong positive clarification of the way ahead.

Baba takes issue with the educational aims that predominate in most of the world today. He insists on education as a preparation for the lifetime search for self-knowledge and for finding the meaning of life. This itself unavoidably involves living in accordance with what is right, good, true, and beautiful, rather than primarily getting qualified to make a good living. He never tires of explaining how vital such an orientation is for any form of education, in order to produce good citizens and a good society and not just good brains.

> Education must determine and delve into the nature and characteristics of spiritual search for the Absolute or the Overself (Paramatma). It must prove its true character by manifesting as a spring of morality, laying down axioms of virtue.[1]

While Sathya Sai's critique of the modern decline in educational ideals and practice has worldwide application, most of his specific advice is directed to the regeneration of educational idealism in In-

---

[1] Sathya Sai Baba, *Vidya Vahini* (Prashanthi Nilayam: Sri Sathya Sai Books & Publications Trust, 1984), p. 21.

dia, whose educational system has fallen out of touch with the rich ancient traditions of Indian civilization. Some words of Baba illustrate the essence of his critique:

> The ancient schools aimed at self-knowledge first and knowledge of the objective world as a corollary. Truly, that is the sign of the educated man—his awareness of his own reality. . . . Among the educated, we do not find signs of self-knowledge, nor do we see another quality that we expect every human being to have, namely, the quality of mercy, of sympathy or compassion.[2]

> Love means the sense of inter-relationship and involvement of the individual with [the] community. This degree of Love is absent now in many highly-educated, highly-placed persons. . . . Education is not merely the gathering of scientific knowledge; it should endow man with heroism in action. It should instruct man on what has to be done and how. It must make man recognize the kinship that exists between himself and others.[3]

Here I want to bring home the crucial relevance of Baba's critique to the West. Since he lays much weight on the need for speaking primarily from one's own experience, I shall air certain issues from my twenty-five years in Western higher education that seem still relevant today.

A very difficult problem for modern youth and anyone meeting the life-determining decisions that sooner or later face most of us is, "What work can I do that is meaningful and right?" Think of the many pressures that tear at one from within and without: the need to make a living and the desire to attain money, status, and even fame, and to succeed in the cynical "eyes of the world"; the desire to live and experience life to the maximum; or the desire to escape from whatever one may fear.

However, critics may often underrate the genuine call of the human spirit felt by many young people in wishing to improve

---

[2] Sathya Sai Baba, Discourse Brindavan, March 23, 1975, *Sathya Sai Speaks*, vol. IX (Prashanthi Nilayam: Sri Sathya Sai Books & Publications Trust, n.d.), p. 199. New Indian edition ISBN 81-7208-161-8: vol. 13, p. 25.

[3] Sathya Sai Baba, Discourse Prashanthi Nilayam, Aug. 29, 1981, *Sathya Sai Speaks*, vol. XI (n.d.), pp. 131ff. New Indian edition ISBN 81-7208-163-4: vol. 15, p. 97.

themselves and bring the world some genuine good. This youthful idealism is often diverted, misdirected, or destroyed by existing educational systems. Both as student and teacher, I went through these problems to some extent. However, very little of what I came across at universities was really of positive help in the decisions of my life.

In turning to the study of social sciences and philosophy in my mid-20s, after already having tried out a range of very different jobs and potential professions, I had genuinely hoped to get further along with the great questions of life. I also worked in several institutions with disturbed and delinquent youth, to find that the quotidian bureaucrats and professional staff (who had little actual contact with these young people) nevertheless had all the say in policy and administration, and were not going to listen to any young foreigner without formal qualifications, even though they were disturbed by the feeling that I saw through obvious errors in their actions.

This and the existential urge I felt to look in every direction, toward science, world literature, religion, and philosophy, as well as the study of unusual cultures or tribes, eventually led me into higher education. I was already studying everything that could offer any hope of learning applicable truths. On the positive side, I found that there was value in the discipline that studying imposes, the scientific systems of research and methods of communication, and the standards of objective excellence. Due to my age and relative experience in life, though, I was less inclined to accept many opinions at face value than to inspect them. What was on offer fell considerably short of what I had hoped for. The main part of what I had to study was to me very largely irrelevant to the real problems of life and society, as far as I already knew them to be.

> Modern education produces only "learned fools"; it does not produce wise men who can meet life calmly and bravely. Its products know how to fill themselves with information, devise tools or handle them for the destruction of fellowmen, or cater to the whims of the senses—but they are helpless to meet the crisis of death, a crisis that is inevitable.[4]

---

[4] Sathya Sai Baba, Discourse Prashanthi Nilayam, Nov. 18, 1963, *Sathya Sai Speaks*, vol. III (Prashanthi Nilayam: Sri Sathya Sai Books & Publications Trust, n.d.), p. 81. New Indian edition ISBN 81-7208-000-0: vol. 3, p. 158.

The need to explore and learn all one can so as to improve one's understanding of the real essentials of life was sorely frustrated by the modern system I met. I found that anyone who goes to a Western university with the genuine concern of knowing oneself, discovering what is right living in practice, or learning about the development of inner vision and universal spirituality, was either ignored as irrelevant or was seen as a bit of a nutcase!

So low had the collapse of cultural values brought us that very little life wisdom was conveyed through so-called "higher studies," and then really only as a historical curiosity. In a few subjects, Socratic philosophy is given lip service but its true spirit, which is to act for the good and according to conscience (the *daimon*) in all things, is *not* really accepted, let alone practiced! The situation seems worse today, if anything. No place is given in the entire system for serious self-inquiry, while questions about the existence of an immortal soul, divine justice, and goodness—with which Socrates principally dealt—are not taken seriously any longer, even in academic philosophy. It has become a sphere of almost nothing but conceptual thought (mainly of a very narrow kind), studied argumentation, and the publishing of theories divorced from one's own actions, other than those required for getting status, income, or the like!

The riddles of the meaning of life and death have led many a keen student into an exhaustive search through the sciences and philosophy, as they did me too. Early on it became evident to me that none of the physical sciences had any answers touching on the vital questions of life as we must live it, or its purpose.

The social or psychological "sciences" and contemporary philosophy were more relevant to self-understanding, yet they also suffered—and still suffer—far too much from the dogmas of scientific materialism and the attitudes it fosters, shortcomings one would have thought were obvious. They usually fail directly to address the human condition as a moral predicament and shrink from open and full commitment to the right and the good, hiding behind the supposed objectivity and neutrality of scientific observers.

The works of C. G. Jung, Jean-Paul Sartre, Erich Fromm, R. D. Laing, Alan Watts, Rollo May, and others were therefore much more fruitful than accepted works in psychology because they recognized the validity of the search for meaning in life. The best of world literature provided a much more illumining source for investigating the purpose of human life and ways of fulfilling the task of personal development. The books, for example, of Dostoevsky, Aldous Huxley, Hermann Hesse, Laurens van der Post, and many another were formative of a much more satisfying and whole form of understanding because of the values they embody and the intelligent breadth of their investigations. Reading in a wide range of esoteric philosophies and mysticisms—despite all the strange aberrations they may contain—often yielded richer insights and inspirations than what was found to be within the pale of scholarly respectability.

Thinkers who deal too often with the *really* basic and "disturbing" questions of humanity, such as why we are here and what we should prepare for and work toward, were often not considered even peripherally relevant where their main contentions were concerned. Such thinkers were of the caliber and scope of Mahatma Gandhi, A. Eddington, A. N. Whitehead, Paul Brunton, Vivekananda, Albert Schweitzer, Sri Aurobindo, Mircea Eliade, and many another lesser-known luminary who brought universal light to varied subjects. The messages of such minds seldom found any place at all either in the syllabi or in research work.

> Spiritual education is not a distinct and separate discipline; it is part and parcel of all types and levels of education. In fact, it is the very foundation on which a lasting edifice can be built.[5]

This suppression of great spiritual thinkers in modern education occurs not least because their work does not give any form of economic payoff or industrial advantage, but surely also because they often emphasize that the scientific mentality has serious limitations of perspective and knowledge, which must be compensated for, or even dominated by, some form of spirituality. Spiritual writers have always raised serious ethical issues neglected by scientists and the crucial question of how mankind should administer the world's goods and nature's fragile resources. Uncontrolled production and selfish consumerism is at long last beginning to be seen to have more and more serious consequences for all beings today, and this

---

[5] Sathya Sai Baba, Discourse Anantapur, Jul. 25, 1975, *Sathya Sai Speaks*, vol. IX (Prashanthi Nilayam: Sri Sathya Sai Books & Publications Trust, n.d.), p. 257. New Indian edition ISBN 81-7208-161-8: vol. 13, p. 98.

awakening has occurred almost despite the climate of modern higher education and the resulting general trend of governments and leaders away from values higher than those of the ballot box.

A key truth that is hardly ever made known in "higher education," is that the greater one's vision becomes, the more one realiszes about the vastness of the unknown and unknowable. This philosophical absolute has been suppressed until forgotten. It is not conducive to good budgetary policy or the "image" of one's particular discipline to dwell on one's shortcomings and what one does not know and may never understand! Instead, almost all intellectuals and scientists nowadays tend to publicize and sell what are but mundane, if informed, opinions, as if they were the genuine article, the truth.

As a teacher partaking in university planning and administration, one has to have some belief that to raise the general level of intellectual achievement is worthwhile. As I explored the situation, my own optimism as to the value of teaching as the most important means of improving the human lot and heading the world toward universal peace and understanding, wore thinner and thinner. This sad situation was not altered either by my continuous research or the ideals and values embodied in the various syllabi. Due to the weight of collegiality and the professorial system, backed by a corporative form of unionism and "closed shop" interests, a more personalized and caring system of tuition and examination, or any broader outlook on world cultures, was not possible. I often considered leaving the university with its undercurrent of the uncaring, competitive ethos, its subtly pervasive pride in status, and its own ever-grinding bureaucratic momentum. Apart from all that, what it gave was a comfortable livelihood.

In the much impersonalized societies of Northern Europe, official "papers" are crucial in almost every walk of life, far more than experience or any other qualities. This was, and for many still is, one unavoidable reason for having to persist in higher studies. Any such traditional system, built up and cemented over generations, takes excessive time and energy to change even minimally. This fact soon acts as a dampener on idealism and enterprise. After dissent and revolt—inner or outer—one can eventually only hope to be effective by joining it and trying to work for the good from within it, to try to neutralize some of the demands of the vested interests of every sort. This was the conclusion I reached, along with other socially-engaged students and teachers.

It was soon clear to me that raising the level of people's awareness of issues that are really important could simply not be done by science or even by improving the research world, for neither have any proven or appreciable effect on individual values or ethical behavior. The results of scientific research can hardly ever be put into practice by individuals for meaningful constructive ends, except in material matters. The social "sciences" provide virtually no information on right living, and only the most exceptional study will demonstrate the benefits of exercising communal values—such as voluntary help out of compassion to the aged, the lonely, the weak, and the deprived. They describe and describe, but prescribe or effectuate nothing of value!

Most of the best that Western intellectualism has to offer still revolves around theories that set out to problematize more than to solve. The social sciences are largely unable to understand or prescribe genuine solutions to social alienation or the modern identity crisis. The cause is surely the lack of dimension in their thought and action, itself due to a mistakenly narrow or "pseudo-scientific" ideal. They are even at a loss to understand or contribute toward solving most types of social disturbance, or compensating people for lack of personal or social autonomy. As Sathya Sai has explained thoroughly, modern education tends to train intellectuals to theorize about what others should have done or should do, rather than analyzing their own activities or getting them to put changes into practice in their own lives. Another name for this, perhaps, is moral bankruptcy.

Universities in the West lack noteworthy programs that lead directly to noble humanitarian activities centered firmly and primarily on genuine values of charity, understanding, and compassion—at least there are no visible efforts. One fares well enough materially in a welfare state such as Norway, which has relatively high public ideals in terms of helping the sick, the needy, and exploited or oppressed people. But nearly all responsibility has been shifted from the individual to the State, and voluntary work is often even looked down on as breaking solidarity with the democratic ideal of "equal work, equal pay"! Consequently, the prevailing mentality is still not to do any work whatever without full remuneration, particularly among professionals and the well-off.

Much in the world still stands on its head; neither the task nor the challenge are over. This fact underlines Baba's constant warnings against bookish scholarship rather than learning what may be valuable to put into practice.

The value of education has to be measured in terms of the virtue it implants, because virtue alone ensures peace and joy. Without it a man is as good as dead, or even worse.[6]

Such ideas vindicated for me my own convictions about the dangers of one-sidedly mental and intellectual education. Sathya Sai Baba's view is that there has been a worldwide decline in educational standards in terms of its most basic values. If one doubts this one should ask why, with higher education more available in the world than ever, so many terrible human problems and real crises are still so far from being solved, often even far from being recognized. More than any other institution, the education a society provides to its members is what forms the character of its individuals, whether for better or worse.

[A]n improved standard of living is no guarantee of happiness. Nor is education or the mastery of information and the acquisition of skills any guarantee of mental equanimity. As a matter of fact, you find the educated man everywhere more discontented and more competitive than the uneducated.[7]

The idea that one can eventually transform a country by improving its educational system radically is very likely to be true. Knowledge of society always has self-knowledge as its reference point, and when the two interact, the starting point must always be oneself. Sathya Sai has made it very clear that the real basis for lasting change is the behavior of the individual and *not* the authorities. To change one's own conduct *before* seeking to edify others is a rule Baba affirms most firmly. Public criticism of the activities of others must not be a substitute for self-examination, following one's conscience, and being really willing to sacrifice one's own interests for the community where necessary. Whatever "system" or organization is introduced on paper and in law, there must first be a sufficient number

---

[6] Sathya Sai Baba, quoted in N. Kasturi, *Sathyam, Sivam, Sundaram: The Life of Sri Sathya Sai Baba*, Vol. IV (Prashanthi Nilayam: Sri Sathya Sai Books & Publications Trust, 1980), p. 161.

[7] Sathya Sai Baba, Discourse Perambur, Madras, April 23, 1961, *Sathya Sai Speaks*, vol. II (Prashanthi Nilayam: Sri Sathya Sai Books & Publications Trust, n.d.), p. 36. New Indian edition ISBN 81-7208-150-2: vol. 2, pp. 21ff.

of individuals willing to put it into practice. No sound structure can be built of flawed bricks.

Baba has many times charged educators with not really demonstrating social conscience in action through selfless vocation and real service to the community. Productivity, technology, and publicity are nowadays, alas, the dominant motives behind most education and science—appealing at bottom mainly to the material self-interest of individuals. Universities have increasingly become little other than providers of a technically-efficient workforce for industry, commerce, and the State, which secure well-paid work for the successful graduate.

In our present science- and technology-worshipping universities, it is most frustrating to observe how life qualities, human character, and moral values are quickly reduced to mental abstractions or even statistics, themes for mere intellectual argumentation, raw material for theses, or simply grist to the formal teaching mill's own standards. This de-humanized, de-universalized, and de-spiritualized modern education teaches little more than some kind of superpolytechnic skills. The only real guiding ideal has become profitability or economic development in place of good citizenship and the service of society and humanity.

> Today's universities have converted themselves to factories which can produce graduates. This cannot be the true purpose of education. Unless education which is acquired helps one to develop discrimination, it is not true education. One should enter into society and serve the nation.[8]

Baba explains with great penetration how the decline in true education is both an effect and an on-going contributing cause of a wider malaise. The world has suffered a long-term decline in simple living of the kind that Baba himself demonstrates daily. The physicalistic viewpoint of science and the pride of intellectual knowhow has accompanied and added to the inner dryness or alienation of the heart. All this is reflected, as I see it, in the very high suicide rate among students, and probably in other groups, too.

---

[8] Sathya Sai Baba, "Education & *Seva*," Nov. 19, 1987. A pamphlet published by Sri Sathya Sai Books & Publications Trust, with Baba's Discourse on Nov. 22, 1987. Reproduced in part in *Sanathana Sarathi*, Dec., 1997, pp. 325ff.

The keenness, constructivity of attitude, and dedication to world improvements, natural to most youth who have not been "system-deadened," is all too often diverted too soon into inadequate or wrong channels owing to the bread-and-butter-with-jam policies that dominate modern higher education. I watched this situation worsen considerably during a mere quarter of a century. Certain colleagues and I were powerless to alter the crushing trend against high ideals that were once the hallmark of university-educated persons. Therefore the Colleges and the University started and guided by Sathya Sai immediately struck me as unique in the world today. Here at last is a system of education that can serve as the top model for all future educators. It is so advanced in outlook that no known contemporary pedagogues have been able to forward a philosophy of such elevating influence.

> Education must strengthen the springs of joy, love, and peace of
> mind that are inherent in the heart; these should not be dried up
> in the dusty years of study. Cultivate these by precept, example,
> and exercise during the formative years.[9]

The above teaching is embodied in the new educational order that Baba is building for India and the world. It is also being realized through his universal program of "Sathya Sai Education in Human Values" for children and youth.

Of the many thousands of Baba's students, many are about to assume positions of influence in India, from which they are to begin to cleanse the nation of its widespread corruption, oppression, and many other moral ills. Baba also says they will even lead the way as an example for the whole world in a new era of spiritual peace and improvements.

To consider the most easily observable manifestations of the Sathya Sai educational program, there are already more than a dozen major institutions raised by him in India. He even personally organizes and supervises the building of schools and colleges. The Sathya Sai Institute of Higher Learning at Prashanthi Nilayam is probably the first fully State-recognized university at national level

---

[9] Sathya Sai Baba, Discourse Anantapur, Jul. 8, 1971, *Sathya Sai Speaks*, vol. IIB (Prashanthi Nilayam: Sri Sathya Sai Books & Publications Trust, n.d.), p. 250. New Indian edition ISBN 81-7208-159-6: vol. 11, p. 163.

anywhere in the world, that sets spiritual instruction as the highest
and overall discipline. Its students often excel academically and win
many national prizes. This institution offers a much wider education
than is available from comparable institutions anywhere. Employers
are nowadays eager to recruit the students, whom Sai Baba has led
to practice strict self-discipline and scrupulous honesty. In 1988, for
example, there were about ten applicants for every available place,
and that was before Baba announced that all study places at his institutions would thereafter be provided gratis. All this is financed by
entirely unsolicited private donations, all public fundraising being
strictly forbidden by Baba. Several of India's states now have a
Sathya Sai College. Many years ago Baba predicted that each state
will have one.

Sathya Sai Education is already represented, mainly through
Sathya Sai Centers, on some scale in forty-two countries of the
world. In some countries the basic education system is gradually
being remodeled on the lines of Sathya Sai Education in Human
Values, for example in Thailand, Ghana, and Mauritius, where it
now forms a model for the national primary school syllabus. There
is already a thriving Sai College in Zambia.

As one example for comparison with other educational institutions in the world, the students of all Sathya Sai Colleges must take
part regularly in free community service work of various kinds. I
have been able to observe the standards of behavior and activity of
students of these institutions in various ways, and have also been
acquainted with a student both before and after he entered the
Sathya Sai College. I can confirm the quite remarkable personal discipline of the students and their great application in all they do. It
strikes any observer as being matched only by their intensity of love
and respect for Baba, himself, and the awe in which they hold him.

These young ladies and men learn in an atmosphere of love and
of care for their fellow-students and teachers, who also share in all
practical tasks with them. Their self-control in talking and comport-
ment generally is impeccable, which can be seen daily at the temple
veranda during darshan.

The talks some of them are occasionally called by Sai Baba to
give in public are always to the point, well-informed, and above all
of a level of spiritual percipience that is unprecedented to hear from
such young people anywhere in the world. Their displays of various
sports, of gymnastics, or group folk dancing and dramatic produc-

tions are of an excellence hard to credit when it is known how few hours of preparation and practice they are given to achieve them, for they have a crowded daily program—from 4:30 A.M. until 9:00 P.M., with very little "leisure" indeed. Yet they thrive on this without wishing it otherwise, as I have been able to satisfy myself is really and truly the case.

THE UNFATHOMABLE
NATURE OF THE AVATAR

Sathya Sai Baba has declared: "My truth is inexplicable, unfathomable. I am beyond the reach of the most intensive inquiry, the most meticulous measurement. There is nothing I do not see, nowhere I do not know the way, no problem I cannot solve. My sufficiency is unconditional. I am the Totality—all of it."[1]

The joy I have had from being aware of the Sai Baba avatar's advent and all that it means is what makes me want to share what I perceive of it. Written accounts by others have helped me in approaching the seemingly-incredible facts in the right spirit of openness. That is one "excuse" for the following reflections on the nature of the avatar. Though I accept that it is impossible to understand anything even approaching the full meaning of his multifarious actions, the fascination and the desire to understand them better seem unavoidable to me.

Even accepting that the first duty is to learn to know oneself, who among those who have already actually "tasted" a little can help but want to know more and more of Sai Baba? Sai Baba has said:

It is impossible for anyone to understand or explain the meaning and significance of Swami. There can be no possible means

[1] Sathya Sai Baba, quoted verbatim by J. S. Hislop in *My Baba and I* (San Diego: Birth Day, 1984), p. 131.

> of approach to this manifestation, from the stage which you can attain. This is an Incarnation, an Embodiment, which is beyond anyone's comprehension. Trying to explain me would be as futile as the attempt of a person who does not know the alphabet to read a learned volume, or the attempt to pour the Ocean into a tiny waterway. You can at best only prepare yourself to receive and benefit by the Ananda (i.e. joy) I confer, the Bliss I grant.[2]

It has been held since ancient times that it is the prerogative of an avatar to organize appearances around himself. The reality "behind" our seemingly sound, yet deceptive, perceptions is not known fully other than by the Creator of Maya, as Baba has firmly assured us. Those with strong determination and steadfastness of faith—or with other comparable achievements—are allowed to glimpse behind one or two of the many veils of his play. There are tests of faith even to the long-term believer, too, as Kasturi and others have shown, providing us with sufficient evidence that close physical proximity to the avatar brings with it extra demands on one's humility, understanding, equanimity, social behavior and many another quality.

That initial hurdle of having faith enough even to take the trouble to approach close enough to see for oneself is seldom overcome without considerable soul-searching and effort. What occurs in Sai Baba's proximity often seems designed to test the readiness of the seeker before divine *leelas* can be witnessed. Without my own drawn-out contact with the swami whom I first met in London, I think I would have been very hard put to make the mental and emotional adjustments for being able to accept and visit the avatar.

Because Sai Baba does not usually explain his actions and—when he does—chooses time, place, and person according to his own inscrutable reasons, doubts can naturally arise about any fact or event in the minds of those who did not themselves witness it. For example, while discoursing at Brindavan before students and others in September 1990—including the world-traveled senior editor, V. K. Narasimhan—Baba exemplified a point by materializing and holding up for all to see a huge white cut diamond that he told them was, "the largest diamond in the world, 1000 carat." After

[2] Sathya Sai Baba, Discourse Prashanthi Nilayam, Oct. 9, 1970, *Sathya Sai Speaks*, vol. VIIB (Prashanthi Nilayam: Sri Sathya Sai Books & Publications Trust, n.d.), p. 55. New Indian edition ISBN 81-7208-158-8: vol. 10, p. 170.

some time he dematerialized it again. Though I did not witness this myself, I was at Brindavan at the time and heard about the incident from Sri Narasimhan directly afterward.

> No one can understand my Mystery. The best you can do is to get immersed in it. It is no use your arguing about pros and cons; dive deep and know the depth; eat and know the taste! Then you can discuss me to your heart's content.[3]

To penetrate one's own doubts, to get some measure of one's own ignorance of the inner Divinity, are both preliminaries to learning something about the "organization of appearances" that veils the truth and surrounds the acts of the avatar. These "invisible" layers of deceptive appearances surround all things, of course, including physical nature. It is the dazzling veil of unknowing or *maya* that hides from us the secret of its creation and the intelligence its organization exhibits. This *maya* operates through the human mind in the shape of our ignorance. Science penetrates some layers of its physical aspect, which is only the most concrete and obvious appearance. But spiritual practice alone can lead to understanding of these facts.

As we can discern from reading about the life of Krishna and comparing that with the acts and events of Sathya Sai Baba's advent, whatever occurs in connection with an avatar can be both deceptive and educative. Which it is will depend, to some extent at least, upon the perceiver's experience, heart, and mind. A strong ego or intellectual achievements (and their common attendant, pride) are evidently of no avail when approaching the avatar! Life in Baba's sphere sooner or later stretches one's understanding well beyond its accustomed routines and explanations, and this in turn makes one set for oneself higher standards of behavior and mental detachment.

By cultivating a discriminating attitude we can be capable of holding on to the truth of the greater vision when further trials have to be undergone. Otherwise we risk being blown away like chaff from the threshing when the avatar may see fit that the wind shall blow.

---

[3] Sathya Sai Baba, Discourse Nellore, July 25, 1958, *Sathya Sai Speaks*, vol. I (Prashanthi Nilayam: Sri Sathya Sai Books & Publications Trust, n.d.) p. 71. New Indian edition ISBN 81-7208-149-9: vol. 1, p. 67.

The main historical sources on the nature of divine avatars, apart from what Sathya Sai Baba himself says, are the ancient Indian scriptures. According to these sources, such as the *Bhagavata Purana,* in hoary ages past, a promise was made by Lord Narayan (i.e., Vishnu), who one must understand simply as being God, the same One and Only God who is worshiped by all peoples whatever the incarnate form or name. The famous vow was that, whenever the world was in danger of falling into unrighteousness and consequent destruction, he would himself incarnate—taking on an appropriate human form and bringing with him whatever powers that may be necessary to effect the reversal of spiritual and social decline. One such avataric incarnation, Lord Krishna, confirmed and reasserted this promise, as one can read in the Bhagavad Gita.

Sathya Sai has explained how an avatar is the descent of God into human form through an act of will, the Holy Spirit remaining totally pure and unsullied while still in possession of all the unlimited divine powers during the entirety of his sojourn among us. He thus never has to undergo any spiritual development whatever. This mystery of the Infinite God within the form of a finite human is yet more impenetrable, Baba says, than that of us souls, born human, who eventually realize our Divinity through good actions, spiritual practices, and self-sacrifice to become (one with) God. Both Gautama Buddha and Jesus Christ attained this union, according to Sathya Sai. Such "salvation" is the potentiality and the actual ultimate destiny of everyone, though it is usually achieved only through many lifetimes in differing incarnations.

Baba asserts that God takes on human form whenever there is a need, or one worthy devotee who needs it, or a general necessity, whether for brief periods or for long lifetimes. Yet the advent of the so-called *purna-avatar,* having *all* the divine qualities and powers to the fullest possible extent, is an extremely infrequent event, according to time-honored Indian scriptures of great antiquity. The last *purna-avatar* is dated by Sai Baba at 5,000 years ago, when—as described in the Mahabharata epic, Sri Krishna brought about the elimination of evil through the great war at Kurukshetra (dated by Baba at 3138 B.C.). This culminated in the major transition of the ages from the Dvapara Age *(Yuga)* to the darker age of the dark-skinned Kali. Baba has stated that Krishna left the body on November 17, 3102 B.C., which affirms the view held by Brahmanic texts and native chroniclers, as also reported accurately to within a few days in the 1880s by Madame Blavatsky in her *From the Caves and*

Jungles of Hindostan. According to Baba, even Sri Rama, many thousands of years previous to Krishna, was not himself the *purna-avatar,* because some of the divine qualities were distributed among his brothers. Baba has also explained that the form and power of an avatar depends on whatever powers are required for the circumstances that prevail in the particular age.

A vast literature on such matters exists in India, it being considered by pundits and shastris within the tradition to refer back to mnemonically-recorded ages and events very long prior to any existing written record. The far-reaching philosophical and theological explanations about the various natures and tasks of embodied divinities of every order that abound in many scriptures, have always left certain issues unanswered and have given rise to questions as to which interpretations on various fine points are correct. Today, however, some of India's most respected theological savants—including her most advanced yogis, swamis, ritviks and pundits of many branches of spiritual learning—have proclaimed how profound and surprising are Baba's interpretations of the symbolism in all aspects of the great scriptural works, even on matters that great saints and savants had to leave unresolved through the ages. Dilemmas and doubts of the most involved sort have been solved for them by Baba, as the relevant literature shows in detail. He has taught and demonstrated most succinctly much about the truth of the origins of Indian beliefs and practices. He even has reportedly quoted verbatim texts of any age and degree of obscurity to learned pundits, interpreting them with complete mastery and not least accompanying them by temporary apports of most amazing ancient artifacts, such as famous diamonds lost from temples and permanent materializations of statuettes of divinities in all sorts of precious metals, from panchaloha to gold.

In front of all the students at his college in 1977, Baba materialized the actual Kasturbam jewel that Krishna once received from his grandmother for his name day, and which he wore centrally on the forehead. It was a very large and bright emerald surrounded by four circles of glittering diamonds. Likewise, he manifested a very large diamond during a talk to some hundred or so Westerners in the Prashanthi Nilayam temple in 1988—something he has done on certain other occasions through the past decades.

One may ask, why do the major avatars only ever take birth in India—why not some other country or as a member of a different race? I am inclined to respond with, "Why not?" and, "Where else could an avatar be accepted so readily?"

Unfortunately, the world still has little more than an elementary insight into the astonishing history and the huge cultural treasures of India from ancient times. Only in the context of the involved history of the many Indian avatars of ancient times can the historical import of this embodiment begin to be appreciated. Many of the legends of India that the Sai Baba avatar actually reinstates by demonstrating them afresh are still regarded as insupportable myth by Western-style historians who are shackled to materialistic thought and the skeptical limitations of natural scientific methods and techniques.

India was the birthplace of *dharma* or right and good living, which is simply to say, true religion. India has moreover always been the chief home of these values, and he has returned there in accordance with the many prayers of thousands of deeply spiritual saints and wise people of India and the world.

India was, moreover, according to Baba's own convincing explanations, the very cradle of religion and human civilization. He has confirmed that Jesus lived in India for many years, wandering from Sind to the holy Hindu temple of Jagannath at Puri during his youth, when he learned both from Buddhists and Brahmins.[4] Most of India's people through history have practiced, experienced, and retained the deep spirituality of its heritage, and this is evidently not lost everywhere today, despite the degradations of modern times.

The constant ministrations of Baba to the destitute, ill, and suffering of India bear out his explanation that a foremost reason for his birth in a very poor family in one of the poorest villages and states of the land was especially so as to succour the humble and needy and to bring them grace and confidence.

Being omnipotent, omniscient, omnipresent, and omnifelicitous, the Infinite Consciousness or God is said to be able to remain without form while yet being able (temporarily—i.e., within space-time) to assume any form whatever that is required. A form is assumed so as to focus the faith and awareness and lead us on toward realization of the otherwise quite unimaginable Formless Universal Consciousness. All incarnations of God, says Baba, are embodiments of one and the same Being, whether under the name of Vish-

[4] See Holger Kersten's *Jesus Lived in India* (Shaftesbury, England: Element Books, 1986) and Andreas Faber-Kaiser, *Jesus Died in Kashmir* (London: G. Cremonesi, 1977).

nu, Rama, Krishna, or Sai Baba. That is why he is acquainted with every detail, known or unknown, of each of their advents and why he is able to appear as any one of these at will for individuals who prefer to worship this or that form of God.

Many individuals have seen Sathya Sai Baba assume the outward appearance of their chosen Deity, or of the guru they follow. It is certainly not without reason that Baba is referred to by most Indian followers as Sai Rama and Sai Krishna. These names can be seen to be entirely fitting when one knows enough both about the childhood and the subsequent lives of Rama, Krishna, and Sathya Sai. No other life story recorded in world history of which I know, can compare with it for perfection of conduct and understanding, for the mystery of events and miracles, or the sheer joy of divine play, unless it be what is known of the childhoods of both Rama and Krishna.

Experiences of an avatar's illusory games of hide-and-seek with the devotee are nowhere in world literature described as intensely and headily, surely, as in the life of Krishna in his relation to his many associates found in the *Srimad Bhagavatham,* the *Mahabharata,* and its component part, the *Bhagavad Gita.*[5] Reading about Krishna's person, about the outward mask or persona of "everydayness" he adopted toward many of the Gopis and to Arjuna, is indeed like reading about Sathya Sai Baba himself, as if the same character were acting in a new great drama. For example, Krishna also gave Arjuna the illusion that he was but a friend, a charioteer and servant, concealing from Arjuna the overwhelming realization as to his true and majestic nature most of the time. Yet, on the battlefield at Kurukshetra, Arjuna was shown the awesome true nature of the avatar, and he realized he had totally forgotten for days and weeks that Krishna was the Cosmic Being. Baba says:

> Since I move about with you, eat like you, and talk with you, you are deluded into the belief that this is but an instance of common humanity. Be warned against this mistake. I am also

---

[5] The *Bhagavatham* has been retold in its true essence by Sai Baba himself in *Bhagavatha Vahini* (Prashanthi Nilayam: Sri Sathya Sai Books & Publications Trust, n.d.). The story of Krishna and the Gita teachings are summarized by Baba in the *Geetha Vahini* (Prashanthi Nilayam: Sri Sathya Sai Books & Publications Trust, n.d.). Books are translated into English.

deluding you by My singing with you, talking with you, and engaging Myself in activities with you. But, any moment, My Divinity may be revealed to you; you have to be ready, prepared for that moment. Since Divinity is enveloped by human-ness you must endeavour to overcome the delusion (Maya) that hides it from your eyes.[6]

Sathya Sai himself visited the sites of Krishna's deeds in the 1960s with a most privileged entourage, which he enthralled by pointing out the exact spots of his various exploits when he was embodied as Krishna. He has explained every apparent anomaly and gap in Krishna's life history, to the satisfaction of the most devoted Hindus, and has also at times added educative details for his students about which no one knew.

In his present advent we can observe for ourselves a perfect model of our own inherent nature. This can enable aspirants to have sufficient insight to inspire them to know and pursue unfailingly what is right. Therefore, it is valid to study the avatar and his actions, to investigate as far as we can this model of perfection in all its facets, and to question honestly when doubts arise. In observing an avatar, Baba makes clear, we are only observing our own true selves, even though we have not realized this perfection ourselves. More than that, Baba says he is ever-present in the inner chamber of every heart, which is how he knows everyone and all about them. Such omnipresence—being present at all times and in everything— is an incomprehensible mystery encompassing all time and space, one that no mere seeker has the authority to claim to understand. We can but observe how completely unhurried and "wholly present in the present" Baba always appears to be.

Let us, despite our limitations, permit ourselves a brief experiment in thought. How would one behave if omniscient, omnipotent, omnipresent, and omnifelicitous? Should one act only as a great mysterious Being beyond anyone's comprehension—or more like a human being whose form one has taken on for the purpose of letting people feel able to approach oneself? That is how I understand Baba's frequent use of familiar conventions such as, "How are you?" and, "When did you arrive?" (though he surely knows—or

---

[6] Sathya Sai Baba, Discourse Bombay, May 17, 1968, *Sathya Sai Speaks*, vol. VI (Prashanthi Nilayam: Sri Sathya Sai Books & Publications Trust, n.d.), p. 226. New Indian edition ISBN 81-7208-156-1: vol. 8, p. 99.

can know at will—both things perfectly well!). How could he otherwise make all the eager new people feel at home—seekers and sceptics, critics and devotees—if he were not to appear in some manner that all can relate to and accept from the start?

As Baba has demonstrated daily, when he asks a question, he is already able to answer it himself. Should he then answer it before it is asked? Well, he has done just that on frequent occasions; the literature abounds in accounts of it. Should he therefore always do that and save one the time and trouble of asking? If he did, then everyone would always have to be mute in his presence, and the "natural" atmosphere would be lost, the sense of participation he creates gone. Clearly he accords with the objective needs (not always the same as subjective "wants") of the particular person, and acts and speaks according to the level of their development, known fully only to him.

This raises the question of the "human aspect" of any avatar, not least Sathya Sai. If God can become human, how can he still be God? For humans are precisely not omniscient or omnipotent beings; they also have preferences and dislikes, and they make errors and have failings. Must the avatar somehow become thus, too, and if so, to what extent? These riddles have exercised theologians in both the Christian and Hindu religions in many ways. By approaching Sathya Sai, we should be able to gain some insight into this and gather some firsthand evidence on the subject.

The subject is many-sided and fraught with pitfalls, so I will only make some few remarks here, based on my own experiences. One test of faith that has confronted me, since actually meeting Baba, concerns his factual accuracy in certain statements. How could an omniscient being say, for example, that, "Cricket was first played in Melbourne in 1898," which I heard him (via his translator) say in a discourse on the origins of sport and its proper aims at one of his colleges in 1987, prior to his distribution of prizes during the annual sports and cultural festivities. However, it is an indisputable fact that cricket was played long before 1898 in Melbourne—and that it was first played in England well before the 17th century! I know without doubt of quite a few similar types of factual error that Baba has made in statements, as well as outright contradictions between assertions made at different times, such as regarding the actual date of Jesus' birth.

Baba is also known to make suggestions and even promises that he does not follow up. He did so with me, asking in a private interview how long we were staying. When he heard the date, he said that he was going to Bangalore shortly and that we should follow him there, himself saying that he would arrange a room for us to stay in. It was evident from the context that this referred to a room in the ashram at Brindavan, where he also resided. When the time came, no room had been arranged for us, and all rooms there were already occupied. No reservation had been made for us then or later on. We had to find a room in a hotel ourselves in Bangalore (some half-an-hour away by taxi). The fact that we got a room in that ashram the next time we visited India does not fulfill his "promise," for it was made in the context of discussing a fixed date. Some sound books on Sai Baba also contain a number of examples of such incidents.

Apart from stark and dismal skepticism, there are two main approaches toward examples of the sort given above: either blind faith or reasoned understanding. The extremely subtle ways in which Baba delivers many of his lessons, often involving tests of faith, makes some devotees reject the possibility that anything Baba does could be in any way less than meaningful or any kind of error at all. They would perhaps quote Baba's reply to questions about his "mistakes": "It is all my *leela*," (i.e., divine play). However, those who quite regularly experience such "human error" on Baba's behalf and cannot find any meaning in these minor events, however much they try, lean to the opinion that the *leela* Baba probably refers to in such cases is none less than his taking on a human form and, along with it, some trivial but quite normal human quirks and foibles. Even if they are intentional "appearances," adopted for some purpose, they remain otherwise exactly like ordinary (though very unimportant) human limitations.

This view appeals strongly to me because, were Baba really all the time a totally infallible and divine power in every smallest thing that anyone can observe, his endearing human closeness might well be lost. If he seemed so unlike us all, it would make the attempt to approach him too awesome for many people, nor would we probably be able at all to identify with him in the sense of seeing him as an example that we really might hope to follow. This very same "human quality" has endeared divine figures from Krishna to Jesus to countless millions. A sensible study of the roles played out by Rama, Krishna, Gautama, and Jesus shows they all suffered at times from human fallibility, at least as judged by any human standards. Rama lost his queen Sita due to a trick; Krishna's diplomacy failed to avert the war at Kurukshetra; Gautama died of eating a poisoned meat offering; and Jesus was crucified and felt his Father had forsaken him.

Even so, there is still no need to doubt that Baba is *in reality* an embodiment of the perfect divine omniscient Consciousness, if we recall that no body is ultimately real, according to Baba himself. The physical body and brain do have certain physical limitations, even though Baba employs his to their utmost capacity. Does it seem likely, for example, that he would simultaneously (want to) be conscious of each single individual's every foolish idea, evil or obscene thought, or banal and trivial word? It is more likely that the incarnate spirit of Baba sometimes simply directs attention now here, now there, according to need.

The name Sathya Sai Baba must refer to a being who is only identified through the body (form) he presently employs as his instrument, yet which his reality far surpasses. Baba's life is itself full of evidence that there are levels of existence beyond the visible "gross matter," where Baba surely sports yet more freely—free of physical limitations. Were I to claim to *know* that Baba is omniscient, it would mean that I would be able to check Baba's consciousness on every single detail, so as to judge whether there was anything he did not know! In saying, "Baba knows everything," one is therefore only stating a *belief*, however many examples of Baba's knowledge we may have witnessed.

Reasoned understanding does allow us to retain full faith, while not denying that Sathya Sai is also prone, by virtue of the natural bounds set by a body, to occasional normal errors of memory in statement of fact, lapses in recalling promises, and even slip-ups in certain of his predictions (as has been documented in a few instances). At the same time, one must not lose perspective; the "human error" factor in Baba seems to be absolutely minimal and of virtually insignificant nature when compared to the enormous demonstration of his perfection and infallibility in all matters of import. It does, however, provide sufficient material for the died-in-the-wool skeptic to hang onto, if he cannot see how to relinquish his hold on the cherished belief that human beings are but animals with better brains! If Baba always appeared in his most Divine "suprahuman" aspect, how would he then avoid becoming an idol of billions of people and be unapproachable for his followers among the poor and needy?

In practice, we cannot always know *when* Baba's acts and seeming mistakes are but tests or lessons that will prove to be of deep significance. To keep an open mind, rather than figuratively to jump from the frying pan of one's beliefs to fiery conclusions, enables one better to wait with equanimity upon events to see what they prove.

No one has been able to subject Baba to so-called "scientific experiments" under strictly controlled observational conditions matching laboratory investigation techniques. This is hardly surprising, for though the immediate physical manifestations could doubtless be examined and recorded by all manner of sophisticated equipment, there is no science that is remotely prepared—theoretically or methodically—to examine such a "hypothesis" as the existence of a full avatar of God. Neither anthropology nor physics, psychology nor comparative religion have anything like adequate theoretical concepts to approach the many new issues that are raised by such a being and the immeasurable extent of the world historical consequences that follow from the hearts and minds that have been inwardly transformed by him.

Conviction in these matters can usually only be reached through an approach combining an unprejudiced mind (even while there are natural doubts) with experience, and the development of faith through expansion of one's vision and life through spirituality.

Those who are genuine seekers, rather than rigid skeptics, will have doubts that are natural to any reasonable person faced with the perplexing phenomenon of the Limitless in limited form, a seeming impossibility. But what is a contradiction to the logical mind is not necessarily fully incomprehensible. The spirit becoming embodied is a less unfamiliar thought than that of the changeless eternal in a changing, temporal form—because we are accustomed to thinking of ourselves, of the human being, as spirit inhabiting and enlivening the body.

I have heard professors at Baba's college tell how, in their regular visits to him, they have never seen anybody at all who is not always in some sort of awe in his presence. Awe, not as fear, but as wonder. His personality is so vibrant, his presence so fascinating and magnetic, that no one can even manage to "speak out of turn," so to speak. They all affirm that, from being the closest companion and friend, he can in an instant somehow withdraw to some imposing distant height, like the imperturbable form of Shiva on Kailas. At a stroke he is seen to be far beyond any normal concerns, more unapproachably majestic than any royal personage. Then, before one knows it, he is with us again, joking, consoling, advising, questioning—as if nothing had occurred. In a moment he shifts, as if from the infinite to the finite, from the Divine to the human.

That Baba is both larger than life and greater than any living person known to the world, can be discerned from studying the kaleidoscope of his activities that make up the overflowing whole image, accessible through the growing flood of literature by those who have some firsthand experience of his person. Even these are but a very small fraction of the total of persons who have received his attention. The actual contact has been relatively little indeed, even in my case, compared to many persons I know or have been able to observe who have written no books, and not least the many students, close assistants, and attendants of Baba.

Why does the omniscient avatar not make known fully and clearly everything about his mission and answer every type of question and apparently valid doubt that arises?

Some words of Sathya Sai may illumine this: "My Will (*Sankalpa*) confers bliss only after assessing the depth of the yearning (*Sadhana*).[7] He insists that the development of faith is the very foundation of any forward steps along the way of spirituality, and that it is a prerequisite of any higher realization or of being fit to receive the grace of the divine.

> You cannot have wisdom (Anubhava) and bliss (Ananda) first, and you cannot postpone faith until you get them. You cannot bargain: "Give me the bliss and then I shall have faith."[8]

> Man today fails to recognise his own true nature. He adores men, but does not realise the humanness in them. He worships avatars like Rama and Krishna, but is not aware of the exemplary ideals offered by them to mankind. Because of his failure to recognise the avatars' exemplary character, man is a prey to all kinds of doubts. Everyone should try to understand the highest human ideals represented by the avatars. He must consider how far he has lived up to those ideals.[9]

[7] Sathya Sai Baba, quoted by N. Kasturi in *Loving God* (Prashanthi Nilayam: Sri Sathya Sai Books & Publications Trust, 1982), p. 149.
[8] Sathya Sai Baba, Discourse Prashanthi Nilayam, Oct. 11, 1962, *Sathya Sai Speaks*, vol. VIII (Prashanthi Nilayam: Sri Sathya Sai Books & Publications Trust, n.d.), p. 141ff. New Indian edition ISBN 81-7208-159-6: vol. 11, p. 306.
[9] Sathya Sai Baba, Discourse Prashanthi Nilayam, Feb. 23, 1990, in *Sanathana Sarathi*, April, 1990, p. 87.

LIBERATION:
THE GREATEST MYSTERY

On our fifth visit to Prashanthi Nilayam in 1990, we were enabled to meet some devotees whose request for liberation from the wheel of life was granted by Sathya Sai and was mysteriously fulfilled some weeks later! We became convinced of the truth of this through personally being witness to a number of events under truly extraordinary circumstances that led up to the granting of this greatest of all possible boons.

Baba assures us that the ultimate aim of life is Liberation *(Moksha)* which he defines as total unity with Divinity and cessation of the individual's karmic cycle of bodily rebirths in the physical world. He insists that not to know or practice anything that leads toward that end is in reality to waste one's entire life. "A person is born to learn how not to be born again."[1] What liberation actually involves is as much a mystery as is the ultimate nature of God. Yet it is supremely desirable, Baba tells us, and so much so that every being in creation will eventually and inexorably achieve it. One who opens both mind and heart towards the moral-spiritual task of complete ego-renunciation, and all that this implies, until complete self-transformation is achieved, will not have to start all over again in subsequent births.

The French painter Paul Gauguin wrote about "the suffering caused by our inability to plumb the mystery of our origin and our

---

[1] Sathya Sai Baba, quoted by N. Kasturi in *Loving God: Eighty Five Years under the Watchful Eye of THE LORD* (Prashanthi Nilayam: Sri Sathya Sai Books & Publications Trust, 1982), p. 1.

future." In my view, Sathya Sai has explained the ultimate reason for birth and the goal of life more convincingly than anyone else. He even demonstrates his assertions through sheer miraculous incidents of many kinds, such as the one I recount here.

I first met Michael Oliver in March, 1988 at Prashanthi Nilayam because his happy personality was most noticeable where he sat amid the large crowds waiting for the daily darshan. I spoke to him at the first opportunity and, during that brief meeting, found him to be a charming person; he seemed especially mature for his 24 years. I was just leaving after a three-month stay, and this was the beginning of Michael's first visit to Baba.

In early October of 1990 we met again at Prashanthi Nilayam: I was sitting inside the men's canteen in conversation with Sri V. K. Narasimhan when Michael entered and, upon seeing us, seemed to light up like a sun and overflow with a loving smile to us. As Narasimhan was near-sighted he did not notice this, and I was so surprised by the intense and visible overflow of this young man's joy that I just nodded, being unable to remember or "place" him. Knowing what I do in retrospect, I would say he must have been in a highly exalted mood at that time, which I think was probably his first day back with Swami again. Afterward I found out that it was the same Michael I had met before, and we had some intense conversations, mostly about Swami and *leelas* that had happened to us.

Sri Narasimhan later told me how impressed he was by the maturity of two articles by Michael, which he had already published in *Sanathana Sarathi* because they were so evidently founded in deep personal spiritual insight and not at all in repetition of others' ideas. He knew Michael and remarked that he always showed that prime quality of happiness, which a genuine devotee must possess, according to Krishna in the Bhagavad Gita.

In the course of our discussions during the following two weeks, Michael told me that during his previous stay, which had lasted about a year, he had at one point begun to have doubts about Baba, and had even left the ashram, because he actually feared to stay in his presence. At Bombay, however, he had been taken ill with a very serious kind of dysentery and was beyond the help of doctors. They thought he was in danger of dying and advised him to leave for the States immediately in the hope of more advanced medical aid there. He had felt terribly ill, believing he was dying, and faced with this he had decided that the only solution was to go back to the ashram, which he did. He became well again directly upon arrival there.

In the course of a few weeks, I learned about his life. Seldom have I heard of a young person who had such difficulties around him while growing up. I do not feel at liberty to go into the details, yet I was truly impressed by his selfless attitude and the way he had risen above all the continuous trials he had faced. He was certain that, during his first (year-long) visit to Prashanthi Nilayam, Baba had cured his mother in the U.S.A. of an illness that the clinicians had declared to be terminal, and that the cure had also included the removal of psychological and other factors that had contributed to it. He had prayed to Sathya Sai for her, while she, being of Catholic background and not believing in Baba, regarded her own recovery as a miracle of Jesus.

Michael soon began working on a centrally-placed exhibit for the opening of the Spiritual Heritage Museum. This contribution on behalf of the U.S.A. was a tall monolith decorated with a mosaic of hundreds of ceramic tiles, designed by Joan Brown, an established artist who directed her team, consisting of her young son, a young American lady named Bonnie, and Michael. One day before Joan's son had to return to the U.S.A., well before the work was completed, Baba had put his hands on his shoulders when on the veranda and had told him that he would soon have cause for much sorrow.

The exhibit had to be erected by painstaking work with improvised tile-cement and other materials (some essentials had been impounded by Indian customs). The team, supplemented with one other member, worked for weeks, often more than nine hours a day and often missing out on meals. Michael told me one day that he, Joan, and Bonnie had quite unexpectedly been called for an interview with Baba. The small group had been with him for half an hour in the small private interview room.

A week or so later, Michael told me about this interview and how Swami had blessed the final draft of his recently finished one-man musical drama. It was based on the Vedas with the setting of *The Wizard of Oz*, and he had asked if he could put on the play in Prashanthi at Christmas. Swami had said, "Christmas?" in a peculiar way, Michael said, perhaps as if he should have known better. He was puzzled and a bit upset and wanted my views on what Baba might have been intimating to him. I did not know the meaning then, but I came to understand it fully later on! From mere hints and Michael's manner, I gleaned that he had learned something else very important at that interview, which I definitely sensed that he had decided he must keep to himself, though he seemed to wish to tell it. That Baba had then agreed to give him liberation only became clear later. Doubtless, he did not talk about the promise of liberation to me, because he was so sensitive as to how others might feel who had not met with *such* grace from Baba.

In mid-October, when Baba reviewed the progress of the museum building work, Michael found that he was able to walk closely behind him throughout the entire visit. He was perplexed that he had had the confidence to join the entourage and that no attendant of Swami had stopped him. There was never a hint of pride or self-advertisement in Michael when confiding in me as a brother about these boons he had received.

One evening we had a long and deep discussion together about crucial events in his life and mine that had brought each of us on our paths to converge there upon Swami's royal highway. Two days later, he also brought his co-worker Bonnie to our room. They stayed for a couple of hours, and Reidun and I had a very enlivening and harmonious time with them. One subject in particular came up, which we discussed at length—namely, what liberation involves! Both Michael and Bonnie were glowing with happiness.

They tended toward the opinion that liberation means final freedom from the human body (no more being reborn at all) and complete absorption in the Godhead forevermore, whatever that may be like. They also both actually said that they were hoping for this for themselves in this lifetime, but told us no more. We discussed Sathya Sai's having once told, after his 60th birthday, that all of those who had accompanied Rama's incarnation, as well as the *gopikas* (cowherd girls) who had been with Krishna, are again incarnate among the devotees of this present avatar. Since these all attained liberation, according to the *Ramayana* and the *Bhagavatha*, we wondered whether one is *never* reborn again after liberation or whether it is freedom from the *necessity* to be reborn, so that one may choose to incarnate to accompany the descent of an avatar. Baba has many times referred to his coming rebirth as Prema Sai, so who can say whether some of those who are liberated during this life will not be reborn to accompany him? (Swami Karuniyananda, who is now a centenarian and is one of Baba's closest attendants, has stated that Baba has said he is to return with Prema Sai.) Obviously, we reached no conclusion on such a great enigma.

The next day (October 25) Michael stopped me while passing in the ashram to confer about what he had experienced that morning. While working on the monolith and thinking about Baba, he had turned around, to find to his amazement Baba standing with his back to him only a few inches away. While Baba stood there talking to some attendants, Michael experienced an upsurge of joy that increased until he was in a very intense ecstatic bliss. This seemed to last for a long time, though he reasoned that it could not have been more than about five minutes. However, when Baba moved away, he said he felt the most terribly depressive feelings, which went on for hours afterwards. He wanted to ask me if I had any idea why he would have felt that, and whether I had ever had any similar experience. I could only say that his guess was most probably better than mine. Such bliss as he had felt sounded to me as if it were close to realization, I told him. During our conversation, I virtually complained to him that having a diamond ring from Swami was unfortunately not at all the same as being given realization.

Michael wondered if perhaps the depression could have to do with dormant feelings that maybe Swami had caused to come up, so as to be finally dispelled. I now clearly see, however, that this was a definite emotional premonition of what was to happen the next day.

Next afternoon, at about 2:15, Reidun and I were in a flat at Roundhouse One when we heard what we thought sounded just like a building collapsing. We saw no damages on the construction work visible from our window, and seeing this was after all Baba's ashram, assumed it must certainly be something else. Not until about 5:30 P.M., after darshan, however, did I hear that there had been an accident at the new museum building, where the big central dome had collapsed. I heard there were many casualties, but it later proved that there were only three! Knowing that Michael had been working long hours in there for weeks, I went to the Prashanthi Hospital with a friend to investigate at first hand.

On arrival there we spoke to an elderly male doctor who said that Michael was indeed there. He had been x-rayed and there were nine fractures and serious internal hemorrhages.

Within moments of hearing he was in fact a casualty, I walked straight into the X-ray room and saw him lying there. I was entirely unprepared for the sight of his condition. I suppose one is never "prepared" to see major injury and the proximity of death. Cuts and sores were visible on his face, arms, chest, and legs, the latter of which he could move even though he had also received a spinal injury. His head was bandaged and there had been injury to the right side of the skull and the brain. One eye was swollen and bloody. Apparently, the only quite painless, uninjured part of his body was the right foot. He was fully conscious and quite himself as he was talking to an American lady from the Santa Cruz group, who seemed to be most sensible and caring. She told him that he must be taken to Bangalore and that she was going with him (which she also did). It was clear from the way he said, "Bangalore?" that he would (at that point at least) rather have stayed at Prashanthi. I only spoke to him to ask if he wanted me to accompany him to Bangalore in the vehicle that was serving as a makeshift ambulance. Michael said, "No!"

I was so shaken up at seeing him thus that I had to leave the room. Evidently seeing my white face when I asked for water, a nurse said, "Don't worry. Swami is here!" I was surprised, for I took this quite literally. It was clear to me that I should not intrude when Baba went in to Michael, and feeling that I was therefore certainly not needed, I left the hospital. Later I learned that Baba had not been there in person. As I was leaving, Baba's car passed me on the road driving up to the hospital, and to my surprise, I saw an orange-clad figure inside. It later turned out that this had been Baba's then 96-year-old attendant, Swami Karuniyananda, whom Baba had sent with *vibhuti* for Michael. Baba himself, it later transpired, had not actually gone to give Michael darshan.

In my poor physical condition, I would not have been much use on the journey to Bangalore anyhow; besides we were booked to leave India two days later. Michael realized, of course, that being moved in his condition was certain to cause him terrible pain and strain, as his subsequent journey indeed proved. The doctor who first treated him told us that Michael had not complained of pain, neither when they had moved him out of the wreckage nor while being moved about under the X-ray machine, despite the fact that he had only been given a very small shot of morphine. He had to be sent to Bangalore at last, because Prashanthi's hospital then lacked facilities to give any chance of saving his life. The doctor strongly doubted that Michael could survive long enough to make the journey.

I met Andrew, an acquaintance of Michael's, on his way to try to find out what had happened. Fortunately he was able to accompany Michael to Bangalore with others in the Volkswagen bus. The journey, normally then about three-and-a-half hours in duration, took over five hours! This was due to road blocks and traffic jams all the way. Michael lay sideways on the back seat of the vehicle with a serum drip attached and evidently also suffering great pain. There were stops for changing a head bandage, which the accompanying medic did. Michael reportedly wanted to be disconnected from the drip, but no one dared to do this. Apparently he pulled off his head bandage himself, leaving gray matter exposed, shortly after which he lost consciousness for the last time at about 9:00 P.M. Upon arrival his death was certified. The correct time of death was in question, and the whole matter was surrounded by inexplicable facts.

In the same accident, both Joan and Bonnie had died, instantaneously killed by masses of falling concrete debris. According to one of Sai Baba's own engineers, the dome-like structure at the top of the central "spire" lacked all-steel reinforcement, necessary because it contained too great a mass of concrete for safety without it. The entire construction job was being done by a firm of private contractors. When a cracking sound was heard about two hours before the accident, they found a fissure in the dome and withdrew all the laborers from work on the building, but for some reason the small American group did not—or would not—leave their work. A Mexican lady, who had become the fourth person in the group and who was herself uninjured, dug Michael out of the rubble. As I did not meet her, I was unable to get reliable information on why they went on working when the danger was quite apparent.

It was said later that Baba himself had very recently warned that it was overweight and would have to be reconstructed, but I do not know to whom or whether he actually said that. However, remarkably enough, Reidun and I, together with a Danish friend of ours, had been invited by one of the ashram staff to go and see the museum under construction, some hours before it collapsed. When we met the man who was to take us there, he told us that the trip had to be cancelled because Swami had given a precise instruction that there were to be no visitors to the museum that day! I can well imagine that we would otherwise also have stayed long and talked with Michael and Bonnie, because their work was in the finishing stages and they were no longer pressed for time! Strangely, Reidun heard from one of the leaders of a large Italian group that they nevertheless *did* tour the whole museum on their own initiative that morning, having heard nothing of Baba's instructions.

In Puttaparthi the next day, we attended the cremation ceremony for Bonnie and Joan on the sands of the dry river bed of the Chitravati, attended by about thirty people who had known them.

During or after the cremation, I realized that a previous wish of mine was being fulfilled, the significance of this being very striking to me indeed, because it again showed me how Baba was aware of my "inner conversation" with him that had taken place many months previously. The background is that our friend Bente had returned to Oslo from India the previous January, after having experienced the death and cremation of a Danish man with a brain tumor. That had been a saga in itself, with a partial cure of that gentleman during an interview. He had been able to walk away from the interview without his wheelchair. Most important, however, he had lost his fear of death, from which he had previously suffered most intensely. Only days later he had fallen ill again, and the Danish group, including Bente, had taken turns at his bedside to help his wife, a trained nurse. There had been a sense of great peace around him over a several-day period, as he slowly sank and also when he had quietly expired. He was cremated on the Chitravati sands, which Bente described as a very natural experience that was thus also spiritually moving.

When I heard of all this, I had begun to think how totally unacquainted I was with death, never having been at a deathbed or even having seen a dead body. I mentally remonstrated with Baba, saying how little I knew of the physical immediacy of death and the destruction of the body. "Why cannot we experience this naturally in our 'civilized' society?" I thought. "I wish I could be better prepared; if only you had let me witness such a death, Swami!" was about what I had said in my contemplations. Well, there I stood on the Chitravati sands with my wish fulfilled! It shows me how careful we must be to be genuine, even in an inner "dialogue" with Baba.

However, Baba had not finished with the saga of Michael, for he was still to demonstrate something more about the reality of liberation through this incident. When we were leaving in a taxi with some friends, we stopped and received a parting darshan from Baba, who was returning to Puttaparthi in a car. On the way, our taxi happened to drive into a resting place simultaneously with one coming in the opposite direction that contained Andrew and the two others who had accompanied Michael to Bangalore on his last journey. So we learned what had happened and our minds were set at rest by them before we left. They told of Michael's ordeal, the journey, and the funeral in Bangalore, where Michael had been cremated with the freely-offered and most comprehensive and loving aid of Baba's service organization, the Seva Dal. Andrew told me that a coconut was broken and the body sprinkled with its juice, according to local custom. However, the smallish coconut had yielded over two liters of coconut water, and the empty halves, having been laid aside in a stainless steel bowl, were found to have produced even more— to the depth of some centimeters!

Michael wrote three very good articles in *Sanathana Sarathi*. These were "Playing Your Role" (November 1988) and "Listening to the Inner Voice" (December 1989). The extraordinary last article, "Removing the Veils," was published (posthumously) in the December 1990 issue. In it one can see something of what his experiences were like in the weeks before his liberation!

About a week later, just after arriving back at home in Norway, I had a very clear dream of Michael, just as I could recall he looked before the accident, quite unharmed, and his face and torso (which were visible to me) were shining with a special inner light or radiance. In the dream I was very happy and also surprised to see him, both so glowing and so well, as I called out, "Here he is!" as if to announce his continued existence to everyone.

Some weeks after our return, a friend from a U.S. Sathya Sai group that Michael used to attend wrote to me from Prashanthi Nilayam. He was able to inform me how Baba had confirmed what many persons already believed, that the three deceased had, at their interview, asked for liberation, and Baba had assured them that he would grant it.

27

THE WAY BEYOND

In the secure joy of just knowing about the advent of Sathya Sai, I may feel the grace of being one who has come through the many sufferings of a lost spirit, to whom divinity was completely veiled, and who has now at least found out about this living God. The deep sense of security in life continues to expand for me in discovering more of its true meaning through Baba. By comparison, the portion of life spent trapped unknowingly in the coils of fruitless and deadening entertainments or passing and futile mundane ends appears now as gray and devoid of charm.

Baba points out the indisputable truth: that since pleasure is but an interval between two pains, to reach equanimity resulting from nonattachment to the body, and from anything whatever in the world, is the only way to attain realization. This way leads, he tells us, to the experience of bliss being the truth. This amounts to renunciation of all worldly desires, while still living in the world and fulfilling one's normal functions and duties. Otherwise, the desires still inherent in the last breath are carried over at death and, presumably through the life-giving *prana* energy in the breath, cause rebirth. The desires that were unfulfilled or unrenounced are present from birth in the form of instinctive and other tendencies (*vasanas*).

The truth of the ancient Indian teaching <u>Neti, Neti</u>, ("which means, literally, not this, not that"), as reaffirmed by Baba, is not always so easy to understand in relation to one's own life, let alone to apply it. The ego-illusion, Baba teaches, though itself an unavoid-

able result of having been born into the world, where we strive for
a livelihood, is also always making us chase unnecessary worldly
mirages in the form of false ambitions and ever-new desires to satisfy. However, this is no Eastern fatalism that excludes the possibility of excellent work to good human purposes. It is primarily a
question of inner liberation.[1]

The search drives us ever onward, from one thing to another.
For example, in my younger days I changed my work often, and
even my profession several times, I left one country for another, and
like most of the young people of my time and background, became
involved in a host of different pursuits, a few good, most middling,
and some bad. In my self-confidence and worldly prowess, progressing toward the fulfillment of the many wants with which I had
equipped—or rather unwittingly encumbered—myself, I reveled in
good health and my strong positive life energy, taking it all pretty
much for granted and mostly accepting the world as it came. Yes,
the proverbial "young and foolish" did apply, though I was also eager to do something useful. I did not really look very far ahead or
see perspectives that I have since learned, and I had no clear idea of
how changed everything becomes for the invalid, how differently
life itself can appear "from the outside," as it were. Nor did I realize the inner gains that really were to be made under such conditions.

Life always seemed to hang a carrot before me or—donkey that
I was—brandish a stick behind—until I was made able gradually to
accept that the renunciation of worldly ambition is the only solution
that gives real peace of mind. The "drive" that had previously been
to improve my situation, my knowledge, and also partly to realize
some ideals that I happened to believe in, brought me ever closer to

---

[1] What the spiritual seeker progressively discovers is that what is sought is
neither "my body, my mind, my intellect, or even my heart." Concerning
the meaning of "neti, neti," Sathya Sai Baba has said, "The true 'I,' which
gives rise to this 'my,' is really the deepest consciousness in everyone and
everything. It is called Chaitanya, the divine consciousness" (Al Drucker,
Bhagavan Sri Sathya Sai Baba: Discourses on the Bhagavad Gita, Prashanthi Nilayam, 1988, p. 3). Further, "Even the great sages, after all their
enquiries and explorations, could only say about the Divine: 'Not this,'
'Not this.' They could not define what *It is*." (Baba, *Sanathana Sarathi*,
Dec. 1987, p. 321).

the end of that road. I was freed decisively from being "driven," by pressures from both within me and outside. It was like getting an early spiritual pension. Before, both my goals and goalposts were often shifting, and it seems that only illness was sufficient to put a stop to this for me. Sooner or later, the limitations inherent in each life situation or circumstance enforced themselves upon my mind or body. Destiny, having first granted me some of my most heartfelt desires, began to make me reduce them. As I have indicated, Baba granted me some fulfillments, too. He has said that either he must grant what we crave for, or we "must realize the very absurdity of it and conquer the worthless yearning."[2] My greatest gain is real and continuing peace of mind! In the dark era of materialism and the dissolution of cultures, it was Sai Baba—in his very existence, his love and his teaching—who lit the way beyond for me. This way is at present as smooth as a highway!

The deeper the shadow in which one may happen to be, the harder it is to see, obviously. Those who imagine they "see the light" in enjoying the worldly entertainments and achievements of life, the satisfactions and comforts, the acclaim even of quite moderate success or riches, cannot have discovered more than a fraction of inner truth, because it would make the transitory nature of such accomplishments transparent.

How the future appears is a reflection of our own mental and emotional projections onto the world as we perceive it. Whether it seems fearful and hopeless or the contrary will of course also depend to some extent on the entire situation from which one has to view it. Inner changes I now feel have enabled me to recognize a tidal change actually taking place in the world saga that is unfolding in this era. Some facts still remain unavoidably true. For example, despite the unheard-of material wealth and technological facilities that abound in some places today, far surpassing even the most fabulous legends of history, this is still countered and even outweighed by poverty, many forms of illness, the ravages of conflicts, and many other untold sufferings of unnumbered millions.

Back in the 1970s, I slid further and further down into the trap of hating, in abstract and at a distance, all those who contributed to the blindly selfish rush of humanity toward the precipice. I even

---

[2] N. Kasturi, *Sathyam, Sivam, Sundaram*, vol. 4 (Prashanthi Nilayam: Sri Sathya Sai Books & Publications Trust, 1960–1980), p. 121.

withdrew into the Norwegian countryside for years, avoiding contact with the madding crowd as much as possible, and with the solace of lake and forest, wrote volumes about an imaginary world, which was to come after the great global catastrophe that I regarded as almost certain. Most lively and dramatic dreams of such events had partly led me to conceive of how, in the aftermath, humankind might survive and learn to make a better society. A number of imaginary features of the society that I described, I later found, to my surprise and joy, to be embodied already in the ashrams of Sathya Sai. There I witnessed, in real life, the climax of my novel: an envisioned, candle-lit procession of many different groups of people from the entire known world, to a great hall where birds flew in and out while music was played!

My escape into novel-writing took place when everything on the world scene was still appearing to grow darker and darker, as morals plummeted, violence spread, radioactive wastepiles and chemical pollution grew everywhere, economic greed caused completely-unheeding ravages of both living and inorganic nature, and the preparations for war in almost every country overstepped limit after limit. Many people today, I know, are similarly and often caught up in much the same anxiety and negativity about the world, which pessimism appears to be quite subjective, from my present vantage point within the sphere of Sathya Sai.

In a similar vein, all predictions, clairvoyant visions, and other scares of forthcoming world catastrophe have been put to shame by Sai Baba. He has on a number of occasions, particularly in 1991, spoken out very firmly to refute all speculations about any future major world disaster. This he did on several occasions to various persons who questioned him, such as leading members of the Sathya Sai Organization in America, including Dr. Hislop and the author and psychiatrist Dr. Sandweiss, among others. Further, he spent some time during his Shivarathri festival discourse in 1991, before the many thousands gathered there, to make a public refutation of rumors that he had previously predicted a world cataclysm. He has on various occasions since the 1970s reportedly said during interviews that there will be no nuclear holocaust. He has also said publicly that there will continue to be natural and human disasters of one kind and another, but that these, such as the Iran-Iraq war or earthquakes, are not really major events on a world scale.

A striking example of a prediction that Sathya Sai Baba did make and that was fulfilled—one that may be tested by anyone who wishes to do so by reading the May 1986 edition of *Sanathana Sarathi*—was on April 10, 1986, when he held the annual Yugadi (Hindu New Year) public discourse. He spoke of what the year of Akshaya (1986-7) would bring and said, "the heat will be excessive and some fire disasters may occur in Vaisakha month" (the Hindu month of "Vaisakha" is from April to May). The Chernobyl nuclear reactor fire disaster actually began 16 days later on April 26, 1986. This disaster was recorded as the hottest fire ever caused by man.

The Hindu new year's day, Yugadi, has often been the occasion for Baba to make general observations about the particular nature of the ensuing year, evidently based partly upon the astrological significance of the different years and the ruling stars or planets. I made a somewhat exhaustive follow-up study of certain types of events foretold by Baba on Yugadi day, 1991. A comparison of the large number and scale of disturbances that actually occurred in the year predicted by Baba, with several years before and since show how remarkably his words were fulfilled.

However, regardless of events and disasters that come and go from year to year, Sathya Sai's perennial lesson is that we all must set strict and intelligent limits on our personal desires. The world can only be changed if enough individuals change themselves; without this absolute prerequisite, it cannot be "fixed up," as if from above, by any government, known type of business or educational organization, party, union, or pressure group. The efforts of individuals at self-transformation may be channeled through organized activities, but it is only the sum of those personal efforts at self-control that can right the ills with which mankind is confronted. When people cooperate in the spirit of divine unity, the resulting whole then amounts to more than the sum of its parts. The removal of selfishness and greed, which is the renunciation of self, is the only motor of lasting change and regrowth. Without this, no amount of ecological or other enterprises will be able to right the disbalances, because the desire for more—when supplied—only leads to increasing desires for yet more. As one would expect, though, Baba has warned of the great threat of pollution and the exhaustion of resources, saying in discourses, for example, that disastrous effects on the earth's ozone layer and atmosphere can only be averted by preventive measures, including the planting of trees on a massive scale.

Though the need for individual self-change and an increase in spiritual values is imperative, it is a futile exercise to try to change others through informing them, for I know that the *only* valid response I can make to the lovelessness in so many places, which Baba calls "living death," is to improve myself, dive deeper into spiritual activities, and care and do more. The world seems already to have plenty of persons publicly pronouncing advice and criticism (of others). That is why my chief interest in practical life now is as a worker in the Sathya Sai Organization.

In India, selfless love in practical commitment is seen in the tremendous achievements by the large voluntary staff at the Sathya Sai Super-Speciality hospital, regarded by various top international experts as the most modern and effective of its kind in the world (with its amazingly low mortality rate for heart operations, of under 2 percent and an infection rate of not greater than 0.8 percent). These are but two of the facets of the many-faceted jewel that shines from Prashanthi Nilayam today and has already regenerated a whole region of Southern India. Sathya Sai's insistence on the avoidance of publicity has so far apparently achieved a virtual international news blackout about these great "developmental" achievements, when one compares with the media coverage generally accorded to almost any small advance in developmental work or international aid.

When I began to study the nature of the Sathya Sai Organization, its activities, structure, and rules, I realized that it is like none other found anywhere today, to my knowledge. Just a few specific points indicate something of its unusual purity of purpose. All arrangements held and service projects carried out are financed, if money *must* be involved, only by the members' anonymous donations. No public collections or profit-taking in any form are allowed. Also, no missionizing whatever is allowed, nor any public advertising campaigns or the like. Telling about Baba through personal contacts is the best means of spreading the news, but we must avoid the sheer futility of evangelizing. Books, films, and videos are, however, often supported by Baba. They provide a relatively neutral source of information for the benefit of seekers. Above all, followers of Baba must lead by being good examples, not empty talkers. The quality of work always takes precedence over mere quantity, and quality means the degree of selflessness, understanding, love, and spiritual aspiration that is in the heart of the ideal Sai worker. The coordinators who lead activities have to regard themselves as "servants of servants," not as masters. All organizational difficulties, including personal conflicts, are to be seen as spiritual challenges calling for self-examination. They are to be resolved only by means of the heart and through full consensus, and not least through prayer to Baba. On several occasions, prayers to Baba to help with some situation met by active workers in our group have had results of a sort that can surely come only from Baba himself.

In the Sathya Sai Organization, and chiefly in the Oslo group, I have experienced an unusual harmony of minds towards the highest of ideals. When all people share a spiritual philosophy and work together toward its realization in Baba's spirit of mutual respect and love, the experience is vital and filled with significance. After having looked into other movements and organizations, I find that the directives Baba has given for his organization are the wisest and most pure for carrying out any sort of spiritual human enterprise. Yet this is definitely not to say that no problems arise. As I know members worldwide have experienced, there occur conflicts of purpose, personality, and ego in the organization. Yet the means of their solution is never far away, not least because of the richness and practical fruitfulness of the teachings that Baba has given as the leading light of all members. The *dharmic* perfection of Baba's own instructions to develop love and a sense of unity, if keenly followed up, ensure protection in the long run from any major error.

Large worldwide organizations with centralized management engender people in high office, or with the VIP mentality, who can lose touch with the aspirations and insights of those who carry out the real work, often unassumingly and with first-hand experience of prevailing circumstances. The organizational tendency is preoccupied with externals, like the number of conferences, meetings, centers, attendance numbers, and membership figures, or the extent of public activity. Though Baba lays most emphasis on the inner life of self inquiry and is ever asking for "quality not quantity," the Sai organization is not wholly free of the above weaknesses, nor of some office-bearers who tend to behave toward other members as subordinates. Sai Baba frequently praises the organization's efforts and service work, but he has also many times pointed out that its members often fall short in many respects, and that things are not always what they are made out to be on paper. Many members do not question properly whether their efforts are really in accordance with his will (i.e., his teachings). Clearly, members at all levels are undergoing tests and subtle, long-term spiritual education because of personal imperfections. This is also what makes the Sai Organization unusual, challenging, and worthwhile. The work is more fruitful as a means of individual and hence worldwide transformation than that of charitable or religious organizations that are supposed to run more like efficient, impersonal machines.

Baba warns us against rushing to conclusions about others and their motives. It is clear that love of everyone and cooperation with others at the most pure level cannot come easily or overnight. The spiritual process is no matter of course but requires very far-reaching self-transformation, the result of much hard work of a sort that cannot be gained by any number of lectures, seminars, or courses. The spirit Baba seeks is clear:

> Some persons suggested that the Presidents of these Organizations may be given a short refresher course of instruction, so that they may carry out their duties (of encouraging units to undertake sadhana and service) more efficiently. This is very much like the move to train whole-time priests for performing worships in the temples! Imagine someone being trained for adoring God! It is not a mechanical process, amenable to the curricula and the timetable of the classroom; it is a spontaneous urge from within, born out of sincere faith and yearning.[3]

In 1988, Baba announced that the World Council that ran the Organization was abolished and all Organization office-bearers were suspended. It was strange to see how nearly all leaders continued in their posts, much as if nothing had happened. Most were eventually reinstated by Baba again. Various incidents through the years suggest that Baba's own testing process is going on and that personal transformation of members is a crucial thing, whatever the Organization may or may not actually be achieving in the way of valuable service to others.

Sai Baba is evidently keen to see people take up his call by joining the Organization in its work, and he often favors his Seva workers in many more or less visible ways. Passive members—those who will not bear duties like attending meetings or doing service—do not stand to benefit in any way from membership in name only. Yet he has also made clear that his mission has a far broader reach than his Organization, further even than to those millions who regard

---

[3] Sathya Sai Baba, Discourse Mysore, Jan. 13, 1970, *Sathya Sai Speaks*, vol. VIIA (Prashanthi Nilayam: Sri Sathya Sai Books & Publications Trust, n.d.), p. 196ff. New Indian edition ISBN 81-7208-158-8: vol. 10, p. 3.

themselves as his followers. If one chooses another spiritual teacher, Baba advises, then follow only him or her. Obviously, not all people or Sai devotees are able to join the Sai Organization, due to various life circumstances or other obligations. But, if one does join, full committment is required, and one must be one-pointed, that is, undivided in concentrating on only the one teacher and involvement in the one organization. Membership gives no rights or privileges whatsoever. Many who visit Baba do not want to do the work involved in active membership, yet surely few other spiritual activities can be compared with cooperative service under the avatar's own wing.

Judging by my own first reactions to the Organization, I know that my reasons for not wanting to join were a kind of lone-wolf individualism and skepticism about spiritual organizations *per se*. I found many other people difficult to get along with, but then cooperation is challenging because it requires effort from *all* parties involved, and so it was always also a question of "what about myself?" At least the rough edges of my ego are gradually being rounded down.

To show me that I should continue to engage in the work of his organization when our best efforts seemed to be without visible progress or results, Baba gave various signs. Pictures of him fell down at very significant moments, concurring with and correcting my thoughts, once in a most dramatic way. Through dreams, Baba directed me in subtle but very definitive ways, such as when he caused me in March 1987 to travel to a European Organization conference in Ghent, near Brussels, despite my back and neck problems: In the dream I chose not to sit down in a vacant space between two persons. Baba glowered powerfully at me and would not speak to me. Though Reidun begged him to do so, he was completely adamant. He caused the diamond ring he had given me to melt down into some awful yellowish plastic waste material. As soon as I awoke (the ring was still O.K.!) I fortunately somehow knew that it meant I must attend the conference, though what useful function I could have there was completely incomprehensible to me. It turned out about six months later that, as a result of my going to Ghent, I was inspired to suggest something as to the planning of Sathya Sai Education in Human Values training in Europe that eased certain clashes of personality and that probably only such a contribution from me could have bridged, all of which I understood nothing of until much later.

284 Source of the Dream

One of several ways in which Baba repeatedly indicates his sat-isfaction with his organization's work here is through the postal ser-vice. We have experienced many times that mail connected with Sathya Sai or his work arrives on a Thursday, which is the traditional day of the Master or Teacher (*Guruvar*), and also the day that both Sai Baba incarnations have directed their followers to hallow as a day of special worship. We almost always hold our Sai organization meetings on Thursdays, when morning mail bearing directly on the evening meeting arrives much more often than on other days! Add to this the frequent arrival of such letters on major festival days, such as the celebration of Sai Baba's birthday (November 23, 1926) or Shivarathri. All this also lends substance to what I once dreamed: "Shiva even sends the mail," (as described in chapter 10, "Dreams from the Source").

Because of its unique aim, methods, and spirit, the Organiza-tion is designed to provide an unmatched opportunity for learning nonattachment from worldly cares and results, and thus for moving toward the goal of life. This involves always being able to keep our minds above any turmoils or trials of the environment, and rise above irritations and injustices that assail us. What happens each moment must be viewed both as an expression of divine intent and as a passing instance. As one learns step by step through life that each experience is a result of the activities of timeless Consciousness everywhere, within and without oneself, one does not attach undue importance to what passes. No details will then distract us from the greater canvas, and no waves will swamp the basic awareness that the soul truly exists, essentially independent of the stream of expe-riences it witnesses.

The goal truly worth striving for is the "other-worldly treasure" that lies beyond the world but which can be appreciated while still in it: Truth-Being-Bliss (*Satchitananda*), the natural condition of the eternal soul within (*Atma*). For me it has been, and still some-times is, hard to have the necessary patience, since spiritual change is *always* gradual, and as Baba says, "Start early, drive slowly, and reach the goal safely!" It has taken a lot of "slow driving" to see any appreciable change in myself. Nevertheless, when I look back ten years, I see how impossible it would then have been for me to ab-sorb and integrate certain insights that have indeed become an in-separable part of my awareness nowadays. At that time, no one could have taught me such things or conveyed to me my present understanding, because a process of growth was required. Though paradise were to fall into one's lap, or infinite truth into one's consciousness, it would not be possible to hold onto it until one becomes pure and nonattached in all things.

There are very many "frontiers of the personality" on which advances have to take place, so that all one's limitations cannot be overcome at once. This makes most personal comparisons either impossible or in danger of being very patchy and partial. It is still difficult not to judge others according to oneself; the personal "glasses" through which we see things at any stage of development are always a source of wrong perception that need cleansing. To learn not to judge conclusively, but just to listen, witness, and remain emotionally and mentally unaffected by praise or blame, success or failure, is the only solution—but it is not an easy one, nor can it be achieved in a short while through any sudden act of will.

The combined flow of inspiration—and also the ego-grinding mill—that Baba's organization provides in relation to members of a very wide variety, has shown me how everyone is each in their personal "karmic soul-capsule," as it were, with each having its own age and time with quite individual juxtapositions of conditions, challenges, and possibilities to match. In Vedanta, these personal conditioning factors are recognized as being the result of personal action (*karma*) in previous times and/or past lifetimes. They regulate one's spiritual ups and downs, one's problems and rewards, and also evidently the amount or quality of the grace that one can receive at any time. To my mind, this has been confirmed by what I have been through in ten years in the organization. In ways that inexplicably seem to have been cut to measure for me, it has been helping me to be more equal-mindedly involved in the present, and to have the sort of carefree faith in the future that children have, without worry or undue thought of any past.

Should one plan ahead for one's life or not? Because Baba has said we ought to be as unattached from "me and mine" as are birds and beasts if we want to attain their natural faith, I decided at one stage, just before our first interview, to try to give up making plans, not least because I felt I had tended to overplan and look ahead too circumspectly. But in the private interview, Baba suddenly asked me, "What is your plan?"

If the plan is rigid it will obviously not work out, because this signals too much attachment to something. On the other hand, if one has no plan whatever it does not mean that one is genuinely nonattached, because one can thereby only drift like flotsam at the mercy of any current. There is evidently nothing to be gained in hanging about, at the ashram or anywhere else, waiting for the grace of God to fall into one's hands, without making any personal efforts. Under Baba's master plan, we in the Sai Organization learn which plans are good (in the real sense) through Baba's subtle guidance and intervention. Having an adjustable plan that changes to accommodate new developments does not mean that one gives up the goal whenever challenges seem very great, for the plan must be so long-term and the goal so worthwhile that it becomes easy to make even major alterations in our lives in order to attain it.

Identifying with an achievement as being "mine" is a trap at the root of this task of freeing oneself from the bonds of the self-centered mind. What I have written about my experiences is, for example, in some respects the result of "my own" labors. Yet the energy to think, conceive, and formulate is not created by myself, only expended through me. That of which I write is not my own invention or creation either; what factual events took place—even the times, places, and circumstances involved—were obviously only influenced by my personal efforts to a very limited extent. Illness confined me to having little more I could do but write. The pleasure of being an instrument is that I can use whatever powers of thought, imaginative presentation, and imagery that God has leased to me (as latent abilities that I have also striven hard to develop) and apply them in communicating events that Baba has arranged on the backdrop that he has likewise provided. Whatever edification about these events and their inherent meanings I have received, he has also provided, through the perspectives of thought required about them and the essential guidance of his teachings.

The great spiritual American writer, Ralph Waldo Emerson, wrote in 1841 of two different kinds of teachers, whether sacred, philosophical, or literary—the first kind, who "speak *from within*, or from experience, as parties and possessors of the fact; and the other class, *from without*, as spectators merely. . . . " The first alone "speak from within the veil, where the word is one with that it tells of," and "[t]he same Omniscience flows into the intellect, and makes what we call genius."[4] Sathya Sai Baba is clearly of this order *par excellence*. His words also resonate within the listener and awaken the beautiful inner life of the deeper heart, which is the same as

---

[4] Ralph Waldo Emerson, *Essays (No. 9) The Over-Soul* (Oxford: The World's Classics, 1902), p. 102.

wider, inclusive consciousness. "The veil" that conceals the inner reality is drawn more and more aside with the progressive discovery of divinity that moving along the Sai highway opens one up for.

Not only are the words of Sathya Sai heard through the ears; they come from him *within*, for example in clear dreams. It is true that dreams show us how the mind, even when idling, creates the most original scenes and sounds, or weaves faces and places, past and present, into the most amazingly detailed concoctions. The mind does this, and we call most of it "mere imagination" or "unreality." That Baba appears amid such dreams, and fashions them to his purposes for the benefit of the dreamer, helps to demonstrate for us something about waking reality as well. Since the mind can create such a convincing world, why cannot it also be the creator of the waking world, too, just as Vedantic philosophy maintains? Baba has often restated that teaching most tellingly: the restless mental action of the mind's desires is what sustains the entire "veil" of creation (*Maya*). When stilled, the mind begins to reveal its own source. This is doubtless also why Baba said to me, "Don't think."

By the "source of dream," I mean the origin not only of sleeping dreams, but also of the much more fantastic dream, the waking dream that we think to be and call "reality" or the universe of space-time. The Creator of all that, in whom we find our very own Identity, I fully believe to be beyond the reach of any mind and to be of unlimited Awareness. Thus, the source becomes the ocean; they merge into One. Indeed, the inability of the mind to encompass the infinite causes it to make everything finite. Its basic nature is to "divide and rule," to distinguish this from that, figure from background, and negative from positive. The way ahead is the way beyond the limits of mind. For me, therefore, Sathya Sai Baba is the very Source of the Dream, the preceptor into whose physical form is poured, as he has himself assured us in many ways, the entire flow of the ocean of Shiva-Shakti power that engenders and plays with the Cosmos.

GLOSSARY

å gjøre deg om. Norwegian phrase meaning "to remake you" or "to make you otherwise."

Advaita. Monism; philosophy of non-dualism.

akasha. The subtlest state of matter (of the five elements): the all-pervasive "sky," ether, or space.

amrit. Known as "holy ambrosia" in the Christian tradition, this sweet, yellowish liquid may form and drip off of holy objects. In Indian religious tradition, amrit is the nector of immortality, as bestowed by Vishnu, in an appearance as the beautiful maiden Mohini, on the race of the devine *devas*, while being withheld from the race of the worldly *asuras*.

ananda. Bliss.

Anubhava. Wisdom. The knowledge gained by one's own experience.

Atma, Atman. Universal Spirit, the spark of God within, the true Self, the soul.

avatar. An incarnation of Divinity in human form.

Ayi. Mother.

Baba. Father, in a number of languages.

Bhagavata Purana. Ancient Indian text on the glory of divine Love, on the glory of God. *Purana* means ancient. *Bhagavata* means Godly.

bhajan(s). Devotional song(s) or singing.

bhakti. Devotion, or one who seeks to realize the Divine through devotional practice.

bodhi tree. The type of tree under which Gautama Buddha sat and attained ultimate realization. Sai Baba planted a sacred *bodhi* tree at Prashanthi Nilayam in 1959, for the benefit of those who meditate under the tree.

buddhi. The intellect, the innate power of discrimination.

chakra. Discus or wheel. Symbol of the wheel of time.

daimon. Socratic ideal of the indwelling conscience.

darshan. The blessing of seeing a holy person.

dharma. All forms of right living, duty, virtue, and good action.

dhi. Thinking. See *Samadhi*.

Ganesha. Elephant-headed form of the Divine; Shiva's son, the "remover of obstacles" who "clears the way" for spiritual progress.

Gayatri Mantra. According to Sai Baba, the Gayatri Mantra is the "mother of the Vedas," expressing praise of, meditation on, and prayer to the Divine—a prayer for illumination on behalf of all humanity. It has five parts: *Om, Bhuh Bhuva Svaha, Tat Savitur Varenyam, Bhargo Devasya Dhimahi, Dhiyo Yonah Prachodayat.* It is often conferred at the age of 12 in the *upayanam* or thread ceremony.

gopikas. "Cowherd girls" who were devotees of Krishna.

Guruvar. Thursday, the traditional Indian "day of the *guru*" or teacher.

Herren-Knecht. Master-servant relationship, as defined by the philosopher Hegel.

japa. Repetition of a holy name or mantra.

japamala. A type of rosary with 108 beads.

jnana. The "universal wisdom" of the discriminative faculty of understanding—the highest, living, self-revealing truth.

jnani. One who masters spiritual knowledge or *jnana.* A wise, liberated person.

Jyothi lingam. A *lingam* that shines mysteriously with a light from within.

Kali Yuga. The current age, the "Age of Iron," filled with darkness and strife.

karma. A universal, inescapable obligation or duty. Action and its effects or results.

kirtan. A gathering for spiritual study, fellowship, and devotion. See *samkirtan.*

laddu. A type of confection or sweet food.

leela. Literally, "divine sport" or play.

lingam. An ovoid or cylindrical holy object symbolizing creation, the ovoid *Shivalingam* form is said to be without beginning or end, and is thus the form of the universe. Sai Baba has created many lingams of different kinds. See also *Shivalingam.*

Mahabharata. The ancient epic by the sage Vyasa, relating the battle of Kurukshetra, between the Pandavas and the Kauravas, in the course of which Krishna imparted the *Bhagavad Gita* to Arjuna. A textbook of dharma and spirituality.

mandir. Temple.

maya. The "veil of creation"; the subtle interplay of the mind's natural "mental projection" and the "objective illusion" of the natural world. Delusion due to ignorance; the principal of appearance that deludes as multiple manifestation.

Mehdi Mood. "The Great Teacher That Was Promised," as predicted by Mohammed, the founder of Islam.

moksha. Liberation; freedom from the birth-death cycle; mergence in the Godhead.

mudra. Hand position with spiritual significance.

muladhara chakra. Sensitive "energy center" at the base of the spine, also called "root chakra." *Chakra* means wheel or discus.

naadi. Ancient palm-leaf manuscripts, such as by Brighu, Kumar, and Shuka.

namaskar. Gesture of greeting with palms folded together near the heart; signifies homage to the indwelling Divine.

Neti, Neti. *Neti* means "Not this." Describes the process of elimination or negation through which one attempts to discover the eternal reality, the ultimate goal or Brahman.

nirvikalpa samadhi. The highest state of spiritual realization.

Om. Also called the *Pranava*, *Om* is the sacred sound held to be that of the original creative urge itself.

Om mani padme hum. "The jewel in the lotus." Sacred Tibetan Buddhist mantra.

Omkara. *Om*, the *Pranava*, the basic sound from which all else issues. Also, a morning ritual of chanting *Om* twenty-one times.

padnamaskar. Blessing of being able to touch the feet of a holy person.

Pak Subuh. The Indonesian originator (familiarly known as "Bapak") of the international and universal spiritual movement in the 1930s called Subud, which is a contraction of three sanskrit words: Susila Buddhi Dharma, meaning "right living according to the will of God." *Pak* means "father" and Subuh is a personal name.

Paramatma. Universal Spirit, the Oversoul, God.

peetha. Literally, a "seat." A type of base upon which a *lingam* may be kept.

pir. Type of base for holding or displaying a *lingam*.

Prakriti. The true or cosmic Mother, or Nature, creation. See *Purusha*.

prana. Vital air, vital essence, "life force" energy in the breath.

Pranava. The primeval sound, *Om*, considered the basis of the universe.

prasad. Food offerings, often sweet-tasting. Consecrated food that has been blessed by a holy person.

Prashanthi Nilayam. The name of Sathya Sai Baba's ashram at the village of his birth, Puttaparthi, in the southern Indian state of Andra Pradesh. Literally, "the Abode of Supreme or Ultimate Peace."

Prema. Universal Love. Pure unselfish love.

puja. Ritual offering or worship, such as placing flowers or fruit on or before holy pictures or idols.

Puranas. Ancient scriptures.

purna-avatar. Literally, "full avatar," having all divine qualities to the fullest possible extent. Krishna was the last previous *purna-avatar.*

Purusha. The Supreme Person, the Divine; spiritual creative urge, the cosmic Father. See also *Prakriti.*

Ramayana. The sacred and classic story of the Rama avatar.

rajas. One of the three "qualities," according to Sankhya philosophy, *rajas* refers to outgoing, aggressive, and vital aspects. See also *tamas* and *sattva.*

rishis. A handful of unsurpassed sages who once lived on the Indian continent; they discovered the ultimate truth through meditation and sacrifice and verbally formulated this knowledge in the Vedas.

Sa. All, sovereign, or divine. From *Sarveswara.*

Sa-ayi. Constituents of the name Sai: *Sa* means "all," and *ayi* means "Mother"—"Divine Mother of All." Also, *aayi* means "Father."

sadguru. The supreme or true teacher.

sadhana. Spiritual practice(s).

sadhus. Holy men, wandering monks or renunciants, literally, "wise spiritual aspirants." Explained by Baba as meaning "good," "virtuous," and thus applying to anyone whose thoughts, deeds, and words concur.

sahib. Sir or master.

sama. Literally, "same." Unaffected, unchanging, steady. Also refers to control of the senses. See *samadhi.*

samadhi. Traditionally regarded as a super-conscious trance-like state. This is refuted by Sai Baba, who defines *samadhi* as perfect equanimity (*sama* = equal, *dhi* = intelligence), whereby one experiences freedom from all duality and serene bliss in all situations (*Sanathana Sarathi*, Aug. 1994, p. 220).

samkirtan. A gathering for spiritual study, fellowship, and singing.

Sanathana Dharma. The eternal religion or wisdom, the combined form and essence of all virtuous living.

Sanathana Sarathi. Monthly journal of Sai Baba's discourses and activities at his ashrams. The phrase *Sanathana Sarathi* means "the eternal charioteer," referring to Krishna, who served as charioteer to Arjuna in the battle of Kurukshetra, as related in the *Bhagavad Gita.*

sankalpa. Divine will.

Sankranthi. Pongal New Year's Day festival.

sanyasin(s). One who has renounced everything and given up all desires toward becoming fully immersed in God.

Sarveswara. The Lord of all, the Source Supreme.

Satchitananda. *Sat* ("being"), *chit* ("awareness"), *ananda* ("bliss") or "Truth-Being-Bliss."

Sathya, sathyam. Truth.

sattva. One of the three "qualities," according to Sankhya philosophy, *sattva* refers to peaceful energies, defined as refined, high-minded, balanced, and inward. See also *rajas* and *tamas.*

seva. Service, especially when performed as worship or adoration of the divine. Selfless service.

Shiva-Shakti. The unification of Divine Mother and Divine Father in one form. Shiva is God; Shakti is divine power or energy.

Shivalingam. The round or ovoid shape denotes the merging of the form with the formless, having no beginning and no end.

sivam. Happy, auspicious, goodness, the Divine.

Smrithis. Sacred Indian scriptures or codes.

So-Ham. Literally, "He is I." *So* refers to He or Divinity, and corresponds to the in-breath; *Ham* refers to the individual or "I," corresponding to the out-breath. Concentrating on the breath while repeating *So-Ham* is practiced as a means of realizing spiritual wisdom.

Srimad Bhagavatham. Ancient Indian spiritual text; "Book of Divine Love." Ancient Indian spiritual text relating events from lives of the Indian avatars and saints.

Subud. An international spiritual movement that originated in Java.

sundaram. Divine beauty, the experience of *sivam.*

swami. Literally owner, master, or Lord. The spiritual teacher to whom one surrenders the ego.

swamiji. Term of endearment for one's spiritual teacher.

tapas. Austerity, self-denial as a spiritual discipline.

tamas. One of the three "qualities," according to Sankya philosophy; refers to sluggish, low, and dark aspects. See also *rajas* and *sattva*.

vahini. "Stream of nectar"

Vaisakha. Hindu month (from April to May).

vasanas. Tendencies, desires, cravings.

Vedanta. The latter part of the Vedic literature, especially the Upanishads, which teach the Higher Wisdom of the monistic (advaitic) philosophy, that all is One and divinity suffuses all and everyone.

Vedas. Holy Indian scriptures that "show the path to the Realm of Eternal Bliss, where there is no Birth or Death." The oldest known religious teaching in the world.

vibhuti. Holy ash. Symbol of the Ultimate, being the irreducible residuum of burning. That unchanging element to which the body eventually returns. Symbol of purity, such as is "worn" by the incorruptible God, Shiva. The physical substance is widely produced in India in various ways, such as by burning sandalwood, rice husks, or cow dung in a sacrificial fire.

Yuga. Era. The current *yuga* is *Kali*. The previous *yuga* was *Dvapara*, which came to a conclusion at least 5,000 years ago with advent of the Krishna avatar and the battle of Kurukshetra (The Mahabharata).

Yugadi. Hindu New Year's Day.

BIBLIOGRAPHY

Sri Sathya Sai Baba has written a collection of sixteen books, each containing the word *Vahini* ("Stream of nectar") in its title. These works include, for example, the longer *Sathya Sai Vahini* (221 pages) and *Bhagavatha Vahini* (300 pages) and the shorter *Dharma Vahini* (89 pages), *Prema Vahini* (81 pages), and *Jnana Vahini* (60 pages).

The discourses that Sathya Sai Baba has held since 1953 are collected and edited in two main series of books; the *Sathya Sai Speaks* series (twelve volumes so far, covering the years 1953 to 1982) and the *Summer Showers at Brindavan* series, covering lectures held at summer courses from 1972 to 1990.

The official biography of Sathya Sai Baba, covering the years from birth to c. 1980, is titled *Sathyam, Sivam, Sundaram,* Volumes I to IV, by Professor N. Kasturi.

Professor Kasturi has also written his autobiography, presenting his own experiences, titled *Loving God* (1982).

Balu, S. *Living Divinity.* London: Sawbridge, 1981.

Baskin, Diana. *Divine Memories of Sathya Sai Baba.* San Diego: Birth Day, 1990.

Blavatsky. H. P. *From the Caves & Jungles of Hindostan.* Wheaton, IL: Theosophical, 1975.

Bruce, R. *Vision of Sai,* vols. 1 and 2. York Beach, ME: Samuel Weiser, 1995.

Brunton, Paul. *The Notebooks of Paul Brunton,* vol 7. Burdette, NY: Larson, 1987.

Budden, John. *Jungle John.* London: Longmans, 1955.

Drucker, Al. *Bhagavan Sri Sathya Sai Baba: Discourses on the Bhagavad Gita.* Prashanthi Nilayam, 1988.

Emerson, Ralph Waldo. *Essays.* Oxford: The World's Classics,1902.

Faber-Kaiser, Andreas. *Jesus Died in Kashmir.* London: G. Cremonesi, 1977.

Fanibunda, Eruch B. *Vision of the Divine.* Bombay: Sri Sathya Sai Books & Publications Trusts, 1976.

Forster, E. M. *A Passage to India* [1924]. New York: Knopf, 1992.

Ganapati, Ra. *Baba: Sathya Sai*, Part I, 2nd ed. Madras: Sai Raj, 1985.

———. *Baba: Sathya Sai*, Part II. Madras: Satya Jyoti, 1984.

Gokak, V. K. *Bhagavan Sri sathya Sai Baba (An Interpretation)*. New Delhi, n.p., 1983.

———. *Narahari: Prophet of New India*. India: B. R. Publishers, 1992; Reprint of 1972 edition. Original publisher: Somaiya Publications.

Haldane, J. B. S. *My Friend Mr. Leakey*. London: Puffin Books, 1937.

Haraldsson, Erlendur. *Miracles Are My Visiting Cards: An Investigative Report on the Psychic Phenomena Associated with Sathya Sai Baba*. London: Century, 1986.

Hegel, G. F. W. *The Phenomenology of the Spirit*. A. N. Miller, trans. London: Oxford University Press, 1972.

Hislop, John S. *Conversations with Bhagavan Sathya Sai Baba*. San Diego: Birth Day, 1978.

———. *My Baba and I*. San Diego: Birth Day, 1985.

Huxley, Aldous H. *The Perennial Philosophy*. London: Triad Grafton Books, 1985.

Isherwood, Christopher. *Ramakrishna & His Disciples*. Los Angeles: Vedanta Press, 1980.

Kasturi, Narayan. *Loving God: Eighty Five Years under the Watchful Eye of THE LORD*. Prashanthi Nilayam, India: Sri Sathya Sai Books & Publications Trust, 1982.

———. *Sathyam, Sivam, Sundaram: The Life of Bhagavan Sathya Sai Baba*. Vols. 1–4. Prashanthi Nilayam, India: Sri Sathya Sai Books & Publications Trust, 1960–1980.

Kersten, Holger. *Jesus Lived in India*. Shaftesbury, England: Element Books, 1986. [Translated from German.]

Kipling, Rudyard. *Kim*. New York: Bantam, 1983.

Krystal, Phyllis. *Sai Baba—The Ultimate Experience*. Los Angeles: Aura Books, 1985. [Reprinted York Beach, ME: Samuel Weiser, 1994.]

Kuhn, Thomas S. *The Structure of Scientific Revolutions*. Chicago: University of Chicago Press, 1962.

Leggett, Trevor. *Sankara on the Yoga Sutras*. Delhi: Motilal Banarsidas, 1990.

Mason, P. and R. Laing. *Sathya Sai Baba: The Embodiment of Love*. London: Sawbridge, 1982. [3rd ed. Bath: Gateway Books.]

Murphet, H. *Sai Baba: Man of Miracles.* London: Muller, 1971. [Reprinted York Beach, ME: Samuel Weiser, 1973 and subsequently.]

———. *Sai Baba Avatar: A New Journey into Power and Glory.* San Diego: Birth Day, 1977.

Oliver, M. "Playing Your Role," in *Sanathana Sarathi.* Prashanthi Nilayam, India: Sri Sathya Sai Books & Publications Trust, Nov. 1988.

———. "Listening to the Inner Voice," in *Sanathana Sarathi.* Prashanthi Nilayam, India: Sri Sathya Sai Books & Publications Trust, Dec. 1989.

———. "Removing the Veils" (posthumous), in *Sanathana Sarathi.* Prashanthi Nilayam, India: Sri Sathya Sai Books & Publications Trust, Dec. 1990.

Prabhavananda, Swami and C. Isherwood. *Yoga Aphorisms: The Yoga Sutras of Patanjali.* London, 1955.

Priddy, R. *The Human Whole: An Outline of the Higher Personal Psychology.* Oslo: privately published, 1991.

Sandweiss, Samuel H. *Sai Baba: The Holy Man . . . and the Psychiatrist.* San Diego: Birth Day, 1975.

———. *Spirit and the Mind.* San Diego: Birth Day, 1985.

Sathya Sai Baba. *Sathya Sai Speaks,* vols. I-XXIII. Prashanthi Nilayam, India: Sri Sathya Sai Books & Publications Trust, 1953–82.

———. "Education and Seva," Discourse of Nov. 19, 1987 at Prashanthi Nilayam.

———. *Preparations for the Presence.* Discourse of Mar. 28, 1975, Brindavan.

———. *Sanathana Sarathi.* Journal. Feb. 1958–1997. Prashanthi Nilayam.

———. *Summer Showers: Discourses on Indian Culture and Spirituality* series. Prashanthi Nilayam, India: Sri Sathya Sai Books & Publications Trust, 1972–1993.

———.*Vahini* (Stream of Nectar) series. Prashanthi Nilayam, India: Sri Sathya Sai Books & Publications Trust of Prashanthi Nilayam, including:

> *Bhagavatha Vahini (The Story of the Glory of the Lord)*
> *Dharma Vahini (The Path of Virtue and Morality)*
> *Dhyana Vahini (The Practice of Meditation)*
> *Geetha Vahini (The Divine Gospel of the Bhagavad Geetha)*

Jnana Vahini (The Stream of Eternal Wisdom)
Leela Kaivalya Vahini (The Cosmic Play of God)
Prashanthi Vahini (The Bliss of Supreme Peace)
Prasnothara Vahini (Answers to Spiritual Questions)
Prema Vahini (The Stream of Divine Love)
Ramakatha Rasa Vahini (The Sweet Story of Rama's Glory), Parts I and II
Sandeha Nivarini (Clearance of Spiritual Doubts)
Sathya Sai Vahini (The Spiritual Message of Sri Sathya Sai) (includes material formerly published as *Paramartha Vahini*)
Sutra Vahini (Analytical Aphorisms on Supreme Reality)
Upanishad Vahini (The Essence of Vedic Knowledge)
Vidya Vahini (The Stream of Spiritual Knowledge that Illumines)

Van der Post, Laurens. *Night of the New Moon.* London: Penguin, 1977.

Wolff, Werner. *The Dream: Mirror of Conscience.* 1952. Reprint: Westport, CT: Greenwood, 1972.

Yogananda, Paramahansa. *Autobiography of a Yogi.* Los Angeles: Self-Realization, 1973, 1981.

Works on or by Sathya Sai Baba published in English in India by Sri Sathya Sai Books & Publications Trust may be obtained from: The Convenor, Sri Sathya Sai Books & Publications Trust. Prashanthi Nilayam, PIN 515 134. Anantapur District. Andhra Pradesh. India. In the U.S.A., they are available through: Sathya Sai Book Center of America, 305 West First Street, Tustin, California 92680. Telephone 714-669-0522.

INDEX

ABOUT THE AUTHOR

Robert Priddy was born in Cirencester, England, and took his Magister degree in 1968 in Oslo, Norway at the University of Oslo. He did graduate research in the sociological philosophy of science, and has been a researcher and university lecturer in philosophy and social science at various institutes. Some of his philosophical publications include *Objectivity in the Study of Human Society* (Oslo: Oslo University, 1968), a meta-social scientific study of social scientific knowledge; *Behaviour, Intention and Meaning* (Oslo: Institute of Social Research, 1969), a critical philosophical study in basic concepts in the human sciences; *Communication and Understanding* (Oslo: Oslo University, 1982), a textbook in language, logic, and the philosophy of science; and *The Human Whole* (Oslo, privately published limited edition, 1991), a study of psychology from a combined Western and Vedantic viewpoint, inspired by the teachings of Sathya Sai Baba.

Since 1987, Robert Priddy has contributed many articles on varied subjects to the international spiritual journal, *Sanathana Sarathi* ("The Timeless Charioteer"), published at Prashanthi Nilayam under the auspices of the Sri Sathya Sai Books & Publications Trust. *Back to the Source* is a compilation and detailed index of over 18,000 authorized sayings of Sri Sathya Sai Baba.

Robert Priddy lives in Norway with his wife. He has made numerous trips to India to be with Sai Baba.